MW00584537

MUSIC EVERYWHERE

UNIVERSITY PRESS OF FLORIDA

Florida A&M University, Tallahassee
Florida Atlantic University, Boca Raton
Florida Gulf Coast University, Ft. Myers
Florida International University, Miami
Florida State University, Tallahassee
New College of Florida, Sarasota
University of Central Florida, Orlando
University of Florida, Gainesville
University of North Florida, Jacksonville
University of South Florida, Tampa
University of West Florida, Pensacola

MUSIC EVERYWHERE

The Rock and Roll Roots of a Southern Town

Marty Jourard

University Press of Florida

Gainesville · Tallahassee · Tampa · Boca Raton

Pensacola · Orlando · Miami · Jacksonville · Ft. Myers · Sarasota

Frontis: Johnny Tillotson is the earliest example of a successful rock and roll performer with deep musical ties to Gainesville. Tillotson was born in Jacksonville in 1939, moved to Palatka in 1948, and enrolled at the University of Florida in 1957. A local disc jockey named Bob Norris sent a tape of Tillotson's singing to the Pet Milk Contest; as a finalist, Tillotson performed at the Grand Ole Opry in Nashville, which led to a record contract with Cadence Records. After graduating, Tillotson moved to New York City, where his career as a performer and songwriter took off. He wrote "It Keeps Right on a Hurtin'" and "Talk Back Trembling Lips," and his recording of "Poetry in Motion" in 1960 reached number two on the chart, with three more of his recordings reaching the Top Ten (www.johnnytillotson.com). Permission of the University of Florida, Smathers Library Special and Area Studies Collections, University Archives.

Copyright 2016 by Marty Jourard
All rights reserved
Printed in the United States of America on acid-free paper

This book may be available in an electronic edition.

21 20 19 18 17 16   6 5 4 3 2 1

Library of Congress Control Number: 2015955715
ISBN 978-0-8130-6258-7

The University Press of Florida is the scholarly publishing agency for the State University System of Florida, comprising Florida A&M University, Florida Atlantic University, Florida Gulf Coast University, Florida International University, Florida State University, New College of Florida, University of Central Florida, University of Florida, University of North Florida, University of South Florida, and University of West Florida.

University Press of Florida
15 Northwest 15th Street
Gainesville, FL 32611-2079
http://www.upf.com

CONTENTS

This is a book about people and music. Specifically, it is about the music played in and around Gainesville, Florida, for roughly a dozen years, and about the people who played it, heard it, and supported it—musicians, students, fraternity members, music and record store owners and their customers, radio station DJs, club and bar owners, hippies, entrepreneurs, hucksters, hangers-on. These people include born-and-raised Gainesville residents, long-term residents, and the uncounted number of people who passed through town, arriving and leaving for reasons of their own—all inseparable from the music. From the early sixties to the mid-seventies, the music and the people combined to create a bustling music scene that thrived and sustained itself in a highly supportive environment. This book is the result of a desire to document events of forty years ago and longer, to show who was there, what they did, and when and where they did it.

Music is a constantly evolving art form, always born from the music that preceded it. The roots of Gainesville rock and roll were nourished by many musical sources, whether live or recorded—church music, folk music, African-American gospel and soul music, white gospel music, country music, blues, Top Forty hits, R&B. For a laid-back small southern town of the time, Gainesville was diverse in the extreme, bringing together people from differing cultures and varied backgrounds—intellectuals and rednecks, liberals and conservatives, racists and civil rights activists, farmers, businessmen, students, and hippies. This clash of cultural forces kept Gainesville vibrant and made for exciting and occasionally violent and chaotic times. Music was an integral part of this culture.

Chronologically this book documents the rise of the Gainesville rock band scene and the social and economic forces that helped bring forth such an abundance of musical activity. Archival research uncovered primary sources of information documenting the music groups and artists who performed in Gainesville from the early 1960s through 1976. Interviews with people who were on the scene as players or as part of the world that surrounded live music provide a personal viewpoint that helps bring to life events from a cultural period that took rock and roll and created rock music.

A welcome source of information was the collective memories of those who joined a Facebook group I created, Gainesville Rock History. This website page became a virtual community of fans and participants of the Gainesville music scene. The result has been the collective sharing of photos and ephemera such as concert advertisements, posters, and tickets, band business cards, radio station playlists, and abundant comments triggered by this sharing. Some of these postings have become part of this book.

At times there are moments in the narrative that could be considered autobiographical, as I describe my involvement or an observation at a particular time. The book is by no means a memoir, but not including my memories and involvement would decrease relevant content. My story will occasionally surface now and again, but in a way that I hope enhances rather than distracts.

This book is a history but also a love letter to Gainesville, as it was a place that encouraged and supported music, bringing plenty of wild rock and roll energy to what otherwise could have been just another small southern college town. Music made Gainesville a more interesting and exciting place to live. In retrospect, the amount of live music you could hear in Gainesville on any given week now seems remarkable: national, regional, and local bands and pop groups playing the university's many venues, indoor and outdoor, day and night; regional and local bands playing clubs, bars, concerts, fraternity parties, lounges, after-hours bottle clubs, dances in the high school gym . . . it was all going on, and it was built around the twin joys of performing music and listening to the music being performed.

The music brought pleasure to those who played it; the music sold lots of beer for the bar and club owners; and the music brought pleasure to an audience that listened, drank, danced, cheered for the bands, and had themselves what southerners call a large time.

Without the popular songs of the moment, there would be no book and nothing to write about. For this reason selected songs trending at the particular time period of the narrative are listed at the beginning of each chapter. To enhance your reading experience, these songs should be revisited, as they inspired the musicians when they were new songs and brought people into the music venues to listen, dance, and keep the musicians working. Social media sites allow virtually all these songs to be heard free of charge on demand, a major change in the music business that cannot be undone.

Several Gainesville musicians have experienced tremendous success as songwriters and musical performers and are members of the Rock and Roll Hall of Fame, an honor that is based on more than simple longevity. This fact supports the theory of Gainesville's providing a unique social and economic environment that consistently nurtured music in a way that produced not just one well-known rock music performer but rather several rock superstars over a span of years. Their stories are here.

No history is truly complete. The narrative that follows cannot be and is not the definitive history of the Gainesville music scene; it is a history of the formative years as understood through my eyes, with the intent of presenting the details of a musical culture that developed in the South and grew to be heard around the world. The stories of Gainesville's rock and roll roots are an undeniable chapter in the history of American popular music. Other books can and should be written about this time and place. I hope this is one of many.

SEE YOU LATER, ALLIGATOR

The year 1955 is described by many music historians as the year rock and roll was born. Among the many pop records released that summer were Chuck Berry's first single, "Maybellene," Little Richard's "Tutti Frutti," Fats Domino's "Ain't That a Shame," and Bill Haley and His Comets' "Rock Around the Clock," a song that spent eight weeks at the top of the *Billboard* charts and helped jumpstart the rise of rock and roll.

That same year a Gainesville musician named Tommy Durden wrote a song inspired by a newspaper article after his eye had been drawn to a *Miami Herald* photo with the headline, "Do You Know This Man?" The suicide victim, discovered in his Miami hotel room, had left the simplest of notes: "I walk a lonely street." Durden was struck with the blues-drenched image of a man walking a lonely street; the following weekend he drove to Jacksonville for a weekly performance on a local television show, where afterward he met with his occasional songwriting partner, Mae Boren Axton. Together Durden and Axton finished his half-written lyric, adding a hotel at the end of the lonely street—a Heartbreak Hotel—and recorded a demo of the tune with local vocalist Glenn Reeves. Later that month, Axton attended a disc jockey convention in Nashville and played the demo for another attendee—Elvis Presley, who was wildly enthusiastic about the song and quickly recorded it, taking care to emulate the vocal phrasing and singing style on the demo, which ironically was Reeves doing his best

Elvis imitation. Tommy Durden later said, "Elvis was even breathing in the same places that Glenn did on the dub." "Heartbreak Hotel" became Elvis's first RCA release, held the top chart position for eight weeks, and was the best-selling single of 1956.

HOME SWEET HOME

In 1955, among the thirty thousand or so citizens of Gainesville, Florida, there lived four young boys whose future involvement with music was anticipated by absolutely no one—they were children, and rock and roll was even younger than they were. Several decades later they would share a singular musical honor, but in the heart of the fifties, the only thing they shared in common was living a few miles apart from one another underneath the big hot Florida sun.

▲▼

In the northwest part of the city lived Otie and Talitha Stills and their son, Stephen, eight years old and in second grade at Sidney Lanier Elementary School. The Stills family had moved from Texas, New Orleans, and Illinois before arriving in Gainesville in the early fifties. "My father was basically one of those entrepreneur types, that would just start up stuff, make a bunch of money, then get bored," Stills recalled. "We didn't get to the beach, but we stopped in Gainesville. He thought it was the prettiest place he ever saw."

▲▼

Four blocks to the south of the Stills's house was the home of Benmont Tench Jr., his wife, Catherine, and their two children, Catherine and Benmont. In 1867, Civil War veteran Major John W. Tench of Newnan, Georgia, traveled to Gainesville to visit his wife's uncle. He found the city to his liking and moved there, where one of his sons, Benmont, had a son, Benmont Jr., in 1919, whose son Benmont Tench III was a fourth-generation Gainesville resident.

▲▼

Three miles northeast lived Benmont's future bandmate, Tommy, the four-year-old son of Earl and Katherine Petty. The Petty patriarch, William "Pulpwood" Petty (1883–1956), was originally from Way-cross, Georgia, but left the state in the early 1920s, a few years after marrying a full-blooded Cherokee Indian and determining that the locals were less than tolerant of his mixed-race marriage. He and his wife and children traveled across the border to north Florida, where in Gainesville his grandson Thomas Earl Petty was born in 1950.

Three blocks west of the Petty house lived Charles and Doris Felder with their two sons: twelve-year-old Jerry and seven-year-old Donny. Donny was a typical southern boy, often found riding his bike in the neighborhood, collecting empty two-cent Coke bottles. After cashing them in at the local drugstore, he would treat himself to an RC Cola and a MoonPie. Don's grandfather, Henry Hampton Felder, was born in 1877 and lived in North Carolina. As a boy, he had decided the state was too cold and left, riding a mule south on dirt trails through the mountains until he arrived at a midland Florida settlement called Hogtown, where he dismounted, spent the night, got up the next morning, looked at the mule, and decided, "I'm not getting back on that thing. I'm just going to live here." His son Charles was Don Felder's father. They came, and they stayed.

What brought all these folks to Gainesville in the mid-1950s?

Gainesville did. For many years, the masthead of the *Gainesville Daily Sun* included this simple motto: *We Like It Here*. It was a small, livable college town where people with diverse backgrounds came together from all across the country.

There was something comfortable about Gainesville. Ninety miles from the Georgia border and located almost exactly between the Atlantic and Gulf coasts, Gainesville was easily discovered by travelers headed south. If you were driving south on US 441 through the middle of the state, you couldn't miss it. For some visitors it was too pretty a place to forget. People liked it, and stayed.

SLEEPY TIME DOWN SOUTH

In the years that preceded the sudden growth in its live music scene, Gainesville was more conservative and relatively idyllic. Gainesville in the early sixties had a population of just over fifty thousand. The passenger train no longer ran down the middle of Main Street—that ended in 1948—but you could still catch the train down at the depot near University Avenue and NW 6th Street.

Prior to 1964, Alachua was a "dry" county, and you could buy liquor only by the drink at a restaurant. The nearest source of liquor by the bottle was Ruby's Restaurant and Package Store, just over the Marion County line, south of Gainesville.

The Soap Box Derby, sponsored by the Boys' Club, was a major annual event, as were the annual Homecoming Parade down University Avenue and Gator Growl, the largest student-run pep rally in the world. Colonel Harland Sanders, founder of the Kentucky Fried Chicken restaurant chain, was the grand marshal one year, leading the parade in his trademark white suit, waving to the crowd.

In the summer the county health department dispatched a flat-bed truck that slowly drove through neighborhoods in the evening, spraying a white mist of vaporized kerosene to control the mosquito population; kids would gleefully run through the fog and follow the truck down the street. After school, children would play outside until dark. In certain neighborhoods each mother had a handbell she would shake to signal when it was dinnertime; you knew the sound of your bell. Children often ran around barefoot. Some older kids would go frog-gigging at night and return home with a bucket of bullfrogs. Rattlesnake Creek ran through part of the city, and younger kids, including this writer, would wade through the shallow water and routinely find and collect ten-million-year-old shark teeth and fossilized shells. Deep pools in the creek held crayfish, water snakes, minnows, and softshell and snapping turtles. Dragonflies hovered about, and the unique sound of cicadas filled the air as you waded about: you were a part of the nature that surrounded you. Gainesville and nature were inseparable.

There was another less idyllic side to life in the early sixties. The Cold War was in full force; the threat of atomic bomb annihilation was always in the back of our minds; and AM radio had periodic tests of the Emergency Broadcast System, a fifteen-second high-pitched tone. Radio dials had a small triangle symbol near the low end; that was where you tuned in if there was a civic emergency: an atomic bomb certainly qualified as one. Public service announcements on television explained what to do in the event of an atomic bomb. Fall-out shelters were in vogue, and some families actually had one, buried in the back yard, a bulge in the lawn topped with a ventilation pipe and metal hatch the only sign of its presence. Communists were seen as wanting to take over the world. The Cuban Missile Crisis of 1962 brought home the fact that Soviet nuclear missiles were aimed at the United States ninety miles away from . . . Florida, the very state where we lived. Fear of the atomic bomb and Communism was a continuous presence in our lives in the late fifties and early sixties.

Like southern cities of the time, Gainesville had a black population firmly separated from whites in all social settings: segregated schools, restaurants, restrooms, and drinking fountains. The College Inn, a popular student cafeteria, displayed in its window a neon sign with a simple, direct phrase in light blue cursive: "White Only." Tradition died hard in the Deep South. There were two white movie theaters, the Florida and the State; the Rose Theater for the African-American community; and two drive-in movie theaters, the Gainesville and the Suburbia. A Saturday matinee at the Florida cost thirty-five cents, where you could watch cartoons, an episode of an adventure serial, and a feature movie such as *Hey, Let's Twist.*

Gainesville's downtown had the look of another era. Although most of the main city streets were of asphalt, much of the heart of downtown Gainesville was paved in red brick from the turn of the century. A statue of a Confederate soldier stood guard in the courthouse square. A series of horseshoes still embedded in the sidewalk across the street led the curious pedestrian around the corner to a building that was a wagon and buggy shop in the 1880s. City buses were green and white, and the fare was ten cents. Cocolas—that's what you called them, or an "I-scold-Coke"—were also a dime, candy was a penny, a pack of Juicy Fruit gum was a nickel, comic books were twelve cents, and gas was sometimes as low as a quarter a gallon. A uniformed service-station attendant would fill the tank, check the oil, wash the windshield, check and inflate the tires, then hand you a six-pack of Coke as a bonus for filling up.

Midland Florida's subtropical climate made Gainesville summers exceedingly hot and humid, with little relief even at night, and at times it rained daily, usually around 2:30 p.m., after all the rain from the previous day had evaporated upward and formed new rain clouds. Spanish moss hung languidly from the widely spread limbs of ancient live oaks. Markets and roadside stands sold watermelons for twenty cents. The Tackle Box out on Hawthorne Road sold fishing supplies and live bait and displayed uncut bamboo fishing poles and raw sugar canes stalks that you cut into serving sizes and chewed. Boiled peanuts were a popular snack. You were living in the Deep South.

Despite the languorous atmosphere, or perhaps because of it, the youth of Gainesville were always seeking an outlet for all that youthful energy. Gregg Allman describes this feeling in his memoir, *My Cross to Bear:* "back then we had so much energy, so much drive, and so much want-to." For some kids this energy, drive, and want-to became focused on playing music.

THE PEOPLE FACTOR

Much of life consists of countless interactions with other people, a multitude of daily encounters that in most cases have no long-range significance or consequence. However, when those of an artistic temperament interact with one another, a creative synergy occurs, with results bigger than the sum of their parts. Gainesville's overall cultural environment eventually became a breeding ground for musicians and rock bands during the sixties and seventies. A perennial influx of new college students every year and the exit of those graduating created a constant sense of ongoing movement and new possibilities for musical collaboration. When musicians hooked up with other musicians sharing similar interests in an environment conducive to creativity, good things would happen.

FROM *HOOTENANNY* TO *A HARD DAY'S NIGHT*

1964

"The Banana Boat Song" » Harry Belafonte

"Wipeout" » The Surfaris

"Theme from Dixie" » Duane Eddy

"The Girl from Ipanema" » Stan Getz and Astrud Gilberto

"Surfin' USA" » The Beach Boys

"Tom Dooley" » The Kingston Trio

"Blowin' in the Wind" » Peter, Paul, and Mary

"The Lonely Bull" » Herb Alpert and the Tijuana Brass

"You've Really Got a Hold on Me" » The Miracles

Near the end of the fifties, rock and roll music and culture seemed destined to become the passing fad so many adults had predicted or hoped for. Little Richard had found religion in 1957 and joined a seminary, and Elvis was drafted in 1958 and served two years in the Army. When Jerry Lee Lewis casually admitted in a British interview that same year that he would soon be marrying his thirteen-year-old third cousin (Lewis was twenty-two and had in fact already married her), the ensuing publicity caused an uproar, leading to the tour cancellation, while stateside Lewis was blacklisted from radio and was back to playing bars and small clubs.

On February 3, 1959, Buddy Holly, Ritchie Valens, and the Big Bopper (J. P. Richardson) died in a plane crash a few miles north of

Clear Lake, Iowa. Later in the year Chuck Berry was arrested for being intimate with a fourteen-year-old waitress and then transporting her across state lines, violating the Mann Act and eventually landing Berry in jail. Payola, a record label practice involving the exchange of cash for radio airplay, came under congressional scrutiny in 1959, resulting in the downfall of Alan Freed, one of America's top DJs and the man who coined the term "rock and roll."

These were the pioneers of rock and roll, and it began to look like the party was coming to an end. However, despite what Don McLean sang in his song "American Pie," the music didn't die the day Holly, Valens, and Richardson did; music simply went elsewhere for a while, mainly just about everywhere.

EVERYWHERE AT ONCE

As the fifties moved into the sixties, varied styles of musical expression rose to prominence in American popular music. The Afro-Caribbean style known as calypso was one trend, presented with great success by singer Harry Belafonte, whose 1956 album *Calypso* was the first album to sell a million copies in a year, aided no doubt by "The Banana Boat Song." Day-O!

During the early sixties, songs that instigated and sustained the popularity of various dance styles raced up the charts, including Chubby Checker's "The Twist" and "Limbo Rock," Major Lance's "The Monkey Time," and the Miracles' "Come On, Do the Jerk." Adding to the dance party was Surf music, twangy guitar instrumentals recorded by artists such as Dick Dale ("Misirlou"), the Surfaris ("Wipe-out"), and the Ventures ("Walk, Don't Run"), and vocal pop hits such as "Surfin' USA" by the Beach Boys and "Surf City" by Jan and Dean. Motown, an independent, black-owned record label out of Detroit, whose slogan was "The Sound of Young America," was beginning to sell millions of records by black artists such as Stevie Wonder and Marvin Gaye. Another musical style adding to the general pop music anarchy of the early sixties was Bossa Nova, a blend of Brazilian samba and jazz that became popular worldwide following the release

of the Stan Getz and Astrud Gilberto recording "The Girl from Ipanema" in 1964, winning a Grammy for Song of the Year and now the
second most recorded composition in pop music history after "Yes-
terday" by the Beatles.

Frank Sinatra, an artist with roots in the forties, was making best-
selling albums with Count Basie and working with a new arranger
named Quincy Jones. In 1962 a style of smooth mariachi-inspired
Latin jazz was introduced by Herb Alpert and the Tijuana Brass with
"The Lonely Bull." Movie soundtracks of Broadway musicals topped
the charts, and 1961's "Hit the Road, Jack" was the second number-
one song from a Greenville, Florida, musician named Ray Charles,
who combined blues, gospel, rhythm and blues, and jazz in a hybrid
style of his own invention called Soul.

Blues, Calypso, Twist, Surf, Soul, Motown, Bossa Nova. If it
seemed that popular music in America was all over the map during
these years, well—it was. But the most popular musical genre among
the counterculture at the time, especially on college campuses, was
folk music.

KUMBAYA

Folk music is a broad genre built of songs that were handed down
from one generation to the next over hundreds of years, transmitted
through performance, and usually with no known composer. The folk
music revival is distinct from the origins of these songs; it began in
the United States in the early fifties and had a strong presence culturally and sales-wise for around a decade. The Kingston Trio was one of
the most commercially successful groups of this genre, formed in 1957
as a calypso group and whose first album included "Tom Dooley," a
folk song that sold three million copies as a single. In 1959 the Kingston Trio had four albums in the Top Ten for five consecutive weeks, a
feat unmatched to this day. Folk music was hot.

Folk trio Peter, Paul, and Mary, Joan Baez, and the Kingston Trio
were established top sellers by 1963. And along came Bob Dylan,
whose "Blowin' in the Wind" was to be a huge hit for Peter, Paul,

The Southgate Singers: (*left to right*) Tom Laughon, Paige Pinnell, John Pierson, with unidentified woman holding albums, 1963. Permission of the University of Florida, Smathers Library Special and Area Studies Collections, University Archives.

and Mary in the summer of '63, topping the record charts and selling more than a million.

The buzzword for the folk scene was *hootenanny*, "an informal session at which folk singers and instrumentalists perform for their own enjoyment." Basically, a hootenanny was a folk music jam session that usually included audience sing-along on the chorus, such as the Kingston Trio's "Tom Dooley" or Harry Belafonte's calypso anthem "Jamaica Farewell." It was tame and pleasant musical fare, but for many adolescent teens seeking an outlet for their hormonal urges and surging youthful adrenaline, folk music was not providing what they were looking for. You could not dance to "Tom Dooley," merely sway a little and softly sing the mournful lyrics: "Hang down your head, Tom Dooley / hang down your head and cry / poor boy you're bound to die." Folk reigned. ABC's *Hootenanny* was the only new music program on television that year, broadcasting college folk concerts to eleven million viewers weekly, including one show filmed at the University of Florida that featured Johnny Cash. More than two dozen magazines about folk music were published in 1963, including *Sing Out!* and *Hootenanny*. The movie *Hootenanny Hoot* featured folk singers Judy Henske and Johnny Cash. One Cincinnati radio station went "100 percent hootenanny" and played folk music "around the clock." An album produced in 1963 of Gainesville "folk artists" featured performances by University of Florida students and faculty members and was called . . . well, you can guess what it was called.

Folk music had become the de facto protest music of society, as rock and roll had been in earlier years, yet folk lacked what rock and roll had: a driving, danceable beat. Folk music's rhythm could best be experienced through listening to Peter, Paul, and Mary's version of Dylan's "Blowin' in the Wind," a recording that also worked well as a lullaby.

Folk music was relatively easy to learn and play, requiring little more than an acoustic guitar, the ability to play a few chords, and a copy of *Sing Out!*, a popular monthly magazine featuring music articles, songs, chord charts, and lyrics.

But Gainesville and the surrounding areas in midland Florida had a musical heritage separate from this folk music revival. Any roadhouse with a dance floor and cold beer was just begging for live music, and musicians in the area were there to provide such a service. One such musician was a product of Florida's musical melting pot.

JIMMY TUTTEN

Jimmy Tutten was playing in and around Gainesville from the midfifties through the sixties. Tutten, who grew up in nearby Waldo, now owns a business named Redneck Trailer Sales in Old Town and is a veteran north-Florida musician with an appreciation of black music and culture, particularly the songs of Jimmy Reed, a popular fifties

Jimmy and the Rockets, circa 1962: (*left to right*) Jimmy Tutten, Jim Garcia, unknown, unknown. Permission of Jim L. Garcia. Reprinted from the *Independent Florida Alligator*.

rhythm and blues recording artist, whose songs have been favorites in the South throughout the years.

"The first place I did anything public was the stage at Waldo High School around 1955," Tutten recalled. "From there we put a group together and played the Recreation Center. Back then I'd written a couple songs. We played Buddy Knox, Little Richard, Fats Domino, all the things that black people came out with, that rock and roll. I liked that music. I always liked the beat of the rhythm and blues that black people had. That was my style, what got me started. Of course you couldn't play that stuff every place you played. We *did* it every place we played, but we usually had to play a lot of that other stuff with it. We had about three or four hundred songs we knew when I finally quit. It *is* a lot of songs. But people would request those songs. Basically, I'd get them off of records, play the records over and over, then you could go to the music store and buy the book that had the words in them. It didn't take long to learn a song that way."

Tutten was atypically open-minded in his musical tastes. "We played a combination of rhythm and blues, rock, and some country. I played at Bobby's Hideaway [in nearby Waldo, Florida] six nights a week. I played a place called the Blue Eagle and for a long time too. It was out in the woods. They were country-western people, and every now and then you'd have a little ruckus out back. I did most of the singing and played the guitar also. I had a Fender and a Gibson, a Fender 'pork chop' [Telecaster], and a Fender amp. I liked rhythm and blues and played blues on my guitar, a little blues and some rock. Jimmy Reed, we did just about all his stuff, 'Honest I Do' and 'Bright Lights, Big City,' songs like that. We were called *Jimmy and the Rockets*. We played up in Georgia, Daytona Beach, Ocala, at the Rancher [Gainesville farming and ranch supply store]—back in the back of it, we'd set up back there."

In the early sixties you can already hear the influence of black music on certain white musicians in north-central Florida who bypassed the traditional cultural boundaries separating the two races and who actively pursued listening and playing music alongside black musicians in the black community. Music was doing what it had done since the beginning of time: bringing people together. In Tutten's words, "I used to go to 5th Avenue and sit in with the black groups there. There was a couple places I played, sit in with black bands. I knew pretty much all the guys that played music there, and they'd tell you, 'Put your back to the wall so you can see what's going on in here. Don't turn your back on nobody in here, except us. We're OK, we'll watch out for you.' Back then when I was doing that, I had a burgundy Gibson Les Paul. That Les Paul weighed twice as much as that Fender 'pork chop.' You stand up on the bandstand three or four hours with that Gibson, and you'd know it.

"There's a lot of respect among musicians. Everybody got along real well together."

THE CONTINENTALS

Local teenager Don Felder was into the guitar playing of Chet Atkins, early rock and roll, and the blues, especially B. B. King. Felder's love of music and interest in playing guitar began in the late fifties and kicked into high gear when his father bought him his first electric guitar setup, a Fender Musicmaster and a tiny Fender Champ the size of a lunchbox, later upgraded to a Fender Deluxe amp more suitable for live performance.

Playing electric guitar became his obsession. Young Don practiced nightly after school, shutting the door of his bedroom after announcing that he was "doing his homework": playing his Sears Silvertone electric guitar un-amplified, so his parents didn't know what kind of homework he was doing. Felder soon began performing in a weekly talent contest at the State Theatre (506 W. University Ave.), preceding the Saturday kids' movie matinee of cartoon, serial adventure, and feature movie. Admission was sometimes free with six RC Cola bottle caps.

Despite the impoverished economics of the Felder household, or perhaps because of it, music was a welcome and constant aspect of family life in their small home on NW 19th Lane. Don's father, Charles Felder, worked at Kopper's, a lumber treatment facility, and after returning home every night, his one luxury was listening to music from a tape library he had amassed by recording albums borrowed from friends, primarily those of swing bands from the forties.

The Felder family also listened to weekly broadcasts on WSM Radio of *Grand Ole Opry* out of Nashville, and these sounds complemented Don's fascination with rock and roll and introduced him to the guitar artistry of Chet Atkins, a regular on the show. Don created his own tape library of songs through borrowing records by Elvis, Buddy Holly, and other dawn-of-rock-and-roll performers and recording them on one channel of his home stereo tape machine, then plugging in and recording his guitar on the other channel, teaching himself the songs by playing along. Felder soon discovered that by tape recording the song at seven and a half inches per second and playing the tape back at three and three quarters, the song dropped in pitch one octave, leaving the song in the same key but now playing at half speed, allowing Felder to figure out difficult guitar passages and solos. In addition to country music and rock and roll, Felder developed a taste for blues guitar from listening to late-night broadcasts from WLAC, a Nashville radio station that featured rhythm and blues music nightly. Both radio stations broadcast with a powerful 50,000-watt signal that could be heard in Gainesville at night and as far away as the Caribbean under proper conditions. The rich musical programming on these two Nashville radio stations, combined with their strong signals, provided inspiration for many southern musicians.

Around 1960 or 1961 a friend told Don of an upcoming local performance by a famous blues guitarist. Felder eagerly agreed to attend, despite rather vague directions as to the location of the venue. Don sat in the passenger seat of the Jeep while his friend drove beyond the city limits in search of the rural locale where B. B. King was playing that night.

"They wouldn't issue liquor licenses to clubs in 'Colored Town,'" recalls Felder, "so the promoters would hold these illegal concerts and bars outside the city limits on these farms, and I saw B. B. King play out there when I was about fourteen or fifteen, and me and the kid who stole his dad's Jeep were probably the only two white guys in the whole place."

Neither Don nor his friend had the five-dollar admission charge, so they listened and watched the performer from a window. In Felder's words, "I saw women crying and screaming 'Tell it like it is, B. B.!' and him standing there with his Gibson 335 or whatever it was he was playing, plugged into a Fender Super or a Fender Concert set on 10. Every knob was on 10 because I saw it when I walked up to the stage afterwards. And he played four sets, and between each set he'd walk back and sit in the back, which was the horse stall, with bales of hay in it. It was in a real barn. I have no idea where it was; we had to ride in this guy's Jeep through cow pastures to get there. So I walked in the back door, and there was B. B., and I introduced myself and told him I'd bought this record, and I loved his playing, and he was so nice and kind."

Felder wasn't merely a white teenager hanging out at an illegal concert venue consisting solely of African-Americans; he was a very blond, very blue-eyed white guy of Germanic ancestry; in fact, few guys around Gainesville looked whiter than Don Felder. Wasn't he frightened to be in what must have been an atypical social situation for a teenage kid? "I never had any trouble with anybody involved with that whole music scene, to tell you the truth. There were a couple African-American churches in Gainesville, and I'd go outside on Sunday and listen, and they played guitars and basses and drums; it had a much more energetic spirit in their music than going to the white church and singing the hymns."

For Felder the next step was as natural as butter on grits. Don formed his band the Continentals, and for the several years of its existence, he remained the one constant as other players came and went, including drummer Jeff Williams, a university freshman who helped the band score coveted fraternity gigs; bassist Barry Scurran, up from Miami; and sax player Lee Chipley. One brief member of this ever-changing lineup was a new kid in town who had lived in Gainesville for a while back in the 1950s. His name was Stephen Stills, and he was looking for a place to stay.

HELLO, I MUST BE GOING

The path of Stephen Stills's childhood seems to embody what scientists describe as Brownian motion: the random movement of molecules that bounce around, influenced by adjacent particles and influencing ones they encounter. The Stills family was constantly on the move as his father pursued entrepreneurial projects that varied from promoting big band artists to land development. Rather than becoming shy and withdrawn with this constant relocation, Stephen was a well-liked and highly social kid who seemed welcome wherever he went. Equally apparent were his rapidly developing musical abilities, absorbing and assimilating the various musical styles he encountered through his many travels.

After his initial few years in Gainesville in the fifties, Stills attended Saint Leo Preparatory School north of Tampa and sixth grade at Admiral Farragut Naval Academy in St. Petersburg. He returned to Gainesville briefly during the 1959/60 school year and left Gainesville in 1960 to attend H. B. Plant High School in Tampa. By 1962 Stills was back in Gainesville and enrolled at Gainesville High School as a member of the class of '63. He is pictured four times in the 1963 GHS yearbook: in his senior photo, playing bass drum in the band, in choir robes front and center in the chorus, and as one-third of a folk group named the Accidental Trio, with classmates Jeff Williams and Nancy Willingham.

Later in the school year he was summoned to Costa Rica by his father to help with a land development project, where Stills attended Colegio Lincoln in San Jose and where he received a certificate of graduation in late 1963. He returned to Gainesville from Costa Rica in the latter months of 1963 and stayed at the Williams home and then at the home of John Scarritt, another classmate. It was mutual friend Jeff Williams who introduced Stills to Don Felder, who recalled Stills as having a rebellious, independent streak and "one of the most distinctive voices I'd ever heard," and they soon began playing together in the Continentals. Stills had to borrow an electric guitar to play with the group: "I was the drummer first, but Jeff couldn't play anything. But he could keep time. And he was the one with the car and the mom that was really understanding."

During the few months that Stills and Felder were both with the Continentals, the group played fraternity gigs (Williams's older brother was a member of Sigma Alpha Epsilon), a dance at Teen Time (Richard Robinson was there: "The band were wearing those Kingston Trio shirts—short sleeves with the V tails worn outside pants"),

Accidental Trio, Gainesville High School, 1963: (*left to right*) Jeff Williams, Nancy Willingham,
Steve Stills.

the Speakeasy on NW 13th Street, the Hootenanny (later known as Dub's), and one out-of-town performance Don Felder clearly recalls: "My mom drove us out to Palatka, and we played some Little Women's dinner at night so we had to stay in a hotel, and she stayed in one room, and me and Stephen and the other two guys stayed in another room. We just piled in."

As Felder's mother slept through the night, her teenage son and his fellow band members drank from a bottle of Jack Daniels and bounced up and down on the bed until the frame broke, an event Stills recalled a dozen years later when he and Felder met at a Miami recording studio working on separate music projects.

Then one day in January of 1964, Stills left Gainesville. "He was just not there," Felder recalls. "He just showed up in town, wound up playing with us, and then vanished. Next time I heard him was his voice on 'For What It's Worth' on the radio, and I went, 'Wait, I know that voice. That sounds like Stills,' and sure enough, it was Buffalo Springfield."

John Scarritt describes Stills's departure from Gainesville: "I gave him a ride to the edge of town, where he hitchhiked to New Orleans. Stephen lived with Jeff [Williams] part time and me part time, and our mothers just loved him."

With plenty of work for bands that played danceable music, local groups such as the Continentals and others were already plugging in and rocking out. The story of another Gainesville group named the Madhatters is a perfect example of how bands would form and evolve as members came and went, with at least one or more players continuing the band identity.

THE MADHATTERS

Many local bands were comprised of University of Florida students who met in classes, dorms, or fraternities, discovered a mutual interest in music, and decided to pool their talents. The Madhatters were one such Gainesville band that played in and around town in the first few years of the sixties, and one member's recollections provide an insight regarding where they played and how they were paid. "There were four of us in the Madhatters," saxophonist Bryan Grigsby recalls. "In September 1961 we played two frats and a local music venue called the Jazz Scene. I think it was a coffeehouse left over from the 1950s, located somewhere on University Ave. We got paid $60–70 a gig that month. I auditioned for that band at a local beer juke called Cason's Grocery, a combination beer joint and grocery store located on Hawthorne Road. Alachua County was still dry in those days, and all you could get was 3.2 percent beer. In December of '61 we played at Camp Blanding. There was a World War 2–era hall there that held dances for the locals. We gradually made more, $100–200 a gig. When Gainesville and Alachua County went wet in 1964, off-campus venues opened up as the local bars were allowed to serve stronger stuff, including Tom's [214 NW 13th St.]—Trader Tom was one of the first to offer topless dancers; the Dungeon, at the corner of University Avenue and 13th Street; the Speakeasy on North 13th Street; the Locker Room, which became the Orleans Club, which became Dub's Steer Room; the University Inn, which offered fancy dining surroundings and a fancy dance floor. There were also black venues located on NW 5th Avenue, such as Mom's Kitchen. We used to jam there after hours. There was a juke out Hawthorne Road called Piero's Blue Eagle and a heavy-duty redneck juke out where Hawthorne Road crosses Cross Creek. It doubled as a fishing camp, and the sheriff's department rolled to it pretty often. Our band had a couple of other names too: the Uniques, which folded into the Playboys, which became the Big Beats, which became the Rare Breed."

The story of this naturally evolving musical ensemble continues with the arrival in Gainesville of a young musician whose last name seems too good to be true. Frank Birdsong played guitar for various bands in the mid-fifties in Kissimmee, Florida, before he enrolled at the University of Florida in 1961. "It was weird how the Playboys got started," he recalls. "I had only been on campus for about three weeks and was living in East Hall men's dorm. One night I was sitting in my dorm room playing my guitar and had the door to the room open. I started playing and humming a song and then, down the hall,

ROCKING THE WEEKEND AWAY

. . . are the Playboys – from left, Randy McDaniel, Frank Birdsong, Lin Thomas, Dick Loper, and Bill Carter. They will play in Club Rendevous tonight and in Broward for the Gator Hop Saturday night. **2-15-63**

Playboys, 1963. Reprinted from the *Independent Florida Alligator.*

I heard a saxophone start echoing what I was playing. This went on for a while until a crowd started collecting in the hall listening to us. I finally went down the hall to see who was playing and that's when I met Jerry White, who was to become our sax player. There was also a guy living on the same floor named Lin Thoms, who played the drums. It didn't take long for us to put together a little combo and start playing around at some of the dorm rec rooms just for fun. We had no name, just a combo. Another dorm resident, Mike Hollifield, could play bass guitar and so we added him to the group."

Later in the year Bill Carter enrolled at the university, and with Carter and Birdsong on guitar, a new sax player, and Randy McDaniel on bass (who didn't own a bass, so the other members chipped in and bought him one), the Playboys were formed, named after Hugh Hefner's new men's magazine. The band emulated the playboy image by dressing in black slacks and white shirts topped with an ascot.

A women's dormitory decided to have a Playboy dance with attendees dressed as Playboy bunnies, and they hired the Playboys to play. Play, boys, play! An article in the college paper ran a photo of the band happily surrounded by Playboy bunnies, and this bit of free promotion brought the group further recognition and higher performance fees, and the Playboys were one of the busiest bands on the university campus in the early sixties.

The Playboys eventually broke up as members graduated college, got married, were drafted, or were fired, and three members were put on academic suspension for flunking because of the inherent conflict of interest between studying and playing clubs until 2 a.m. Two members stayed in town and were joined by saxophonist Bryan Grigsby of the Madhatters, and guitarist Jim Garcia, who previously played with Jimmy Tutten of Jimmy and the Rockets and later with the Big Beats, becoming the house band in a club north of town named the Hootenanny. The Big Beats had also broken up, and the band's drummer, Paul McArthur, along with Garcia and Grigsby, joined the two remaining members of the now-defunct Playboys, McDaniel and Carter, to form the Rare Breed, who played around town for several years, recorded several singles, acted as a backup group in the studio and on stage for singers, and became the house band at the Orleans, the new name for the night club called the Hootenanny before it was called Dub's.

This convoluted story is typical of how it worked: bands formed, merged, broke up, fired members, and lost members, with no plan other than a love for performing music. The university brought students together, and some of these students were musicians freshly arrived in a college town that supported live music. Musical friendships were inevitable, and in a college town with thirteen thousand students, it happened over and over again.

THE BRITISH ARE COMING

Following a massive promotional campaign and plenty of hype from Ed Sullivan, on February 9, 1964, the Beatles performed five songs on the *Ed Sullivan Show* for seventy-three million viewers. The girls screamed, the guys stared, the critics howled, the parents shook their heads in puzzlement and outrage, and a large number of teenage boys were immediately fascinated with the idea that you could create such a reaction simply by playing music. And the Beatles quickly rose to become the most successful and influential pop music group of all time.

The Beatles' American television debut was a jarring experience visually and musically. Everything about the group was fresh and different: the hair, the collarless matching suits, the symmetric stage appearance with McCartney's bass guitar pointing left, Lennon's guitar pointing right, Harrison in the middle, and drummer Ringo behind and above. The overall look, the music, and their onstage chemistry combined to form a total entertainment package that had never been seen or heard before.

A glance at the Top Ten albums at the time of the Beatles' arrival provides us with the context of their American debut. In late January of '64, the best-selling album in the country was *The Singing Nun*, a record by a Belgian nun whose folk-style song "Dominique," sung entirely in French, had topped the singles chart the previous month, possibly the strangest song to ever do so. Three albums by the folk trio Peter, Paul, and Mary were in positions 2, 6, and 10. Elvis Presley, now ten years into his career, held two chart positions with the soundtrack for *Fun in Acapulco* and an album of previous hit singles. Pop vocalist Barbra Streisand and folk icon Joan Baez were also in the Top Ten, which was rounded out by the soundtrack album from the movie *West Side Story* and a record by Los Indios Tabajaras, a guitar duo from Brazil with the million-selling single "Maria Elena."

You get the picture? There was no picture; it was more of a slide show, and it was smack in the middle of this disparate collection of musical expression that the Beatles landed.

One result of their appearance on the *Ed Sullivan Show* remains a singular achievement. Here is a list of the five best-selling pop singles for January 18, 1964:

1. "There—I've Said It Again!"   Bobby Vinton
2. "Louie, Louie"   Kingsmen
3. "Popsicles, Icicles"   Murmaids
4. "Forget Him"   Bobby Rydell
5. "Surfin' Bird"   The Trashmen

Three months later, on April 4, 1964, the five best-selling pop singles were, in descending order, "Can't Buy Me Love," "Twist and Shout," "She Loves You," "I Want to Hold Your Hand," and "Please Please Me."

The Beatles had taken over the entire Top Five.

HEY, LET'S GO

The impact of the Beatles (1960–1970) on popular music and on popular culture has been well documented, and we can confidently acknowledge that the four lads from Liverpool changed rock music forever. Tom Laughon, a member of folk group the Southgate Singers and later lead singer of the Maundy Quintet, sums it up by way of example: "We all went from The Kingston Trio to being asked, 'Are you a boy or are you a girl?'"

There are few precise moments that are a tipping point in social history, and the Beatles' debut national television appearance is one of them. Locally there was a similar example of how the times, they were a changin,' as illustrated on a page of the May 1, 1964, *Florida Alligator* college newspaper. Adjacent to an advertisement for Elvis Presley's fourteenth movie, *Kissin' Cousins,* is an ad for *Muscle Beach Party,* starring former Mouseketeer Annette Funicello and former teen singing idol Frankie Avalon. Accompanying *Muscle Beach Party* is a British newsreel from December 1963, *The Beatles Come to Town.*

Elvis Presley, a surf movie with two stars from a previous musical era, and the Fab Four, all on the same page. Pop culture was about to turn a corner.

In August the Beatles released their first full-length movie to commercial and critical success. Following its release, *A Hard Day's Night* screened several times daily in Gainesville for months, and the Beatles had now sold eighty million records worldwide.

The transition from folk music to rock bands had begun, and all across America teenagers wanted electric guitars for Christmas. The massive Sears mail-order catalog offered several pages of musical instruments, and these pages became dog-eared and pored over by young future rock and rollers. If you were persistent and your parents finally gave in, there were several local music stores ready to help you out. The wheels of rock and roll were back in motion.

LONDON CALLING

"She Loves You" » The Beatles

"Glad All Over" » Dave Clark 5

"My Love" » Petula Clark

"A World without Love" » Peter and Gordon

"Don't Let Me Be Misunderstood" » The Animals

"I Had Too Much to Dream" » The Electric Prunes

"Dirty Water" » The Standells

"Wild Thing" » The Troggs

"Good Thing" » Paul Revere and the Raiders

One spring afternoon in 1964, a fourth-grade teacher at Gainesville's P. K. Yonge Laboratory School gave in to his students' pleas and allowed them to put on a classroom concert. The teacher was well aware of a recent trend in popular music that had captivated the interest of his students.

After the class returned from the cafeteria, four members of Frank McGraw's class put on Beatles wigs (from Jolly's Toyland) and stood in front of their classmates. Three held brooms as if they were guitars, with a fourth student sitting on a chair behind the trio, a pencil poised in each hand as the drummer. McGraw reached down and placed the needle of the record player on the 45 single of "She Loves You." As the song began playing, the four students sang along: "She loves you, yeah, yeah, yeah," shaking their heads wildly with each "You know you should be glad / Ooo!" At the song's final "YEAH!"

the Faux Four bowed in unison just as the real Beatles had on the *Ed Sullivan Show* a few months previously. The audience burst into applause and laughter; the band members removed their wigs and became fourth-graders again. Seemingly in an instant, the Beatles had become part of the American cultural mainstream.

What was going on here? A few months ago few Americans had heard of the band, and now their music was on center stage around the globe. The British had invaded our country, once again, but this time with music and fashions.

LOVE ME DO

A cultural phenomenon known as the British Invasion had begun. Ed Sullivan quickly responded to the unprecedented success of the Beatles' appearances on the show by rapidly presenting more English pop groups. The next group to appear was a London band named the Dave Clark 5, who performed "Glad All Over," a song that recently knocked the Beatles "I Want to Hold Your Hand" off the top of the British charts. Other English musical acts soon followed: the Rolling Stones, Freddie and the Dreamers, Gerry and the Pacemakers, the Searchers, Herman's Hermits, the Animals, Billy J. Kramer with the Dakotas, the Bachelors, Peter and Gordon.

British pop groups had absorbed various aspects of American blues, rhythm and blues, rockabilly, and rock and roll music, added contributions from their own vast musical heritage, and then sent the result to America as a hybrid of both cultures. The songs and lyrics sounded fresh to our American ears, as did the names of the groups: "Groovy Kind of Love" by the Mindbenders; "Doo Wah Diddy Diddy" by Manfred Mann.

British culture was also arriving in America through the cinematic successes of *Mary Poppins*, *My Fair Lady*, and secret agent James Bond, starring in his latest movie *Goldfinger*. British fashion became the rage—miniskirts; Oh! de London perfume; the skinny silhouette of supermodel Twiggy; long bangs, heavy eye shadow, and straight hair on women; the fashions of London's Carnaby Street; Beatle boots;

and English Leather cologne. Within the year Gainesville's southern culture was inundated with British pop groups on the radio and television and British fashions in magazines and on the clothing racks of department stores. Roger Miller's 1965 song "England Swings" hit the Top Ten with lyrics extolling all things British: "England swings like a pendulum do / Bobbies on bicycles two by two / Westminster Abbey, the Tower of Big Ben / The rosy-red cheeks of the little children."

British culture differed enough from American culture to be appealing while not being totally alien; after all, the English spoke English—more or less. In the first few years following the Beatles' arrival, many Gainesville bands did their best to emulate the British styles in music and dress, with some band members affecting a British accent.

FOLLOW THAT DREAM

Tom Petty was among the many who were transfixed by the Beatles' performance on the *Ed Sullivan Show*. As Petty commented in the documentary *Runnin' Down a Dream*, "It all became clear. This is *what* I'm gonna do, and this is *how* you do it."

Petty was already hooked on rock and roll, in part through his encounter with Elvis Presley three years earlier. Tommy's uncle Earl owned and operated Jernigan Motion Picture Service, a business whose services included filming special events, parades, and football games and providing technical support for movies produced in and around central Florida. When Mirisch Productions arrived in July of 1961 to shoot several scenes for Elvis Presley's upcoming movie *Follow That Dream,* Earl Jernigan invited his eleven-year-old nephew along to meet Presley and watch the filming.

As Petty recalled, a line of white Cadillacs pulled up to the movie site in Ocala. As car doors opened and the passengers began exiting one by one, Elvis finally stepped out, recalls Petty, "looking like nothing I'd ever seen before."

After being introduced to Elvis and receiving a brief nod from the King, Tommy watched as Presley was forced to shoot one simple scene over and over, because of the large group of fans who broke through each time the filming began of Elvis driving up to a bank building and stepping out of the car. Petty returned to Gainesville deeply impressed.

Tom's neighborhood friend Keith Harben had a sister who was an Elvis fan and had just moved out of the house, leaving behind her collection of Elvis Presley 45s. Petty traded his slingshot to Harben for the box of records.

And that was that. "The music just hypnotized me," he recalls. "The hook was in really deep. I'm in about the fifth grade, and I'm playing 1950s records, and it's all I want to talk about. Even the other kids thought it was weird. I didn't have the faintest dream of being a musician—I just loved to listen to it."

It was the early Presley recordings that got Tommy all shook up, songs such as "Heartbreak Hotel," "Jailhouse Rock," "One Night," "Hound Dog," and "Don't Be Cruel," all golden oldies by the mid-sixties.

What was a young boy to do?

C'MON, LET'S GO

The answer of course was to start a band, an idea made abundantly clear a few years later with the success of the Beatles, four guys singing and playing as a group. This group approach was sort of new as an idea. Most early rock and roll acts were singers—Roy Orbison, Chuck Berry, Elvis, Fats Domino, Little Richard. If there was a band involved, they were usually second-billed to the singer: Bill Haley and His Comets, Gene Vincent and the Blue Caps, Buddy Holly and the Crickets. A self-contained band performing their own songs and playing under a collective name such as the Beatles or the Kinks or the Who was a relative novelty as a musical entity. As Petty recalled, "the minute I saw the Beatles on the *Ed Sullivan Show*—and it's true of thousands of guys—*there* was the way out. *There* was the way to do it. You get your friends and you're a self-contained unit. And you make the music. And it looked like so much fun."

Tom Petty was only one of many Gainesville teens that watched the Beatles on television that February night in 1964, but the difference was Petty acted almost immediately. "Within twenty-four hours, everything changed. I wanted a group. I set about scouring the neighborhoods for anybody that owned instruments, that could play instruments." He located a few neighborhood kids with similar interests who gathered at his house, plugged into the one guitar amplifier, chose a song they all knew, and began to play. This sound, he recalled, was the biggest rush of his life. They were making the music.

Thus, in 1964 the Sundowners were born: Dennis Lee, drums; Richie Henson, guitar; Robert Crawford, guitar; and Tom Petty, guitar and vocals. With a repertoire of four songs—"House of the Rising Sun," "Walk, Don't Run" by the Ventures, and a couple more—the Sundowners played their first gig at a high school dance. None of the band members was old enough to drive, so Dennis Lee's mother brought the group and their gear to the school in her station wagon, waited for the end of the show, and drove them home. At later gigs they asked that she drop them off down the street so no one saw that a mom was driving them around. The band rehearsed at Tommy's house, in a backyard shed covered from floor to ceiling in carpet to deaden the sound—unsuccessfully. "The cops would come daily," Petty recalls. "From complaints. They were really nice. They'd say, 'You can play another hour, and then you're gonna have to knock it off.' This would go on every day."

Obsessed is a term mentioned by several of the musicians profiled in this book, including Petty. "We were working guys. We were either practicing or playing all the time. We were obsessed with it. *Completely.*" The Sundowners practiced constantly and immediately found work every weekend, playing fraternity gigs and high-school dances.

Petty soon switched from guitar to bass, playing a Gibson EB-2 through a Fender Tremolux amp, both bought by his father, Earl, in a rare and genuine show of support. The group wore Beatle boots bought at the local self-service shoe store, and Mrs. Lee sewed band uniforms for each member: pink collarless jackets and ruffled shirts.

Worn with tight black trousers, the Sundowners were striving to emulate the look of the first wave of British groups that appeared on television in later months, such as the Dave Clark 5 and the Kinks.

HERE COME THE LEADONS

Faculty members hired by the university occasionally arrived with families that included musicians, and they came from all regions of the country. The Leadon family is one such example. The University of Florida had hired Dr. Bernard Leadon as a professor of aerospace in early 1964, and with his arrival from San Diego, the population of Gainesville increased by eleven—Dr. Leadon, his wife, Ann, and their nine children.

Bernie Leadon was the eldest, born in 1947 in Minneapolis, where his mother played piano and demonstrated sheet music songs at a music store; Leadon recalls her as being a great "stride pianist," a style that required considerable technical skill. Yet it was country and bluegrass music that fascinated him, especially banjo, admitting he was "obsessed with it, eaten up with it."

Already musically proficient at the age of seventeen and searching for musical companionship, Bernie Leadon arrived one day at Lipham Music, the main music store in town, and asked for the name of the best local guitarist. The answer was Don Felder. Bernie called the Felder home and was told that Don was on his way home by bus from a gig in Palatka; Leadon drove to the bus depot to await Felder's arrival.

The two players became immediate friends and soon found they were both highly proficient on guitar but in differing styles. Felder played rock and roll electric guitar, and Leadon played country and bluegrass on acoustic guitar and banjo. Each taught the other what he knew, a mutually beneficial situation all around, as Felder recalls: "Bernie and I had two bands; we had the Maundy Quintet or whatever we were doing for a weekend band, and then during the week we had a bluegrass band. Bernie was a phenomenal bluegrass player; taught me how to play bluegrass flat-top and mandolin. We had three guys: Bernie, me, and this really tall guy who worked for the Florida Fish and Game Commission named Dale Crider. He played mandolin. We'd go on Monday or Tuesday night to play these little bluegrass country gigs just for fun. What little I learned about bluegrass I learned from Bernie. That was his primary and deep-rooted musical heritage and background. When we first met, he didn't even own an electric guitar, so we went down to Lipham's. He bought a Gretsch Tennessean, and I bought a Martin acoustic and eventually traded it and got another D-35. But we kind of shared our music together."

Crider recalls Leadon as "the first 5-string banjo player in shorts . . . barefooted."

PINK PANTHERS

Another recent Gainesville arrival was a high school sophomore from Bloomington, Indiana, named Sumner Wayne Hough, who practiced drums at ear-splitting volume in his music room, playing along with records of surf bands. "Boomer" Hough soon joined forces with singer Tom Laughon, whose father was pastor of the First Baptist Church, and along with bassist Willis Harrison and guitarist Sol Varron, the Pink Panthers were born, playing dances at the university and at the Woman's Club for Cotillion and Junior Assembly social functions. The band was named after the stuffed pink panther Boomer had won for his girlfriend at the state fair, and it shared the stage at all of the group's performances.

The image of a band was an important aspect of a group's overall appeal, and the current trend in the pop world was matching uniforms, so the sewing skills of yet another Gainesville mother became part of the fabric of local rock and roll history. "My mom made us pink Nehru jackets to look like Beatle jackets," Laughon recalls, "and we had white turtleneck shirts, and Beatle boots, and we looked like crap. We even wore wigs while we were letting our hair grow out."

Pink Panthers performance at Club Rendezvous, May 22, 1964. Permission of the University of Florida, Smathers Library Special and Area Studies Collections, University Archives.

BEING BRITISH

Eventually Sol Varron and Willis Harrison left the group, and Bernie Leadon, Don Felder, and bassist Barry Scurran joined Laughon and Hough to continue the Pink Panthers' gigs. With the Beatles and the British Invasion in full swing, the name Pink Panthers sounded hopelessly out of date, so the band searched for a more English-sounding name. Leadon's Catholic upbringing brought to mind Maundy Thursday, the day before Good Friday. *Maundy* did sound British but wasn't enough for a band name. Tom Laughon began scanning names of currently popular groups, and when he got to the British-sounding Sir Douglas Quintet, he suggested adding the word *quintet* to *Maundy*.

Maundy Quintet, circa 1966: (*left to right*) Bernie Leadon, Barry Scurran, Don Felder, Tom Laughon, Boomer Hough. Permission of Tom Laughon. *Above*: Most working bands had business cards.

Ironically, Texan Doug Sahn had chosen the name Sir Douglas Quintet for his group for the same reason: it sounded British. Other American bands that chose British names included the Buckinghams and the Beau Brummels. Being English was suddenly where it was at.

The Maundy Quintet played the current popular songs and other favorites, focusing on the Top Forty hits that blared from radio speakers across the nation. The band learned songs by the Beatles, the Zombies, Lovin' Spoonful, Booker T. and the M.G.'s, the Animals—whatever was danceable and on the pop charts or had once been on the charts and was familiar to both band and audience. When the group added local teen whiz-kid David Mason on organ, making them a six-piece band, they kept the Maundy Quintet name, explaining that you got a bonus when you hired the Maundy Quintet—a free sixth member.

With "Maundy Quintet" boldly painted in Old English script on the sides of the band van, parked daily in the Gainesville High School parking lot as Boomer attended classes, the group presented themselves as a possibly English group without actually claiming they were. What was never in doubt was the band's musical skills.

HAIR TONIGHT, GONE TOMORROW MORNING

In Gainesville in the mid-sixties, it was almost impossible to wear your hair below your ears while still in high school. "That was the craziest part of the Maundy Quintet," Boomer Hough remembers. "Bernie was at GHS, I was at GHS, but you couldn't have long hair and go to school, so we wore wigs on stage; we went to May Cohen's [department store] in Jacksonville and bought some wigs and wore them. And Bernie was trying to grow his hair out long, and he got thrown out of GHS because of his hair, and that made the front page of the *Gainesville Sun*. Then we started using this stuff on our hair, Dippity-Do. We'd grease our hair back so that we could grow it out long. As long as it didn't go over your ears, you were allowed to go to high school at GHS. So we would start to grow our hair out to some degree and put this stuff in our hair to keep it so it wouldn't go over our ears."

Another musician who owned a wig for the same reasons was Jim Lenahan, who in junior high played drums for the Diplomats, then the Road Runners, followed by the World Shattering Agents and the Certain Amount. Lenahan had been performing since the age of five, singing on local radio shows and on the Glenn Reeves television show in Jacksonville, the same Glenn Reeves who ten years earlier had sung the original demo to "Heartbreak Hotel." When the Certain Amount disbanded for the summer as two members left town on student break, Lenahan and keyboard player Trantham Whitley wanted to keep playing and hooked up for the summer with the Sundowners, who had a regular gig out at nearby Keystone Heights on the pier. Sundowner Tom Petty had already met Lenahan through a common bond: "I met him in high school, and he had long hair, and he was one of the five or six guys in town with long hair, so you would kind of group together so that you wouldn't get your ass kicked. Because there was the real danger of rednecks beating the shit out of you." Petty had somehow convinced the high school administration that his own long hair was a job requirement for playing rock music, and they agreed, although getting harassed by certain students for having long hair continued.

Playing an out-of-town gig was a step up for any band, even if it was just a few miles away in Keystone Heights. Regional bands in Florida played a much wider area of the state, and when they came to Gainesville, local musicians took notice.

Ron and the Starfires was one such band, based in Auburndale, 120 miles to the south. The band played frequently in Gainesville, averaging twenty gigs in town each year during the mid-sixties, mostly at fraternities. Lenahan remembers them as a white soul band playing mostly rhythm and blues, with a set list that included songs by Jimmy Reed, James Brown, Ray Charles, and other black artists, as well as songs by Jerry Lee Lewis and Lonnie Mack, eventually adding songs made popular by the British Invasion. By every account they were an excellent live band. "Petty and I went to see Ron and the Starfires at the Gainesville American Legion Hall in 1965," Lenahan recalls, "and sat right in front of the stage. We were awestruck at how good they were and kept talking about it all through the set. When they took a break, Tom and I were walking out, and Ron and lead guitarist Carl Chambers stopped us and wanted to kick our asses. They thought we were laughing at them during the set. I assured them that we thought they were the best band we'd ever heard, and we became fast friends after that."

INTOLERANCE

The presence of the University of Florida was one of several factors that made Gainesville a liberal oasis in a conservative state, but even still, the city population included those who were extremely conservative. With roads from nearby rural towns such as Archer, Newberry, Hawthorne, Waldo, and Williston all converging in Gainesville, there was often quite a mix of people routinely in town, farmers and professors and businessmen, whites and blacks, young and old, the highly educated along with the barely literate. Along with this convergence came variously expressed hostile attitudes toward race, hair length, and fashion choices. Stated more directly: there were some intolerant people in Gainesville and the surrounding areas who expressed their disapproval with physical violence. *Redneck* was not a term applied to every rural Floridian, just to the violence-prone and actively intolerant among them.

It was hard to tell whom rednecks hated more: African-Americans because of their color, or white males who had long hair. It appeared that the latter drove rednecks the most crazy. Everybody knew that being African-American was not a choice, but growing your hair long was. "Ain't you a cute girl" was the least of what you'd hear. The routine went roughly like this: you were insulted to your face as a "sissy," a "girl," or a "queer," instant fighting words to a redneck, and when you didn't respond with an offer to fight, you were perceived as weak or afraid, emboldening them even more. And so it went. One

GHS graduate now in the Rock and Roll Hall of Fame recalled being grabbed by one of the high school varsity football players and hung upside down by his heels from the second-story school walkway because of his long hair. Based on this action and the relentless threats from other students to "kick his ass after school," he carried a tear gas pen with him for protection.

This was no joke. In certain areas of Gainesville up through the mid-seventies, you showed up with long hair at your own peril. You were careful where you went around town. This oppressive atmosphere inadvertently created a strong bond among long-haired musicians and encouraged an instant sense of community.

But despite the constant threat of harassment, hair continued to grow, and Gainesville bands continued to form and find employment. Bands were playing all around town at fraternities, bars, college dances, roadside lounges, teen dances, and gym sock hops: the Druids, the Playboys, the 5 of Us, the Birdwatchers, the Casanovas, the Henchmen, the Limits of Persuasion, the Epics, the U.S. Males, the Centurys, and regional acts such as Leesburg's the Nation Rocking Shadows and Ron and the Starfires.

PLUG ME IN

Bands needed musical equipment to perform: electric guitars, bass guitars, drum sets, an organ or electric piano, and microphones and speaker cabinets and a sound system for vocals. Gainesville's music stores were only too happy to oblige. The Beatles indirectly helped sell millions of dollars' worth of musical equipment through inspiring the creation of bands that wanted the same brand and model instruments and amplifiers as those used by the Fab Four.

Lillian's Music Store (112 SE 1st St.) in the heart of downtown was the oldest music store in Gainesville, a small mom-and-pop business with a genteel clientele of piano teachers and students, stocked with sheet music and a few acoustic guitars, a piano or two, and glass-paneled wooden counters displaying the usual assortment of metronomes, tuning forks, and Marine Band harmonicas. Lillian's was where you might go to buy a spare guitar string or a graded piano instruction book, but that was about it.

West of downtown at 1226 W. University Avenue was Marvin Kay's Music Center, a small annex of the main music store in Jacksonville. Nestled in a row of small storefronts that are still there today, Marvin Kay's sold electric guitars, amplifiers, drums, and related musical gear for the rock musician. Located a few blocks east of 13th Street—the name of US 441 as it ran through the city—Marvin Kay's was a convenient stop for out-of-town bands, and with the university campus just a block away, the store catered to the nearby student population.

But the place to be, the store where most Gainesville musicians eventually found themselves hanging out, was Lipham Music.

TALK TO BUSTER

Lipham Music eventually became known as the social hub for most every rock and roll musician in Gainesville and midland Florida, a music store located at 1004 N. Main Street, in the south corner of the Gainesville Shopping Center, a business where at various times three current Rock and Roll Hall of Fame members worked behind the counter: Tommy, Don, and Bernie.

Buster Lipham was born in El Paso, Texas. In the early fifties the family moved to Midland, Texas, where his father, T. V. (Theron Velford), worked at Wimple Music. Sent by the store's owner to a music trade show in Chicago, T. V. met C. Asbury Gridley, a dapper man with a pencil-thin moustache, who dressed like a Hollywood actor and who owned several Gridley's music stores in the South, including one in Gainesville, Florida. Gridley was looking for someone to manage and eventually purchase the stores. T. V. agreed to manage them, and the Lipham family soon relocated from Texas to Tallahassee, Florida.

Keeping track of five stores in two states kept T. V. Lipham constantly on the road, accompanied by young Buster, but he was soon given an ultimatum by Mrs. Lipham: choose one store or find a new wife. With marriage intact, the Liphams moved to Gainesville in

1954, where Gridley Music (1025 W. University Ave.) prospered; by 1960, he had moved to the larger space in the new Gainesville Shopping Center and after a year or so renamed the store Lipham Music.

As a longtime dealer in the major music brands and with generous floor space for the latest music gear, Lipham Music was perfectly positioned for what happened four years later: a vast demand for musical gear triggered by the bands of the British Invasion and the Beatles' global success.

"That was a beautiful time," Buster recalls in 2012, as he glances through photos of the showroom floor from the mid-sixties. "The Beatles made rock and roll happen for everybody. Everybody was going to be a star. We had more garage bands than you could shake a stick at. We sold Farfisa Combo Compact Deluxe organs, Hofner basses, and Rickenbacker guitars like crazy. It was 1967 when Tom Petty was working for us . . . everybody hung out at the store on Saturdays."

Buster was a warm, personable, energetic, and shrewd businessman intent on expanding the store to meet the explosive demand for rock and roll musical equipment. Having grown up in Gainesville, Buster was a part of the local community and comfortable in dealing with the wide variety of clientele of different ages, backgrounds, and musical interests who patronized the store. Certain aspects of his approach to business enabled many young players to get their hands on top musical instruments and begin playing in bands and earning money. Lipham was an enabler of rock and roll in the best sense of the word.

It was simpler time with a level of trust unimaginable today. The music store offered credit terms to teenagers, and with a small down payment you could go home with musical gear, and generally speaking, you had a year to pay it off.

The weekly visits to make payments brought you to the store often, and while you were there, you would meet and hear other musicians as they tried out guitars and amps, developing an informal sense of community among players. Drummer Stan Lynch recalls

Lipham Music guitar rack, late sixties. Permission of Buster Lipham.

that the weekly payment amount wasn't specified; you paid what you could, and the amount would be duly noted on a card along with the date of payment.

A teenager walking around Lipham's was akin to a kid in a candy store, gazing up at the very same brands and models of musical instruments played by the Beatles and the Rolling Stones and the Kinks, hanging on the wall behind the counter by the dozens: new Fender, Rickenbacker, Mosrite, and Gibson electric guitars and Martin acoustic guitars. On a shelf overhead were stacks of drum sets: Ludwig and Gretsch and Rogers and Slingerland. On the showroom floor were rows of amplifiers by Fender, Gibson, Sunn, Standell, and Kustom, a brand whose over-the-top metallic-sparkle tuck-and-roll Naugahyde covering was reminiscent of custom hot-rod upholstery.

The back half of the store was a piano and organ showroom run by T. V., and Buster gradually took over the rock band side of the business as his father concentrated on piano and organ sales, later moving that part of the business across the street in a separate location, opening up even more floor space.

The musical gear came in and soon went out, every guitar amplifier emblazoned with a Lipham Music logo on the grille cloth, a promotional gimmick similar to the license plate frames automobile dealers included on each new car. A band onstage became an advertisement for the music store. Buster took promotion a step further. "I had a deal with bands. I said if you buy your equipment from me, and you have a band van or trailer, I'll pay to have it lettered with your band name, as long as I can add, 'Equipped by Lipham's.'" By Buster's count he had seventeen bands driving around Florida and the southeast with the store name on the van.

Lipham Music supplied the tools of the trade to a thriving band scene, and although it was undoubtedly a for-profit enterprise, the store provided much more than merchandise and is inseparable from the story of Gainesville's rock and roll roots. The musicians and the store served one another; players met other players there, heard other players there, and lusted after the same shiny new guitars that hung behind the counter saying, "hold me . . . try me . . . buy me!" The store made money. The music scene had a place you could hang out.

IT WON'T BE LONG

The year 1964 was a very good year for the Beatles. With a song at the top of the U.S. record charts when they arrived in February for their television appearances, four short months later the Beatles had every reason to feel fine with the release of their first full-length movie, *A Hard Day's Night,* which consisted of following the Beatles around London as they went about the business of being the Beatles, including several staged performances of the band playing songs from the soundtrack album. The movie also introduced a new aspect of the band: they were funny lads, with none of the posh mannerisms of the British upper class, and each member had a distinct personality. The Beatles were the real thing and were charting their own individual path through the pop music marketplace. And they made it look so simple: two guitars, bass, and drums. Sing and play.

With the Beatles showing what was possible, everything was in place for Gainesville teens if they wanted to start or join a band. You decided on the name—which was better, Sound Dimension or the Kensington Squires?—you worked on the band image, learned songs, and, of primal importance, learned to play guitar or bass or drums or how to sing. You learned this by copying the records as closely as possible, or you asked someone who knew how to play the song to show you the chords. And there were so many songs to choose from.

The architecture of the basic rock band—drums, bass, guitar, and vocals—became the musical foundation of countless hit records in the years that followed, and this basic instrument lineup continues to this day. Additional layers of sound were available: 12-string acoustic or electric guitar, saxophone and trumpet, orchestral enhancements (strings), sitars, organs, and pianos and other keyboard instruments added texture and variety, but underneath it all was the foundation of drums and bass and electric guitar. Bob Dylan brought this rock band sound to his "Like a Rolling Stone" in the summer of 1965, alienating his folk audience while scoring a number-two single (just below the Beatles' "Help") and attracting a large new audience all at once.

In the two years following the Beatles' appearance on Ed Sullivan, British music groups and acts were a dominating presence in the airwaves in both radio and television. Along with these British sounds was a quickly evolving American pop music scene with its own rich variety: black Motown acts such as the Supremes, Stevie Wonder, the Four Tops; white pop groups such as the Beach Boys, the Young Rascals, the Four Seasons; psychedelic pop by the Electric Prunes; and the garage-band sounds of the Standells' "Dirty Water." A bold new world of sound was coming from home as well as from across the Atlantic.

All during this heady time Gainesville was, as usual, teeming with teenagers and college students who listened to the AM radio and bought singles and albums down at the Record Bar or Top Tunes or at variety stores like G. C. Murphy or Woolworth. You could dance to these songs, and bands who learned them could get work at the fraternities, teen centers, recreation centers, and parties, maybe even at the grand opening of the new Sears in the Gainesville Mall. For musicians there were plenty of places around town you could play. Go ahead—start a band or join one. Bring your dad along to Lipham Music, have him talk to Buster, and maybe you could leave the store with a new set of Ludwig Hollywood drums identical to Ringo Starr's kit, eventually paid off through the money you earned playing at Westside Recreation Center or at the Place or the Woman's Club.

There was a lot to like about being in a band. Making money indoors at night was a lot more fun than making money outdoors during the day, delivering papers or mowing lawns, especially in the summer. To the bored and frustrated teenager, there didn't seem to be a downside to learning to play guitar or drums or bass, forming a band, and then getting paid to play cool songs.

There wasn't a downside. All around Gainesville and all across the country, rock bands began to form.

PEOPLE GOT TO BE FREE

1967–1968

"Light My Fire," "Hello, I Love You" » The Doors

"Kind of a Drag," "Mercy, Mercy, Mercy" » The Buckinghams

"For What It's Worth" » Buffalo Springfield

"Ruby Tuesday" » The Rolling Stones

"Incense and Peppermints" » Strawberry Alarm Clock

"Hello, Goodbye," "Hey Jude" » The Beatles

"Purple Haze," "Foxy Lady" » Jimi Hendrix

"2's Better Than 3," "I'm Not Alone" » Maundy Quintet

"The Little Black Egg" » The Nightcrawlers

"What a Man" » Linda Lyndell

"Time" » The Tropics

"Get Together" » The Youngbloods

"Born to Be Wild," "Magic Carpet Ride" » Steppenwolf

"(Sittin' On) The Dock of the Bay" » Otis Redding

The British Invasion of the American record charts included not only the pop groups mentioned but also solo artists such as Tom Jones ("It's Not Unusual"), Petula Clark ("Downtown"), Dusty Springfield ("Son of a Preacher Man"), and Lulu ("To Sir, With Love"). The initial influx of music from England, triggered by the success of the Beatles, lasted about two years before the American record charts were again dominated by American acts, including new rock groups with eccentric and sometimes flat-out comical names such as the Box Tops, the Cyrkle, the Left Banke, the Turtles, Count Five, the Electric Prunes, and Strawberry Alarm Clock. It was all a bit zany and a clear indication that what you listened to was different from the music appreciated by your parents. They listened to the Vogues' "Turn Around, Look at Me," and you listened to the Human Beinz' "Nobody But Me," with its opening lyric of thirty "no's," and there was no mistaking one musical style for the other.

Pop and rock music was straying into new territory. The Beatles had been carefully packaged by manager Brian Epstein as a wholesome pop group, singing songs about being in love ("P.S. I Love You"), losing love ("Don't Bother Me"), giving love ("All My Loving"), and the clearly stated desire to hold hands in "I Want to Hold Your Hand." Ed Sullivan played it safe through his booking of the Dave Clark 5 ("Glad All Over"), Gerry and the Pacemakers ("Ferry Cross the Mersey"), and the Searchers ("Sugar and Spice"). But then songs expressing a wider range of feelings came along, in the form of the Kinks' "You Really Got Me," described by some rock critics as the first "hard rock" song, and the Rolling Stones' "(I Can't Get No) Satisfaction," hardly reassuring words for the parents of a teenage girl. The innocence of the Beatles' "I want to hold your hand" was replaced by the Rolling Stones' blunt suggestion "Let's spend the night together," a lyric that Ed Sullivan requested be changed to "Let's spend some time together" for the group's television appearance. Mick Jagger initially refused but finally agreed, on camera rolling his eyes with each chorus. He knew the Rolling Stones' appearance on the *Ed Sullivan Show* was instant nationwide exposure, and Ed knew it too. There was no bigger weekly show on television.

With the British Invasion firmly ensconced in the American cultural mainstream, another cultural force was rising up, but this time from within. This force had a lasting effect on music, fashion, and politics: the hippie.

Gainesville was rather cosmopolitan for a small college town, in large part because of the presence of the University of Florida and its large and diverse student body and faculty, and because Gainesville was a pleasant, affordable place to live for those of artistic temperament. True to the adage that birds of a feather flock together, the presence of artistic types attracted those of similar nature, and an arts culture began to develop. Although geographically tucked away in the deepest part of the South, Gainesville was far from being isolated from current cultural trends: the adults, students, and young people of Gainesville read the newspapers, listened to the radio, watched network television, and were as aware as anyone in the country of the new youth movement growing in San Francisco, more specifically in Berkeley.

GET TOGETHER

A Human Be-In gathering at Golden Gate Park on January 14, 1967, was billed as "A Gathering of the Tribes." Attendees were asked to bring "flowers, feathers, incense, candles, banners, flags." Twenty thousand people showed up, and speakers included LSD advocate Timothy Leary and the Beat poets Allen Ginsberg, Lawrence Ferling-hetti, and Gary Snyder. Local San Francisco bands performed, including Jefferson Airplane, Santana, Steve Miller Band, the Grateful Dead, and Quicksilver Messenger Service. An added bonus was the widespread availability of "Owsley Acid," provided by Owsley Stanley, the first private individual to manufacture vast quantities of LSD and whose product was well known in the Bay area for both purity and consistency. The people gathered and danced, faces were painted, bands played, bubbles and minds were blown, and self-appointed guru Leary advised the stoned crowd to "turn on, tune in, and drop out."

The Be-In was influential as a prototype for rock music festivals of the sixties, and the event's large attendance confirmed the existence of a growing hippie counterculture. Gatherings known collectively as the Summer of Love occurred later in the year, when young people on summer vacation descended on the Haight-Ashbury section of San Francisco and other major cities and created a sense of community through their shared antiestablishment views and an evolving fashion sense that brought them together as a separate culture while alienating mainstream society, including the government and most parents.

A growing disconnection between the Baby Boomer kids (those born between 1946 and 1964) and their parents had been dubbed the Generation Gap. "Don't trust anyone over thirty" became a half-serious slogan among young people seeking a different approach to living from that of their parents. One mode of expressing this difference was by embracing the hippie lifestyle. But what was the ethos of this new social being?

The values of your standard-issue hippie were hard to quantify, but there were overarching themes, often summarized in bumper-sticker slogans on the back of a VW bus. A belief in nonviolence ("War Is Not Healthy for Children and Other Living Things"), peace and love ("Make Love, Not War"), freedom of personal expression in speech, dress, and grooming; political and social equality for all races, sexes, and sexual orientations; a rejection of the Cold War mentality of Us versus Them ("One Planet, One People, Please"); organized resistance against the Vietnam War ("Hell No, We Won't Go"); exploration of communal living from communes to group housing; alternate experiential viewpoints as expressed by writers such as Carlos Castaneda (*The Teachings of Don Juan: A Yaqui Way of Knowledge*); alternate architectural concepts such as Buckminster Fuller's geodesic dome; living in harmony with nature; experimenting with psychedelic drugs and marijuana; sexual freedom through nontraditional relationships; a rejection of materialism; and a sense of tribalism—to name just a few. To paraphrase the opening song of the 1968 Broadway musical *Hair,* this was the dawning of the Age of Aquarius, and peace will guide the planets, and love will steer the stars. Many of those who participated in the hippie culture of the sixties were sincere in the belief that the world would soon become a better place if and when everyone realized that love was better than hate, and peace was better than war. Details on how to convince others of these beliefs were sketchy. Although this was naiveté in the extreme, what was wrong with promoting these ideas rather than the opposite?

A subset of the hippie culture was the Jesus Freak, a devoutly religious hippie whose goal was to convince you to confirm Jesus Christ as your personal savior, preferably right now and on the spot. This involved admitting that you were a sinner and that Jesus Christ was the Son of God and died for your sins. Getting someone to agree to these two statements was the Jesus Freak's mission, and they diligently worked the rock festivals and other counterculture gatherings. It was a tough crowd because most hippies were there to get high and engage in sinful behavior with other like-minded souls. There was serious competition from the Hare Krishna people, who shaved their heads, wore orange robes, and chanted and danced in public, accompanied by finger cymbals. It was a wild, wild West of religious belief.

Gainesville's relatively liberal atmosphere and a rising student activism helped create a large, very loosely organized hippie community in town, easily identified by their hair, clothing, and lifestyle. For several years a downtown shop called the Roman Sole offered leather goods and custom sandal designs, made by a craftsman who wore sandals and a beard and went by the name of Jesus. No one in Gainesville knew his real name.

Rent and food were cheap, and living arrangements were casual. An area behind Mac's Waffle Shop at 912 West University Avenue was known as the hippie "ghetto," and other cheap housing was available just north of campus. Finding a place to live could be as easy as going to the Krispy Kreme doughnut shop and asking if anyone had a place to stay, as Melanie Barr recalls during a 1970 visit: "I walked in with two guys too, yet the first person we asked said we could stay at his apartment. It got a little scary since a few hours after we were there, someone said the cops were outside, and in a panic some green things were flushed down the toilet. It turned out to be a false alarm!"

By 1968 Gainesville was the site of civil rights demonstrations and student-led antiwar protests, and the city had been named "The Berkeley of the South" by University of Florida professor Marshall Jones. Doran Oster, a twenty-one-year-old folk musician who lived in Gainesville at the time, remembers that feeling: "I think everybody back then, or at least people my age, felt like the government was either trying to draft you and get you killed or trying to arrest you for drug use to put you away for many years. And our relationship with the government was very tenuous."

As the turbulent world of late-sixties political activism began to unfold, rock groups continued as a mainstay of entertainment, and many local and regional bands stayed busy playing all around the Sunshine State and beyond. One of these bands was the Maundy Quintet.

THE MAUNDY QUINTET

The Maundy Quintet is a significant band in the story of Gainesville's rock and roll roots if only for the fact that guitarists Don Felder and Bernie Leadon eventually became members of the Eagles. But there was more to the band than that. Beyond the overall excellence of the Maundy Quintet's musicianship and live performance, the band was a self-contained business entity, and a closer look reveals how most aspects of the music business were being covered from within the group.

First, Don Felder and Bernie Leadon were brilliant musicians, and that talent made it easier to get work. Felder was adept at learning songs very quickly, duplicating the original guitar parts on records, and showing up at rehearsals with a song already figured out before the rest of the band had learned it—an invaluable skill for anyone making their living playing in a cover band. Leadon exhibited formidable skill as an instrumentalist and as a songwriter, quickly writing the two tunes the band was to record for their single. Boomer Hough was a drummer well versed in the latest pop styles through listening to the radio and records and playing along on drums. While still a senior at GHS, Boomer was hired as a disc jockey and was on the air from 3 to 4 p.m. daily after school at WUWU, one of the Top Forty AM radio stations in town. He recalls the first record he played was "Somebody to Love" by Jefferson Airplane. Boomer's simultaneous role as band member and radio personality raised awareness of the Maundy Quintet and increased his status around town, and with this increased standing among teens Boomer was soon promoted to hosting the coveted afternoon drive program. "They moved the station to the new Gainesville Mall," Boomer recalls, "and that's where it really took off because the Gainesville Mall was the biggest thing in Gainesville, and [station owner] Leon Mims had put this radio station right in the mall for everybody to walk by and actually watch you broadcast. It was great. I remember interviewing the Beach Boys, Graham Nash of the Hollies, and Buddy Ebsen, who was there to perform at Gator Growl. The crowd around that window in the Gainesville Mall was huge, and it went all the way across the mall to Kinney Shoes. I was the one that got to interview all these people because of the popularity of my afternoon drive shift." In other words, Boomer was the local star interviewing the national and international stars.

Maundy Quintet bassist Barry Scurran had moved to Gainesville from Miami to attend college, and as social director of his fraternity and eventually president, Scurran was well positioned to book the group at fraternities in town and in Tallahassee, and then throughout the state and in the Atlanta area.

Tom Laughon had begun singing at an early age, first with his family at home and later in talent shows in the family group at church camps, and eventually as a member of local folk music groups Tryon and then the Southgate Singers. "The harmony singing, that was the base mark of the Maundy Quintet," he recalled. "I don't know if it was from the church, or that we were in folk groups. Barry could always go up to a high falsetto; I was lead singer but basically in that baritone range; Felder sang lower than me. The band did four-part harmonies. And that's what set us apart."

Since the band insisted on excellence in all areas, top quality musical gear was part of the band image, and the Maundy Quintet had seen another band that had the right stuff. "Our equipment went from hodge-podge at first to Fender stuff. We had Fender Showman amps. There was a group called the Nation Rocking Shadows; they were the band that had amazing equipment, and that influenced our guys. They all wanted the best. All I wanted was the best sound system. We each had our own microphone on stage. Even Boomer would sing one or two Ringo songs. We spared no expense. Fender guitars— Don and Bernie both had three guitars each; Don had Gibson Les

★ THE NATION ROCKING SHADOWS....
LEESBURG....WHAT CAN WE SAY ABOUT THE
SHADOWS THAT YOU DON'T ALREADY KNOW.

The Nation Rocking Shadows and their wall of Fender equipment.

Pauls. Don was really into jazz riffs. He also liked a lot of hollow body guitars."

During the summer of 1968, the band played Ondine's, a celebrity nightspot in New York City, where bands such as the Doors and Buffalo Springfield had appeared. Playing a New York City club was an eye-opener for this top Florida cover band that was making up to one thousand dollars a night performing songs as close to the original recording as possible. "Before we came to New York, we were doing covers," Laughon recalls. "We were on the circuit, playing the fraternities in town, and Barry would get us gigs down in Miami at the World, a club with four stages. We'd play with the Byrds, the Turtles, pretty good bands. We were getting some good bucks. But when we went up to play Ondine's, the bands there weren't playing what all the bands were playing in Florida. They were doing original stuff, or would do an amazing interpretation of a Beatles song. And that's when Barry,

Bernie, and Don said, 'Man, we gotta get some original stuff.' That's when we came back and really started interpreting songs differently, and when Bernie and Don said we needed to record a single. Bernie wrote '2's Better Than 3' and 'I'm Not Alone' very quickly; it really wasn't a collaborative thing. He worked with Felder on both of them for a very short time—Don helped him with some of the riffs—and a week later we did the two songs live, and then we went down to H&H Productions in Tampa and recorded them. They came out on a 'vanity' label called Paris Tower, so there was no label promotion of the record."

Felder recalls the sessions and the resultant increase in prestige of a band with their own record: "There was a guy named Jim Mueller, one of the leading local disc jockeys at night, and we would go out there and play live on the radio, and Jim would run a two-track and record it, and then every night that we weren't there, he'd say, 'Oh, and here's the local Gainesville band, the Maundy Quintet' and play '2's Better Than 3' over the air, and finally we started getting enough response and action so we said we need to make this into a record, and that's when we went down to Tampa and literally recorded everything live except the background vocals. I think the lead vocal was live—it may have been an overdub—and we ordered and pressed five hundred copies ourselves. It wasn't a legitimate record deal with a record company; it was a guy that had a studio and a lathe that could cut master discs for pressing records, and we just paid him a few hundred bucks to make this record for us. And then we sold them at gigs and went around to record stations ourselves and did interviews and got them to play our records, and Boomer was a huge asset for that because he was working at WUWU."

Having their own record provided a huge boost for the band's local and regional status as well as their performance fee. "2's Better Than 3" was the most popular record for several weeks on the Gainesville radio station charts in 1967.

Listening to the two songs today provides the expected wave of nostalgia but also evidence of the high quality of Bernie Leadon's songwriting and Don Felder's arranging and guitar skills. The band had a distinct sound with a British undercurrent enhanced by an English-inflected vocal sound and harmony, especially the harmonies on "2's Better Than 3," and Leadon's brief banjo solo on "I'm Not Alone" predates his banjo work on the Eagles' "Take It Easy" by five years. Both these recordings sound fresh more than forty years later and are an example of what Gainesville cover bands could do when they put their minds to it. There seemed to be a lot of potential lurking in some of these garage bands playing around town.

HELL NO, WE WON'T GO

Meanwhile, the outside world was intruding on this burgeoning rock and roll culture, and it wasn't all peace and love. For American males eighteen years or older in 1967, the outside world included the likelihood of being drafted into the army and sent to Vietnam. Bernie Leadon was certainly more interested in holding a guitar than a gun. "I had a six-month draft deferment when I was nineteen, and the lady who was the head of the local draft board called up my mom cold, right out of the phone book, and said, 'Your son is going to be classified 1-A next month, but I happen to know there are vacancies at the Army Reserve Center [National Guard], and if I were you, I'd consider sending him over there.'"

Leadon agreed and signed up. "I left on Valentine's Day 1967 and went to Ft. Benning, Georgia, for basic training. When I came back, I was ready to leave town to seek [my] fame and fortune."

Leadon eventually found both. Following his arrival in Gainesville in '64, several of his friends living in San Diego had moved up to Los Angeles, including Chris Hillman, who was currently playing bass in the Byrds, a popular rock group that had released six singles. Their latest hit was the presciently titled "So You Want to Be a Rock 'n' Roll Star." Soon after Leadon's return from basic training in the late summer of '67, he received offers from two bands to move to Los Angeles, "bands that had record deals with members that had left, and they were going to make a second record. I decided to join the one on Capitol Records [Hearts and Flowers] because that was the label of the Beatles, the Beach Boys, and the Kingston Trio. The same producer who helped us make our record worked with Linda Ronstadt, so I played on Linda Ronstadt records. Pretty soon I was touring with her, making more money with her than I was with my little band. I changed bands every year the first four years I was out there. I worked with Ronstadt, with Dillard and Clark, and that led to the Flying Burrito Brothers with Chris Hillman, what a lot of people called the first country-rock band."

POP FESTIVAL

The year 1967 continued to be a year of rapid change in popular culture. In June the Monterey Pop Festival was held in California and thus began the establishment of outdoor pop music festivals that continue to this day. Among the acts that performed onstage at Monterey were Jefferson Airplane, the Who, Janis Joplin, Buffalo Springfield, the Mamas and the Papas, and the Jimi Hendrix Experience, whose leader's flamboyant stage act and revolutionary guitar playing brought the group instant acclaim.

The songs on Hendrix's debut album, *Are You Experienced,* were studied carefully by guitarists around Gainesville, who, in learning them, quickly realized that trying to copy Jimi Hendrix's guitar solos on "Purple Haze" and "Foxy Lady" was another thing altogether compared to playing three-chord rock songs such as "Mustang Sally" or "Good Lovin'." How did Hendrix get those sounds? And where did he get those clothes?

One aspect of his sound aside from his virtuoso technique was his use of Marshall guitar amplifiers and effects pedals such as the Arbiter Fuzz-Face and the Uni-Vibe. You could buy all this music gear at Lipham Music. As for clothes, they certainly weren't available at Stag 'n' Drag or the Young American shop on University Avenue; you probably had to get them in New York City or London. But that became unnecessary after a local store opened that offered the fashions and lifestyle accessories of the new counterculture. The store was named the Subterranean Circus.

SUBTERRANEAN CIRCUS

In the fall of 1967, Bill Killeen stood in front of a vacant warehouse at 10 SW 7th Street and contemplated his recent decision. Killeen's arrival in town is the story of a new Gainesville resident with an entrepreneurial spirit who saw opportunity in the thriving youth culture of the city. His timing couldn't have been better.

Originally from Lawrence, Massachusetts, Killeen was the editor and publisher of the *Charlatan,* a college humor magazine he had started in the early sixties while a student at Oklahoma State University. After moving to Austin, Texas, he continued publishing, eventually relocating in Tallahassee, another college town. Monthly visits to Gainesville to sell copies of the latest *Charlatan* on campus led him to solicit local ads. "I realized that Gainesville was the place with the most advertising potential, and it had a bigger and hipper student body than Florida State University, so I moved down here in 1965." *Charlatan* eventually became the number-one college humor magazine in the country, published from 1963 to 1967. One issue included a discreet nude photo of his girlfriend, Pamme Brewer, who happened to be a student at the University of Florida at the time, resulting in her suspension as a student and a subsequent controversy that brought national attention to the magazine, the university administration, and Bill Killeen, who was happy to trade verbal barbs with the school administration through his letters to the editor in the *Florida Alligator.*

With seed money from the recently defunct magazine, Killeen rented the 7th Street location for seventy-five dollars a month. He then flew with friends to New York City to buy stock for the store in Greenwich Village, returning with hundreds of posters, buttons, pins, clothing, smoking accessories, and other hippie boutique items.

The Subterranean Circus was an immediate success, a tribute to Killeen's awareness of current social trends and the vast untapped market in Gainesville for all things counterculture. If you lived in Gainesville and had an *Easy Rider* movie poster on your wall, and if you wore bell-bottoms, a peace-sign button, and sandalwood beads, chances are you bought them all at the Sub Circus.

Dozens of posters printed in bright fluorescent ink glowed under ultraviolet lighting on the walls of a back room, creating an unforgettable visual effect for first-time viewers. The front counter offered a wide selection of incense, water pipes, roach clips, more than a dozen brands of rolling papers (from six-cent packs of Zig-Zag Wheat Straw to the premium Rizla rice paper at sixty cents, reserved for the wealthy hippie), and handcrafted leather goods made by local artisan Dick North, who offered items such as leather sandals, carry bags, belts, brass peace signs on leather thongs, and other accessories. A display board on the counter held novelty buttons with various mottoes: "Turn on, Tune in, Drop Out"; "Draft Beer, Not Students"; "Stamp out Reality"; "Ban the Bra." A magazine rack near the entrance offered the latest underground comic books such as Robert Crumb's Zap Comix and Gilbert Shelton's Fabulous Furry Freak Brothers, along with alternative periodicals unavailable anywhere else in town, such as *Rolling Stone, Crawdaddy,* Paul Krassner's the *Realist,* and the *Village Voice.*

In a southern college town where clothing ran more toward the preppy styles at Stag 'n' Drag and Donegan's or casual wear from Sears or J. C. Penney, the Sub Circus offered the latest styles available in Haight-Ashbury in San Francisco or New York's Greenwich Village, including the definitive hippie fashion statement, bell-bottom jeans. "We sold bell-bottoms when no other stores knew they existed," Killeen says. "One salesman sold fifty pair the first day he worked for us. Then there was Nehru shirts and Cossack shirts. We sold so many we couldn't stay supplied and eventually hired eighteen women to make them, under Pamme's direction."

Killeen bought the adjacent building and opened Silver City for clothing and fashion accessories, featuring a long curved stairway built by Ron Blair, a local musician and a skilled carpenter. The Sub Circus and Silver City became Gainesville's one-stop destination for hippie accoutrements (and were in business until 1990, when the buildings were razed and the property became a hospital parking lot).

For a small southern town to have such a store in 1967, during the early years of the hippie counterculture, was an example of Gainesville's acceptance and support of new social trends and newly opened businesses. The Sub Circus was known by most patrons as a "head shop" that sold everything you needed to smoke marijuana except the marijuana. Killeen preferred the term "boutique." Business boomed.

The soundtrack accompanying this rapidly evolving cultural hubbub was the phenomenal amount of pop music being produced on both sides of the Atlantic. The young musicians of Gainesville were busy doing their part to contribute to this banquet of sound, and the first step in almost every case was playing these songs in a cover band.

RODNEY, TOM, RICKY, DICKIE, AND TOM

By late 1967 Tom Petty had left the Sundowners and was playing bass as a member of the Epics with drummer Dickie Underwood and the two Rucker brothers, Rodney on vocals and Ricky on rhythm guitar.

Guitarist Tom Leadon, a younger brother of Bernie, joined the band a year after Petty. In Leadon's words, "Rodney came by with my brother Chris and invited me over to the rehearsal at Petty's, so I went over there and listened, and they took a break, and I was showing Ricky how to play "Feel a Whole Lot Better," by the Byrds, that Bernie had showed me. We were sitting outside in the side yard. I was just there listening and showing them a song, but the introduction had been made. The next day I walked back there and knocked on his door, and I remember being a little nervous because I didn't hardly talk to Petty at the rehearsal, but he came to the door and asked me in, and we just sat and talked, and basically I went over there practically every day after that for about three or four years. We were pretty much inseparable.

"I started hanging around with the Epics and would work the lights for them and after a couple months they asked me to join, and Tom told me later he was pushing for that. He felt he needed a good musician, someone who could really play guitar, and I was only fourteen. The Ruckers were like eighteen, nineteen years old, but I knew more about guitar than they did, and when I joined the band, I was figuring out the records and showing everybody the chords and notes. Why else would they hire a fourteen-year-old player? So that's how I met Petty." The Leadon and Petty households were a few blocks apart, so Leadon walked to rehearsals.

The band played extensively around central Florida, driving in a van to gigs and occasionally staying overnight at hotels. The Rucker brothers were older than Tommy and by all accounts were your basic wild-eyed southern boys. "That's where I kind of grew up, in the Epics, watching these guys," Petty remembers. "They were nuts, just *nuts*. Just completely bonko, wild, partying, drunk. They were just crazy. But they had a really good drummer. Dickie Underwood. The guy just played the most *solid* beat. He could just keep time all day long. He just played great. I loved playing with him."

The Epics: (*left to right*) Tom Petty, Rodney Rucker, Dickie Underwood, Ricky Rucker, Tom Leadon.

LIPHAM MUSIC COMPANY,
in the Gainesville Shopping Center,
specializes in outfitting top
area bands. The Taxmen, the Epics,
and the Maundy Quintet chose
their guitars from such names as
Gibson, Fender, and Gretch.
They chose from a large
stock of Sure microphones and
Kustom sound cabinets. If
your band is just getting started,
or if your're an established
band in need of new equipment,
come in, look over, and
try out the equipment at **LIPHAM'S.**

Gainesville High School 1967 yearbook ad for Lipham Music. The Taxmen: David Mason, organ; Jim Forsman, drums; Dean Lowry, guitar; Larry Lipham, bass. The Epics: (*left to right*) Rodney Rucker, Tom Petty, Dickie Underwood, Ricky Rucker. Maundy Quintet: (*clockwise from top*) Bernie Leadon, guitar; Don Felder, guitar; Barry Scurran, bass; Tom Laughon, vocals; Boomer Hough, drums.

Jim Lenahan was between bands, as out-of-work musicians often described themselves, when Ricky Rucker asked him to join the Epics as lead singer, although Rucker put it more bluntly. "I was partying with Tom and the guys all the time. At one of these parties Ricky informed me that I had just joined the band, and if I didn't like it, he would kick my ass. I had no doubt that he could do it too, but I wanted to join anyway. That was how I replaced Rodney as vocalist."

"Mudcrutch grew out of the Epics," Lenahan recalls. "Ricky got the idea for the name 'Mudcrutch,' and they changed it, keeping the same lineup. Eventually they got pissed off at Rodney for missing too many rehearsals. He was always going off hunting. They finally told him it was either hunting or the band. He said, 'No problem. Hunting!' Then Dickie quit the band and joined the army, and Ricky got a job teaching. Suddenly the lineup was Tom Petty, Tom Leadon, and me. We needed a drummer, but we also wanted to play, so we worked up some folk/country tunes and played one drummerless gig at a coffee shop in town called the Bent Card. That country element, which was very much Bernie Leadon's influence, continued in Mudcrutch after we found [drummer] Randall Marsh and [guitarist] Mike Campbell."

The Bent Card was sort of a time warp, a coffeehouse modeled after the early sixties folk music venues of Greenwich Village and located in a church building across from the college campus. The decor was Vintage Beatnik, with wooden spools for tables, a bass fiddle leaning against a wall in the corner, a small stage, and a casual atmosphere. The name referred to the warning on an IBM computer punch card not to "fold, spindle, or mutilate."

The great process of natural selection was clearly in motion. Some members of a band remained members until something more interesting came along—a girlfriend, a job, the chance to shoot a deer—while other members thought of little else besides playing music. A number of Gainesville musicians had already made the commitment to play music, period. There was no plan B for Don Felder, Stephen Stills, Tom Petty, or Bernie Leadon.

ELECTRIC NIGHTS DOWN SOUTH

In 1968 change was in the air, politically, culturally, and musically as the pop music revolution continued with new sounds and new sights. The university presented cultural and musical events funded by various entertainment budgets and open to the public throughout the school year. Up until 1967 the Lyceum Council, staffed by university administrators and faculty with student representatives, chose the musical artists who performed the one or two major concerts per quarter or trimester, with the final decision made by faculty. Most students, however, were not interested in the soft sounds of

Mantovani, Al Hirt, Glenn Yarborough, or the Brothers Four, all of whom had appeared in previous years. In the summer of 1967 Student Government Productions took over from the Lyceum Council in choosing and presenting music acts at the University of Florida, eliminating faculty input and control.

This shift in campus government was instrumental in bringing popular rock and pop acts to campus. In 1968, the university presented the Hollies, Ray Charles, Ian and Sylvia, the Fifth Dimension, Dion, the Four Tops, and Peter, Paul, and Mary. A dance billed as a "Freak-Out" at the Reitz Union ballroom featured two local acts, City Steve (a five-piece psychedelic band that included my older brother Jeff on guitar) and Gingerbread, a group with Don Felder on guitar, Chuck Newcomb (formerly of the Jades) on bass and vocals, and drummer Mike Barnett and organist and woodwind player John Winter, two former members of an Ocala band called the Incidentals. Strobe lights and loud live music were combined in an attempt to recreate a psychedelic drug trip, a concert trend that had begun in San Francisco at Fillmore West concerts.

A writer for the *Florida Alligator* college newspaper was clearly unimpressed as well as unclear as to the names of the two groups: "For those of us who had the fortitude to attend the Men's Interhall Council dance Saturday night, let me congratulate you for going. Of course, the dance was the worst 'Freak-Out' the campus has yet seen. If any real hippies from San Francisco had bothered to show up, the hippie movement might have ended last Saturday night. The main problem was the music. Aside from the fact that 'City Steve and his Gingerbread Men' [sic] made vague attempts at making music, they would have done well to play charades."

While the counterculture was taking root, clearly not all young students endorsed the hippie lifestyle and values. This was still the Deep South, and in a college town with nineteen thousand enrolled students at the University of Florida, not everyone was buying in to the Age of Aquarius.

THE MUSIC GOES ROUND AND ROUND

In 1968 there was plenty of live music in town. Local bands included Styrophoam Soule, the Rare Breed, the Epics, the Brothers Grymm, the Wrong Numbers, Airemont Classic, U.S. Males, and the Centurys. Regional bands such as Tampa's the Tropics and the Split Ends from St. Petersburg played clubs and fraternities. James Brown brought his soul revue to Citizens Field. John Fred and his Playboy Band, a Louisiana-based group with a chart-topping single, "Judy in Disguise (With Glasses)," the title a spoof on the Beatles' "Lucy in the Sky (With Diamonds)," played at the Place (811 W. Univ. Ave.), a teens-only club that had opened the previous year in the former Rebel Lanes bowling alley. Also playing at the Place was Noah's Ark, a regional group that included drummer Bobby Caldwell, later with Johnny Winter and Captain Beyond. Ian and Sylvia, the Four Tops, and the Fifth Dimension all played the Florida Gym. The Bent Card coffeehouse presented folk groups the In-Keepers and the Relatively Straight String Band.

The biggest show of the year, however, was on April 10 at Florida Field with the Beach Boys, Strawberry Alarm Clock, and Buffalo Springfield, whose band members included Neil Young and a twenty-three-year-old Stephen Stills, who after hitchhiking out of town four years earlier had returned to Gainesville with his own rock band and performed the Stills-penned Top Ten single "For What It's Worth."

It was not much of a homecoming, he recalled in a 2001 interview: "I wore a green Pierre Cardin suit, and a paisley scarf as a tie. I was very much the 'British pop star.' Most people didn't know that I was there, and nobody paid any attention, and there was no review. Nobody cared. It was a Beach Boys show. I think some of my running buds were in Vietnam, and a couple more were off in other colleges, or had moved away. But I was a townie."

A month later Bernie Leadon arrived in nearby White Springs to perform at the Florida Folk Festival, as noted in the 1968 program: "Bernie Leadon, who was raised in Gainesville, is bringing his group 'Hearts and Flowers' all the way from California. The group is made up of Bernie who plays banjo, guitar, mandolin and dobro; Larry Murray, Waycross, Ga., the lead singer and David Dawson, Honolulu, Hawaii, plays Appalachian autoharp. They have two Capitol records out now."

North-central Florida is far from Southern California, where Stills and Leadon were both living at the time, yet both musicians returned to Florida and performed at large musical events as a normal aspect of their careers, another example of the region's deep musical culture.

Less than a month after Buffalo Springfield performed at Florida Field, the band broke up, with a farewell live performance at Long Beach Arena on May 5, but in the ensuing years Stills and Young would repeatedly cross musical paths. Bernie's group Hearts and Flowers also broke up the same year—bands tended to break up— and he soon joined musical forces with Doug Dillard and Gene Clark to record *The Fantastic Expedition of Dillard & Clark*, with Leadon co-writing six of the nine songs on the album. Meanwhile, Tom Petty was beginning to write songs for his band the Epics, a group that would eventually evolve into Mudcrutch.

NOT SO BLACK AND WHITE

Rock and roll's roots were nurtured in a varied musical soil that included country music and rhythm and blues. Chuck Berry's first single, "Maybellene" (originally "Mabellene"), was essentially a rewrite of an old country fiddle tune called "Ida Red." Berry, who practically invented rock and roll guitar playing, loved country music, as did Ray Charles, whose 1959 hit "What'd I Say" was a hybrid of Latin, rock and roll, and rhythm and blues styles and had a profound effect on the Beatles early in their career, as they performed the song during their months in Hamburg. Midland Florida was a distinctly rural area, and country music was very popular. Even if your tastes ran toward rock or Motown, you could often hear a Buck Owens or George Jones tune wafting from the radio of the pickup truck next to you at a red light. Drop your car off for repair, and the radio behind the service counter might be tuned to WDVH, the local country music station. Bernie

Leadon was a bluegrass and country flatpicker fanatic; his bandmate Don Felder listened to blues and jazz guitarists as well as the current pop hit parade. Music, to a musician, was simply music, an inclusive art form. Certain songs could be labeled country, blues, or gospel, but there were as many that were hybrids of all three.

Gainesville had a large black population culturally and geographically separated from whites and in several distinct neighborhoods. The Porter's Quarters neighborhood was created in 1884 by Dr. Watson Porter, a white Canadian doctor who sold the land exclusively to blacks. With the train depot located nearby, many early residents worked for the railroad and nearby businesses. In the southwest area of town and bordered by Depot Avenue, sw 4th Avenue, South Main Street, and sw 6th Street, Porter's Quarters was home to many black-owned businesses.

Despite the separation of the races, music brought blacks and whites together, beginning with the discovery by white musicians that they could play with black musicians on the so-called other side of the tracks and, generally speaking, were welcomed.

The majority of this cross-cultural musical collaboration occurred on NW 5th Avenue between 6th Street and 13th Street, another primarily African-American neighborhood. "Where the music was, was around 5th Avenue," recalls musician Charles Steadham. "It was at Mom's Kitchen, Sarah's Place, and Red's Two-Spot." Originally named Seminary Avenue, NW 5th Avenue was located in the heart of Gainesville and was the business and social hub of Gainesville's African-American community.

Mom's Kitchen, a restaurant at 1008 NW 5th Avenue, offered live music on occasion, and directly across the street from Mom's Kitchen was a club called Red's Two-Spot that also presented black musical acts. Charles Steadham recalls playing there at various times with the Georgia Soul Twisters, Lavell Kamma and His 100-Hour Counts, and Weston Prim and Blacklash. A culinary highlight of the neighborhood was Y. T. Parker's Barbecue at 1214 NW 5th Avenue. Parker served barbecued pork, beef, and goat and was renowned for his dozen or so hot sauces that ranged from mild to Super Saber Jet.

The Allegros: (*left to right*) Dave Jackson, vocals; Harold Fethe, guitar; Bobby McKnight, Hammond B3; Frank (last name unknown), alto saxophone. Courtesy of Harold Fethe.

Sarah McKnight owned a business variously named through the years Sarah's Place, Sarah's Restaurant, and Sarah's Sandwich Shop at 732 NW 5th Avenue, a trolley-car diner and lunch counter with a wood-frame building attached to one side that served as a nightclub-styled music venue that served beer and presented blues, rhythm and blues, and jazz every Tuesday, Thursday, Friday, and Saturday. Harold Fethe, a white college student, often sat in on guitar with the all-black house band at Sarah's. The drums and Hammond B3 organ were permanent fixtures, and the house drummer Walter "Fat Papa" Hill was by all accounts a supremely funky player and equally known for his astounding "mouth-trombone" solos. Fethe recalls, "It was a predominantly African-American audience and band, playing soul top-40 repertoire. I learned about Sarah's from band mates in my fraternity-circuit rock band. Hung out at Sarah's for a year or so, got invited to play one night, got the job offer, and quit the frat-rock band. Not that we used names much, but I believe Sarah [McKnight] and her husband Bobby called the rear room The Allegro Lounge and the band The Allegros. I played there from '64 through '66, blues,

R&B, some funky jazz, usually chosen by a series of drop-in singers or the house organist. We played 'Mercy, Mercy, Mercy,' 'Summertime,' 'Georgia,' 'A Change Is Gonna Come,' songs with an emotional message or a danceable pulse or both. I remember Lee Dorsey's 'Workin' in a Coal Mine' and Nat Adderley's 'Blue Concept' were my favorites on the juke box."

Fethe was one of several white musicians who were drawn to black rhythm and blues and black music in general. Jimmy Tutten was also a white musician who played the 5th Avenue area, as was Linda Rowland, a white singer who while growing up in Gainesville attended both white and black churches.

Rowland eventually began singing in a local band called the Mark IVs that included saxophonist Charles Steadham, a white musician with a similar passion for black music. Linda changed her stage name to Linda Lyndell, Charles Steadham became Charlie Blade, and they both began playing extensively around the South, primarily as the only white members of all-black rhythm and blues acts. Charlie went one step further to virtually reinvent himself as a light-skinned or mixed-race African-American, dyeing his hair and goatee jet black and straightening it in a "process," wearing sunglasses at all times, and taking on the cultural mannerisms of an African-American saxophone player in a rhythm and blues band. Lyndell so impressed local audiences with her soulful singing that Gainesville businessman and club owner Wayne "Dub" Thomas took an interest in her career and financed some demonstration recordings. The producer of these demo tapes brought Linda to Memphis to record for Stax Records, where she released two singles, the second one, "What a Man," reaching number fifty in the *Billboard* rhythm and blues charts.

This unlikely career achievement, being white and having a hit on Stax Records, was marred by racism: Lyndell was an attractive white woman who had embraced African-American culture both professionally and socially. With the attention she got from the press—a white woman who sings with soul—she received death threats from white supremacist groups such as the Ku Klux Klan and retired from performing soon after. One listen to "What a Man" makes it obvious

Linda Lyndell, circa 1966. From the collection of Charles Steadham.

that she had the voice to make it as a soul singer. Blade continued his role as a white musician playing in black rhythm and blues acts. By 1969 he had assembled a Gainesville band called the Midnight Playboys, featuring vocalist Weston Prim. The band was renamed Weston Prim and Blacklash and played for years in and around Gainesville at black venues such as the Cunningham's Country Club and the Village Gate and at the university. "Linda did a television show with us on WUFT-TV," recalls Steadham, "because we were an integrated band.

It evolved from when integrated bands were not in demand to when they were. It was a time of transition. But again, the music was ahead of the general public." Lyndell and Steadham continued working together, often the only white players in black bands. "Linda and I used to commute from Gainesville to South Florida to play on some weekdays and on weekends. During the week she had to be back at work in Gainesville at eight in the morning, and I had to be in class at UF. We would commute to Ft. Lauderdale to play with this band, Lavell Kamma and the 100-Hour Counts, leave there at three in the morning, and I'd drive ninety miles an hour on the turnpike and get Linda back to work just in time—thankfully there was no traffic at that time of night."

Soul bands, as black rhythm and blues acts were sometimes called, were very popular at Gainesville's fraternity parties because you could really *dance* to the songs. One regional group from Chapel Hill, North Carolina, was a particular favorite in Gainesville and other college towns: Doug Clark and the Hot Nuts. Geared for the college crowd, they specialized in bawdy party tunes just this side of obscene. Singer Doug Clark's signature tune was "Hot Nuts," with a chorus that consisted of "Hot nuts, hot nuts / Get 'em from the peanut man. / Hot nuts, hot nuts / Get 'em any way you can," followed by Clark's apparently endless supply of risqué couplets along the lines of "See the girl dressed in green? / She goes down like a submarine" or "See that guy from Florida State? / That's where they teach you to masturbate." They often dressed outrageously; one New Year's Eve gig they performed in pink jockstraps and transparent raincoats. At the stroke of midnight, they removed the raincoats. The group played Dub's and the Rathskeller in Gainesville many times.

Meanwhile, the line between black and white music was being blurred with groups such as Sly and the Family Stone ("Dance to the Music"), Booker T. and the M.G.'s ("Green Onions"), and later with the Allman Brothers Band, all three groups with a mixed-race lineup. Society may have drawn racial boundaries, but apparently music was not willing to cooperate.

CLUB DELISA

SAT. JULY 30

3317 Bennington Rd.

9:00 P.M. 'til 1:00 A.M.

ADMISSION $2.00

1966

LAVELL KAMMA
"MR. KNOCKOUT"

LINDA LYNDELL
THE NEW QUEEN OF ROCK 'N ROLL

The DYNAMITES
CY HIGHTOWER *Plus* TED JOHNSON

THE COUNTS
100 HOURS
6 PIECE
ORCHESTRA

Concert poster, 1966, Club Delisa, Houston, Texas. From the collection of Charles Steadham.

You simply could not determine a musician's color solely through the sound of their musical expression, especially in the South. Anyone listening to Wilson Pickett's vocals on "Land of 1,000 Dances" would rightfully assume that Wilson Pickett was black—he was—and based on the feel and sound of the music behind his vocals, one would reasonably assume that his exceedingly funky backing band was also black—but they weren't. Of the nine musicians backing Pickett on the song on May 11, 1966, seven were white boys with an astonishing facility for playing soul music, members of the FAME Recording Studio rhythm section, down in the Muscle Shoals area of Alabama, white guys who played with a black feel. Or was it simply playing with feeling?

It was commonly known among Gainesville bands that to play fraternities, your set list would be enhanced by songs such as Eddie Floyd's "Knock on Wood," Pickett's "Mustang Sally" and "Land of 1000 Dances," "I Feel Good" by James Brown, and if you really wanted to get down and stay there, "Tighten Up" by Archie Bell and the Drells or "Walking the Dog" by Rufus Thomas, among the dozens of rhythm and blues classics to choose from. There was a strong presence of black music just below the surface in the Gainesville music scene that white players absorbed both directly, by learning songs by black performers, and indirectly just through living in a town in the Deep South with a large African-American population that, while segregated, resided near the center of town rather than in an outer district. Gainesville had soul.

Although white players with a love and a feel for black musical styles were generally welcomed at black musical venues, black musicians could not necessarily show up at white venues expecting a similar level of acceptance. Gene Middleton was a black singer who performed occasionally at Dub's, backed by the Rare Breed, the (white) house band, whose sax player Bryan Grigsby recalled how "Middleton was allowed to sit with us between sets, but he had to come in the back door."

There were exceptions. Bobby Griffin, a black musician, played piano at the upscale dining room of the University Inn, a motel that allowed black and interracial dining groups. Owner Nat Pozin, whose social attitudes were not the norm, could not purchase a house in the adjacent Kirkwood neighborhood because it was a "restricted" community—no Jews allowed. Gainesville was a relatively liberal town, but there was still prejudice to spare against Jews, hippies, blacks. You could take your pick.

I CAN HEAR MUSIC

1969–1970

"Aquarius/Let the Sunshine In" » The 5th Dimension

"Crimson and Clover" » Tommy James and the Shondells

"Get Back," "Come Together" » The Beatles

"Honky Tonk Woman" » Rolling Stones

"Everyday People" » Sly and the Family Stone

"Proud Mary," "Born on the Bayou," "Bad Moon Rising," "Green River," "Travelin' Band" »
Creedence Clearwater Revival

"In-a-Gadda-Da-Vida" » Iron Butterfly

"Mama Told Me Not to Come" » Three Dog Night

"All Right Now" » Free

"Evil Ways" » Santana

"Ride Captain Ride" » Blues Image

Songs! The entire Gainesville music scene was built around songs: Top Forty songs on the radio, songs on albums, original songs performed on stage by bands and other musical ensembles. The late sixties was a golden age of rock and pop music and the rise of the rock band as a musical entity.

As the counterculture marched for equal rights and against the war in Vietnam, a sonic revolution was occurring in the recording studio and on the concert stage. New sounds were being created through multitrack recording techniques, and record producers such as Phil Spector and George Martin became integral parts of the creative process. Musicians expanded their sonic palette by experimenting with the sounds of sitar, and through sound-modifying electronic effects such as the wah-wah pedal, fuzz tone, and the Echoplex tape-delay unit, as well as a variety of new electronic keyboard instruments and synthesizers.

The sound of every musical instrument contributed toward the overall sound of a performance or recording, and bands were beginning to expand beyond the core of drums, bass, and a couple guitars. Keyboards were a common addition to this core instrumental lineup, but it wasn't just "organ" on a specific song; it was a Vox Continental on the Doors' "Light My Fire" and Sir Douglas Quintet's "She's About a Mover"; it was a Hammond B3 on "Green Onions" by Booker T. and the M.G.'s, and a Farfisa organ on Sam the Sham and the Pharaohs' "Wooly Bully" and the Swingin' Medallions' "Double Shot (Of My Baby's Love)." Keyboard manufacturers recognized the new market for instruments beyond the traditional large home consoles and began offering portable organs specifically designed for easy transportation and live stage use. There were new sounds emanating from the electronic sound labs at universities, involving combinations of tone oscillators and filters and envelope generators: synthetic music made purely through electronic means.

A pioneer in this new field of electronic sound synthesis was Robert Moog, inventor of the first widely used music synthesizers. By 1970 Moog had designed and manufactured the Minimoog, an affordable and portable monophonic synthesizer model suitable for onstage use that was such a new concept in both design and sound that the company was having trouble convincing music dealers it was a musical instrument. A Moog sales representative named David Van Koevering said he'd try, and his first stop was Gainesville, Florida, and Lipham Music. "I go to Buster Lipham," Van Koevering recalled, "and he laughs at me. He says, 'You want me to sell that thing? Show me how to do a violin, show me how to do a flute.' And he said, 'If you can prove to me that musicians will do this, you come back . . . and I'll sell them.'" Bob Turner, a musician who worked at the store, saw the potential and encouraged Buster to stock the instrument. He eventually

Buster Lipham and Robert Moog, circa 1970. Permission of Buster Lipham.

did, and the synthesizer became an immense success. Lipham Music was the first retail outlet in the United States to sell the Minimoog.

Musicians and producers alike experimented with new instruments such as the synthesizer and also through creative approaches in the recording process. "Crimson and Clover" by Tommy James and the Shondells is one such example, a song that reached number one in the United States and six other countries. The instrumental track includes a guitar played through an amplifier with a tremolo circuit, an effect that can be described as turning the volume up and down very quickly, in this case in time with the song's tempo. In the studio, someone got the idea of plugging a microphone into a guitar amp as James sang, "Crimson and clover, over and over" over and over. Anyone who had heard this song in late 1968 can recall the singular sound of that vocal: [pronounce this exactly as written for maximum effect] "Crim-m-m-m-son-n-n and clo-o-o-o-ver-er-er-er, oh-oh-oh-oh-ver-er-er and oh-oh-ver-er-er-er-er-er." Singers in cover bands would duplicate this effect using just their voice when performing the song onstage. It was hilarious.

SOUNDS UNLIMITED

Although we now take for granted the basic lineup of a rock band, in the late sixties the band as a distinct musical entity was new, compared to the traditional pop recording session consisting of a vocalist backed by hired session musicians playing an arranger's music charts. The goal of a rock band was to produce a singular musical expression comprised of the collective musical talents and personalities of each band member. In the late sixties bands were becoming a rising presence on the record charts, and the successful ones had a distinctive sound they retained from record to record. The Byrds' vocal harmonies along with the electric twelve-string guitar style of Roger McGuinn were integral to the Byrds' musical identity; records by the Kinks were identifiable through Ray Davies's vocal sound and brother Dave's massive "power chord" guitar riffs; the overall sound of Creedence Clearwater Revival's music arrangements and John Fogerty's vocals were unique to the band. Bands were artistic entities bigger than the sum of their parts. The good bands sounded like no other.

SOUTHEAST POP MUSIC CONTEST

Having already presented live music in the parking lot of Lipham Music just for the fun of it on occasion, in the summer of 1969 Buster Lipham concocted an event that was either a showcase of regional musical talent or simply brilliant self-promotion. It was probably both and led to a memorable musical performance by a newly formed band out of Macon, Georgia. "We'd been having bands playing out in the Lipham's parking lot," Buster recalled, describing the occasional weekend events that promoted both band and store simultaneously, "so we came up with the idea of why not just have a contest. We called it the Southeast Pop Music Contest.

"We had three divisions—B, A, and AA: an entry level, just kids getting started; and then we had the guys who were playing, but hadn't made any kind of a circuit; and then we had the guys who

THE ALLMAN BROS. BAND
GENERAL ACCOUNT

5010

64-1137
612

DATE _March 22, 19 70_

PAY TO THE ORDER OF _Lipham Music Company_ $_200 00_

Two Hundred and 00/100 _____ DOLLARS

the PEOPLES BANK
MACON, GEORGIA

THE ALLMAN BROS. BAND
GENERAL ACCOUNT

FOR _Eighth Weekly Payment_ _Duane Allman_

⑆06 12⑈ 1137⑆ 0 11 248 8⑇ ⑈00000 20000⑉

Check payable to Lipham Music signed by Duane Allman. Various band members signed these weekly checks. Permission of Jack Weston.

were playing around pretty well. And we had a six weeks' elimination series of shows."

The winners got more than a trophy. "Gibson gave a Les Paul and a bass away; Fender gave amplifiers and a Stratocaster away; Sunn gave amplifiers away; Strobodelic gave strobe lights away; and remember, this was in 1969; I was given thirty-five thousand dollars' wholesale worth of merchandise to give away. All the vendors were very supportive of the event and the concept. Things were really rolling back then."

The final round of performances took place in the Gainesville High School auditorium, 1900 NW 13th Street, during the last few days of August 1969, over Labor Day weekend. Nestled among the finalists such as Noah's Ark and Frosted Glass was a group from Macon that had been playing together since early May: the Allman Brothers Band.

Brothers Duane and Gregg Allman were born in Nashville but had grown up in Daytona Beach. As members of the Allman Joys in the mid-sixties, they played Gainesville fraternities and the American Legion Hall. The Allman Brothers Band was now signed to Phil Walden's Capricorn Records, had just recorded their debut album, and was on a short tour in support of its upcoming release. When the band agreed to compete in the contest, they had still been an unsigned act and were now disqualified because of their record contract. They played the contest most likely as a favor to Buster, with whom the band had developed both a business and a personal relationship. Most of the band's stage gear and guitars had recently been stolen, and Buster Lipham had advanced the band thirteen thousand dollars' worth of instruments, guitar amplifiers, and accessories. Secured by nothing more than a handshake, the loan was repaid through weekly checks written to Lipham Music by various band members a couple hundred dollars at a time. Thus began a long-term friendship between the Allman Brothers Band and Buster Lipham.

LIVE AT THE . . . GHS GYM

When the Allman Brothers Band hit the stage as the last act to perform, it was immediately apparent this was not just another rock band. (I was present and will attest that the performance embodied a level of musicianship far above that of any other group.) The overall effect of the six-member band was that of a single musical entity performing songs that combined dual-guitar interplay with passages of free-flowing jazz-like improvisation over a rhythm section of organ, two drummers, and a bassist. Their first song, "Mountain Jam," was an instrumental based on Donovan's "There Is a Mountain," and when Duane Allman stood at the front of the stage for his slide guitar solo on the song, we could see Allman playing well beyond the highest fret of the guitar neck with perfect intonation; how did he do that? The band then played the first two songs from their upcoming debut album, the instrumental "Don't Want You No More" segueing into "It's Not My Cross to Bear," a slow blues vocal. The audience, having just heard two instrumentals, quickly scanned the stage for the source of this singing on the third song, wondering if a vocalist was singing backstage, because the voice was obviously that of an African-American; but no, it was Gregg Allman at far stage right, half-hidden behind his long blond hair and the console of a Hammond B3 organ.

Recalling this performance forty years later hasn't changed the opinion of those present regarding the chemistry, interplay, and unity of this group, who had been together less than six months.

Allman Brothers Band playing the Southeast Pop Contest, Gainesville High School auditorium, Labor Day weekend, 1969: (*left to right*) Jai Johany Johanson, Berry Oakley, Butch Trucks, Dickie Betts, Duane Allman. Not pictured: Gregg Allman. Photo by Joel Berger, courtesy of the Allman Brothers Band Museum at the Big House.

In addition, drummer Jai Johany Johanson was African-American, making the Allman Brothers Band a multiracial band as was Booker T. and the M.G.'s and Sly and the Family Stone, a rarity in any part of the country and virtually unheard of in the Deep South. Everything about the band was different. The Allman Brothers Band performance that day set a local standard for musical excellence.

The band was to record only three complete albums with the original members: their eponymous debut release, *Idlewild South*, and their masterpiece, *Live at the Fillmore*.

What the Allman Brothers Band brought to the ears of Gainesville musicians was not necessarily their specific approach to playing, which was a jazz-like style of rock and blues guitar improvisation at virtuoso level; it was more about the power, precision, and unity of their overall sound. This was a *band* in the best sense of the word, working together to create their own sonic universe. This was the ultimate goal of every band. The Allman Brothers Band showed us that the elusive "next level" so often referred to was there for the taking. They raised the bar for every musician and every band in Gainesville, and those of us lucky enough to have heard the original band in high gear knew what all the fuss was about.

REALLY GOOD FRIENDS

In 1969 a new Gainesville band called RGF began playing around town. Neither a typical cover band nor one with a particularly southern identity, RGF included two Miami transplants, Doug D'Amico and Thomas Patti, Gainesville guitarist Jeff Jourard, drummer Mike Hitchcock from Starke, and bassist Ron Blair, a "navy brat" whose family was based at various times in Jacksonville, Hong Kong, and most recently Japan, where Blair had lived just prior to his arrival in Gainesville.

RGF were what was known as a Cock Rock band, with an image and musical style that celebrated sexual aggressiveness and carnal pleasure, but in the case of this band accompanied by a sort of playful wink. Musically the group was deadly serious, but with original songs such as "Orgasm," "Cock," and the randomly named "Narcotic Puppy Fuck #2," it was a band with a sense of humor. Drawing from a wide variety of American musical genres, RGF played heavily rearranged rock versions of folk and blues tunes such as "John Henry" and Howlin' Wolf's "Wang Dang Doodle," and hard-driving covers of "Dancin' in the Streets" and "Jailhouse Rock." If the term *Americana* had been coined at the start of the seventies, RGF would have been in a subgenre called Americana Cock Rock. With two singers, two lead guitar players, a drummer playing a massive drum kit that included two bass drums connected in-line, and a bassist who played a Dan

RGF at the University of Florida Arts Building courtyard, summer 1971: (*left to right*) Ron Blair, Michael Hitchcock, Jeff Jourard, Randy Kidd, Doug D'Amico, Thomas Patti. Photo by Kathleen Grey.

Armstrong Plexi bass guitar through four Acoustic 360 bass cabinets, RGF were easily the loudest band in Gainesville and modeled themselves around hard rock groups such as the Who, Led Zeppelin, MC5, and the Stooges, bringing to the stage an eclectic mix of material with the underlying theme being Big.

The origin of the group's name reveals much about the camaraderie amongst fellow musicians and band members and provides an example of how the music scene was inclusive within its members but treated outsiders with irreverence. As RGF guitarist Jeff Jourard recalled, "We didn't really have a band name; Love Cannon was one candidate, but we got a gig playing with Celebration, so our no-name band agreed to play for free in the Plaza of the Americas, on a weekend non-school day. The band showed up at noon, and there was no stage, no electricity, and someone noticed an outlet on a light pole, so we pulled up the band van, and someone was standing on it, trying to get an extension cord plugged in. Celebration band members Alberto de Almar and Gerry Greenhouse were hanging around watching. Then this blond-haired kid in a plaid short-sleeve shirt and an ROTC haircut drove up on the grass in a sports car, with two giggly sorority girls, a Big Man on Campus sort of guy, and he was being cool and asked Alberto, 'Hey, is this a band? What's the band's name?' 'The Fuck,' says Alberto. Doug said 'No, it's the Good Fuck.' Now, *fuck* was a really aggressive word at the time. Hitchcock says 'No, we're the Really Really Good Fuck . . . no, the Really Really Good Fuckin' Fuckers,' and the guy gets mad and says, 'You guys are crazy' and finally leaves. So we called the band Real Good Fuck but shortened it to RGF so we could get gigs."

Reactions to the name varied from amusement to moral outrage to bemusement, as drummer Mike Hitchcock recalled: "One day the Allman Brothers were in town playing, and I was in Lipham's talking to Berry Oakley. We were just talking music, and he said, 'Oh, you're a drummer. Well what's the name of the band?' and I said, 'Real Good Fuck,' and he said, 'I wish you all the luck in the world with the name of a band like that.'"

When the group drove up to Boston to play some shows, they caught the attention of another rock band just starting out—Aerosmith, whose bassist, Tom Hamilton, recalls a show at Boston University that the two bands played: "Another band we liked was RGF [Real Good Fuck] who wore cool clothes and were very professional and great-looking."

THE RAT

In 1969 the first University of Florida on-campus beer hall opened, offering food, beer, and live music in what was Johnson Hall. The Rathskeller, known as the Rat, opened up with waitresses dressed as German fraüleins serving beer while a ragtime music group named My Father's Moustache entertained with banjo strumming and corny turn-of-the-century songs. The German beer hall theme and ragtime band were eventually dropped and replaced by a steady booking of local, regional, and national acts. In 1971, still struggling with how to spell their name, Jacksonville band Lynard Skynard played the Rat for fifty cents admission; in 1972 they returned as Lynyrd Skynyrd and admission was a dollar—twice as much as the year before. Things were looking up for the band, eventually inducted into the Rock and Roll Hall of Fame in 2006.

Local groups such as Mudcrutch, Road Turkey, RGF, Celebration, Riff, and others were often paired with the headlining acts, who over the years included Dion, Pacific Gas and Electric, Rotary Connection (with singer Minnie Riperton), Doug Clark and the Hot Nuts, Blues Image, the Swingin' Medallions, Jerry Jeff Walker, Alex Taylor, Cowboy, and Archie Bell and the Drells. In 1972 and on the cusp of her career, Bette Midler played the Rat for three nights; admission was one dollar and fifty cents. The Allman Brothers Band played three shows at the Rat in May of 1970 for one thousand dollars per night, then returned in August for a show without Duane, who was in Miami recording the *Layla* album with Eric Clapton. The Rat continued to book bands, including U2, who played there in 1981 in support of their first album—admission was four dollars. By the time the venue was destroyed by a fire in 1987, it had been the scene of thousands of live musical performances through the years.

APPEARING . . . EVERYWHERE

There was plenty of room for music in Gainesville—literally. Outdoor concerts were common for several reasons; the mild weather made it a natural setting, and the two-thousand-acre college campus was a vast and sprawling affair, with multiple locations that routinely presented live music.

The J. Wayne Reitz Union was undoubtedly the mother ship of the university's entertainment offerings, a large student multiuse facility that presented music indoors and out. With a student population of twenty thousand in 1970, there was a large captive audience eager to enjoy live music as a break from pesky classes and exams, with events free to the public. If you were there on a particular Sunday in February 1970, you could hear RGF play loud hard rock on the Union Terrace, choose the softer rock sounds of Frosted Glass in the Cafeteria, enjoy the acoustic guitar and poetry reading of John (you know—of John and Ed, who recently opened for Biff Rose at the Rat), or sit in the Browsing Library and listen as Doran Oster sang and played folk music on the dulcimer and banjo. According to Union officials, the entertainment was an experiment at offering many styles of music at the same time. The university understood the importance of music as a part of student culture, and this event was yet another example of Gainesville's supportive musical infrastructure.

Another popular meeting place for students and city youth was the Plaza of the Americas, a large grassy area in front of the UF Library and the site of many, many concerts, political rallies, and other gatherings over the years. As reported by the *Florida Alligator* on February 16, 1970, "One thousand UF students celebrated St. Valentine's Day by participating in a love-in, rock festival held in the Plaza of the Americas Saturday. The activity, which ran from noon until 8 p.m., featured the sounds of 'The Two Shades of Soul,' 'Dead or Alive,' 'Emergency Exit' and 'Celebration.' Forty-five participants remained to sleep overnight in the Plaza on blankets and sleeping bags. Andy Kramer, an organizer of the love-in, said, 'We came together for peace within ourselves and to make the world better for everybody.' Another coming together is tentatively planned for Saturday, in the Plaza. All participants are asked to bring old clothing and food which will be donated to Neighborhood Houses, Inc., a non-profit organization that works in ghetto areas."

Kramer was a UF student who emceed many such events and was connected to the hippie community. Forty-five people sleeping overnight at the Plaza drew no attention from police or campus authorities. Dogs and frisbees, body-painting, dancing, sleeping outdoors— the love-in rock festival was just one of many similar events held at the Plaza.

Two of the love-in bands are of particular interest to the Gainesville story. Celebration was a popular local group fronted by vocalist Deborah Shane, one of the few female performers on the rock music scene around town, whose performance of Laura Nyro's "Poverty Train" was a highlight of their concerts, as was the playing of guitarist Alberto de Almar, whose technical prowess was held in high regard by the audience and fellow musicians; he later studied flamenco guitar in

Spain (and currently performs in that style). Most of the members of Celebration lived in a house in the southwest part of town on a small pond with its own alligator, and they practiced incessantly: the tribal living aspect of the hippie lifestyle brought a unity to bands that lived and played together. Celebration was often the opening band for national headliners that came to town, and the group played frequently at the Rathskeller.

Dead or Alive was a three-piece group that included Randall Marsh, a drummer from Bushnell, Florida, and a nineteen-year-old guitarist from Jacksonville named Mike Campbell. Both musicians had quickly relocated to Gainesville after graduating high school. "I moved up to Gainesville, after one semester at Hillsborough Junior College," Marsh recalls. "I hated Tampa and that whole scene, and I had a friend in Gainesville, so I popped on up there. I put up a card at Lipham's, and Mike called me, and he and the bass player, Hal Maull, didn't have a drummer, so the three of us jammed some and hit it off. We couldn't have been together more than a year. We basically were a psychedelic jam band. We'd do a little bit of a song, and then do these long jams, playing at the Plaza."

Marsh and Campbell soon moved into a dilapidated tin-roofed two-bedroom Florida cracker house north of the city limits, shared with a third roommate, William "Red" Slater, who slept in the kitchen pantry. The house had no hot water, and the stove was used to heat water for baths as well as cooking, but with each of them contributing twenty-five dollars a month, the rent was covered, and the isolated location made it ideal for young rock and roll musicians. The house and property became known locally as the Mudcrutch Farm, despite only two members of the group living there. "We had the farm before Mudcrutch," recalls Marsh. "We were out there being Dead or Alive. One day in 1969, the bass player, he took a lot of psychedelics. He said, 'I'm not gonna do this anymore. I'm gonna get a sailboat and sail around the world,' and he did. Mike and I tried to keep the band together and find other people, and it didn't work, so we both said, 'Well, we better try getting in bands independently.' I went down to

Mike Campbell of Dead or Alive playing his infamous Guyatone guitar, 1969. Permission of William "Red" Slater.

Lipham's and put up another card, and Petty and the guys ended up coming out to the farm after I had a first audition at Lenahan's place. They said, 'It sounds good, you're in, but we'd like to have another guitar player,' and I said, 'Well, my roommate is back there,' and brought him out, and they saw his shitty little guitar and went, 'Oh God, now we gotta suffer through an audition with this guy,' and then he plugs in and starts playing."

THIS MAGIC MOMENT

Tom Petty clearly recalls this meeting, in the documentary *Runnin' Down a Dream*: "And I heard him yell, 'Mike, can you play rhythm guitar?' and this voice comes back and says, 'I think so,' and into the room walks Mike Campbell . . . and he's carrying this eighty-dollar Japanese guitar, and at that point we all kind of looked at the ground like oh no, this guy is bound to be terrible. And Mike kicks off 'Johnny B. Goode.' And the song ended, and we said, 'Hey, you're in our band.' And we were fast friends right away."

Tom Leadon also remembers this meeting with similar humor: "The Epics and all the bands who were working, like the Certain Amount, we all had really good equipment; we had Fender amps and Fender reverbs and Gibson 335 guitars. So Tom and I just kind of looked at each other when Mike came out with that guitar and kind of rolled our eyes. He didn't look like a professional player, and Mike was really surprised because he told me later he thought we wanted to jam, and yet when he sat down, we started showing him all our original songs and told him what we were looking for was a rhythm guitar player to replace Ricky [Rucker]. While I was showing him all the chords, strumming and telling him, 'This is G, D'—we did a lot of country rock songs Tom had written—and Mike is trying to remember all these progressions to songs he'd never heard, and he was doing pretty well. We're thinking, 'This is going well,' and right at the end of the rehearsal, or I guess you could say the audition, Randall said, 'Mike, why don't we play "Johnny B. Goode?"' We knew Johnny B. Goode, but Mike played the lead, and he played it great. He sounded like Chuck Berry. I had heard a lot of Chuck Berry from Ricky Rucker. I kind of knew what the two-strings-at-a-time guitar lead was about, but Mike had it down. He did an impressive job, and we finished the tune, and we asked the two of them if they wanted to be in the band,

and they said yes, and we were all really happy, and that's how Mudcrutch started."

With the new lineup of Petty on bass and vocals, Campbell and Leadon on guitar, Marsh on drums, and Lenahan on vocals, Mudcrutch began nightly rehearsals and soon began playing a club that was just down the road a piece: Dub's.

A HOT TIME IN THE OLD TOWN

The role of Dub's as a significant part of Gainesville's rock and roll history can be traced directly to the personality of the club's namesake, one of several Gainesville entrepreneurs who supported the local music scene while profiting from this involvement.

When James Wayne "Dub" Thomas (1932–1990) bought the Orleans from Tommy Hicks in 1966 and renamed it Dub's Steer Room (steaks were a specialty), the location at 4560 NW 13th Street had been a dining and dancing destination since the 1950s. The Kit Kat Dinner Club, the Hootenanny, and the Locker Room were some of the names at the address over the years, and in late 1964 a full-page ad in the *Gainesville Sun* announced the grand opening of the Orleans, described as "away from the hubbub of downtown Gainesville." Live music had been a feature over the years, and this policy continued after Dub's grand opening with the Playboys, a group that had evolved from the previous house band in the Hootenanny. "We were the house band when Dub brought in the first topless dancers," recalls Playboy's guitarist, Frank Birdsong. "It's difficult to play when your jaw is hanging down on your strings."

Dub was born in Oklahoma and raised in a suburb of Los Angeles, where he later found work as a bouncer on the Sunset Strip. Initially planning a career as a criminal investigator, in 1954 he switched gears and moved to Gainesville, where his activities included owning the In-N-Out Hamburger stand and Dub's Athletic Center ("Come Get in Shape with Fat Boy Dub"). His involvement with the music community began soon after he bought the six-hundred-capacity club, renamed Dub's in reference to his mother's nickname for him, "J.W.," pronounced by her as "Dub Yah!" when she was angry.

Gainesville's vast student population was Dub's target clientele, and highly aware of the club's previous reputation as a low-class roadhouse where there were lots of fights, Dub made changes. "Nine years ago when I bought this club," he recalled in a 1974 interview, "in the first week we had twenty-two fights. It was a hell of a transition period to get the fighting crowd out and make the students feel comfortable. After that first week I imported two ex-professional boxers from up north. Eventually we established the fact that if you came in here and caused trouble, you were going to get the shit beat out of you. It took us about two months to get that message across." Dub then hired five bouncers to ensure the main activities at Dub's were drinking, dancing, and hooking up.

Dub was consistently aware of the latest trends in entertainment, musical or otherwise, and the evolution of the music and other forms of entertainment he presented mirror the pop culture trends of the times. Musician Jerry Shell (the Trojans, the Better Half) remembers one popular event: "Dub's was still considered on the outskirts of town in 1968, when it rose to fame as the host of the Thursday Night Mini-Skirt Contest, the parking lot jammed, and cars with Georgia tags lining the shoulders of US 441—basically an amateur strip show for $100, huge money then, and decided by applause, whistles, and yells, with intoxicated males chanting in unison, 'No skin, no win' to urge the contestants on. Bands like the Unicorn Horn and a trio Dickie Betts had with his first wife, Dale, on keyboards, played hooch music for the contestants."

Dub managed every aspect of the club, hiring and firing employees and bands as he saw fit, and was generally respected and liked for his personal warmth, sense of humor, and ability to recognize musical talent—a sort of benevolent dictator, if you stayed on his good side. This attitude was not a common trait among club owners, as guitarist Michael Lowe recalled: "It's the only place I ever played where we got an unasked for bonus because they had a good turnout for the week.

Dub's Thursday-night miniskirt contest, March 1972. Reprinted from the *Independent Florida Alligator*.

Hell, forget the unasked part; it's the only place I remember getting a bonus at all."

In the fall of 1970 Mudcrutch began playing the club six nights a week, five sets a night, each member earning a hundred dollars weekly. It had been a long road to the present band lineup and an offer of steady work as a professional musician. Tom Leadon recalls the summer leading up to their first gig at Dub's: "Tom and I got a job at the Plants and Grounds Department at the university, and we spent a hot summer there slaving away. I was on the paving-the-streets crew and painting bus stop benches. We'd spray paint the crosswalks and arrows. It would be one hundred degrees with humidity, and the sun would be shining down on the white paint, and you put the reflective glass beads in that paint, and the sun would be hitting them. That was the hottest summer I ever spent in my life; you worked for eight hours and made like fourteen dollars. Tom was on the crew working down at Lake Alice.

"We practiced every night at least five nights a week, and it was really hard because we'd be at Plants and Grounds all day long, come home from that, then go out to the Farm [rehearsal house] and practice for a few hours, day after day. We went right from that into Dub's. Tom had already been fired or quit the job—they had a little falling out, a little tension there. He wasn't on the job anymore, and he came out and got me, and we'd practice a little bit. We were already doing originals—'Save Your Water' we were doing. 'Possibilities' was a co-write between Mike and Tom. One we did, even with Ricky and Rodney, it was called 'Get Me out of This Place.' That was one of the tunes we showed Mike and Randall the day they auditioned.

"The condition he hired us under was we learn a bunch of cover tunes for the dancing crowd. With Mike and Randall we'd only learned about ten or fifteen songs, and they were all our original songs, so we needed a bunch of cover tunes. The first night we played all the songs we knew, and then we played them again!

"The reality of working around Gainesville was you needed to do cover tunes. We had no problem with it. After we made it through the first night, which was mainly getting over the shock of the topless dancers, we met there the next afternoon, and Mike Campbell brought his reel-to-reel tape recorder over, and we started putting quarters in the jukebox and playing songs and taping them on his tape recorder, and then we learned most of the songs on the jukebox that we thought we could pull off with our instrumentation. We met down there every day for a week or two. We'd play our set and take a break, and they'd start playing the jukebox, and it'd be all the same songs!

"Lenahan sang lead. We did 'Ride Captain Ride' by Blues Image, 'Black Magic Woman,' 'Evil Ways'—Santana was really big at the time—one or two Badfinger songs like 'No Matter What.'"

The club's topless dancers lived nearby, as did two members of the band, and the party often continued into the wee hours at Mudcrutch Farm after the last set.

ROCKIN' IN THE RAIN

During the summer of 1969, the Woodstock Music and Art Fair weekend in upstate New York expressed the hippie culture on a grand scale. Widely regarded as a pivotal moment in popular culture and music history, Woodstock featured more than thirty bands, who played for a crowd of four hundred thousand people. The movie *Woodstock* documents this massive muddy celebration that included Jimi Hendrix; the Who; Crosby, Stills, and Nash; Santana; Sly and the Family Stone; and many others.

In June of 1970 Gainesville had a music festival of their very own held at Florida Field, the university football stadium. Celebration '70 starred Sly and the Family Stone with special guests Grand Funk Railroad and seven other bands. Sly had scored chart success with "I Want to Take You Higher," "Dance to the Music," and "Stand" and played all those and more in the pouring rain, preceded by Grand Funk Railroad, a rock trio relatively forgotten today but who in 1970 sold more albums than any other American band.

It was raining all day at this event, which presented a broad cross section of musical styles from different musical eras. James Cotton performed somersaults as he played harmonica and sang Chicago electric blues; the Youngbloods performed their hippie anthem "Get Together"; Grand Funk Railroad played their many hits; the show lost twenty thousand dollars; and the college Athletic Department was furious with the condition of the playing field, which had been

FALSTAFF
BREWING CORPORATION
and
THE UNIVERSITY OF FLORIDA
STUDENT GOVERNMENT
present in concert

CELEBRATION '70
SLY & THE FAMILY STONE

YOUNGBLOODS
JAMES COTTON BLUES BAND
CROW
TEN WHEEL DRIVE
GREAT SPECKLED BIRD WITH IAN & SYLVIA
EWING ST. TIMES
MECKI MARK MEN

special guest appearance:
GRAND FUNK RAILROAD

Florida Field — Sat. May 16th 4:00P.M.
General Admission: $5.50 — Tickets on sale at:
J. Wayne Reitz Union Box Office &
The Record Bar

Falstaff Brewing Corp. St. Louis, Mo.
Entermedia Future Corp. N.Y.

Celebration '70, better known as Super Show, held at Florida Field football stadium, May 16, 1970.
Reprinted from the *Independent Florida Alligator*.

"destroyed by partying hippies" and was eventually replaced with Astroturf.

It was a time of outdoor shows. Later that year Johnny Winter performed at the Suburbia Drive-In, backed by three previous members of the McCoys, including Rick Derringer, whose classic "Hang on Sloopy" had been a hit five years earlier. This concert was another musical coup for the city, to have two of the best blues and rock guitarists on the current scene performing at night in front of the same outdoor movie screen where you watched dusk-till-dawn horror movies as a kid. You could hear music seemingly anywhere in Gainesville if you waited long enough.

MUDCRUTCH FESTIVALS

Why not throw a little festival yourself? Mudcrutch hosted outdoor music festivals on several acres at the Mudcrutch Farm. Tom Leadon remembers this brief period at the end of 1970 and the start of the next year as home-grown events that attracted large crowds, with several bands and free food by the Hogtown Food Co-Op, an organization created by a group of community activists and hippie entrepreneurs recently arrived from Cleveland, who called themselves the Candle People. Among them was Jeffrey Meldon, an attorney who became an effective conduit between the mainstream business community, local government, and a growing hippie population of Gainesville. Meldon approached several businesses for donations. "Dan Ryals of Ryals Plumbing had scaffolding, so that's how we got the stage together," Meldon recalled. "There was no fee to get in, but we went to Baskin-Robbins and got empty ice cream containers and put them at the entrance. People put enough money in the buckets, so we said, 'Next time let's do a weekend event where people can put out sleeping bags and tents and just hang out.'"

Two more festivals at the Mudcrutch Farm attracted even more attendees and more bands—and an unexpected visit from the landlady, Leadon recalls. "We did the second one, and we did the third one about a month later, and the next day the landlady and her husband showed up and looked around the place, and we hadn't had time to clean up the wine bottles and trash and everything that was all around the property, so they evicted us, and we moved out to Earleton, on the west side of Lake Santa Fe, the four of us right on the lake. That was a good period of growth for us musically because we played all the time."

GETTING BETTER

1970–1971

"American Woman" » The Guess Who

"Mama Told Me Not to Come" » Three Dog Night

"Venus" » Shocking Blue

"Travelin' Band" » Creedence Clearwater Revival

"Clean Up Woman" » Betty Wright

"Groove Me" » King Floyd

"Joy to the World" » Three Dog Night

"Brown Sugar" » Rolling Stones

"Maggie May" » Rod Stewart

"Black Magic Woman" » Santana

"Get Ready" » Rare Earth

"Up in Mississippi" » Mudcrutch

It was not a difficult task to be in a band in Gainesville, as bands were forming like rain clouds on a summer day. However, being a good musician in a good band took more work.

What did "good" mean? For bands whose sole purpose was to play cover versions of popular songs, the answer was obvious: play the song as closely to the original recording as possible. Just as an infant learns to speak through listening and imitation, so learns the musician. In both cases a new language was being explored, and most musicians began their musical journey through mimicry, by listening and then copying what they heard. The two greatest pop groups of all time, the Beatles and the Rolling Stones, both began their careers as cover bands. The first Beatles album consisted of six cover songs and six originals; the first Rolling Stones album contained nine cover versions and three originals. Musicians learned by copying.

As simplistic as this may sound, there is much more to the process. By the late sixties rock and roll records were becoming more sophisticated in both sound and structure. Recreating these songs could be challenging and required an increasing level of craft. Learning five or six chords on guitar and then determining which three you needed to play "Mustang Sally" in the key of G was no longer enough.

EASIER SAID THAN DONE

Consider the musical challenge of learning the Beatles' "Nowhere Man," a song that begins with an unaccompanied three-part harmony vocal that remains throughout the song, features background vocals on the bridge, and a carefully crafted guitar solo with a rich, warm sound ending in a bell-like harmonic. "White Room" by Cream was in two time signatures, 5/4 and 4/4; the vocal varied from full voice to a delicate falsetto in each verse; and accurately replicating Eric Clapton's guitar parts required a fuzz tone, a wah-wah pedal, and the technical skill of . . . well, of Eric Clapton, one of rock's top guitarists. Playing the guitar parts to "Louie Louie" by the Kingsmen or the Troggs' "Wild Thing" was no big deal, but any guitarist attempting to emulate Clapton, Jeff Beck, Jimi Hendrix, or Jimmy Page on stage had some serious practicing to do. The dance crowd had heard these songs on the radio countless times—that's why you were playing them and why they were comfortable dancing to them—and audience and band alike knew how closely your performance came to matching the original version. Intangibles such as enthusiasm, stage presence, and the overall look of the band certainly counted for something, but the bottom line was getting your sounds and performance to closely match those of the original recording, the first step to better bookings and perhaps a step toward creating music of your own.

An unspoken competition was in effect regarding which band played the most authentic rendition of a particular song and came closest to duplicating the vocal or instrumental sound of a musician or vocalist. The process of observation, analysis, and emulation is a primary process in learning to be a musician, and that is exactly what each member of the band had to do.

With so many songs to choose from, what did a band play to make the audience happy? It depended on what was popular in your part of the world. In Southern California these favorites would certainly include surf instrumentals by Dick Dale, the Surfaris, and the Ventures and beach-oriented hits by Jan and Dean and the Beach Boys, a reflection of the popular culture in that part of the country. North-central Florida had a musical culture of its own that did include surf music—in the mid-sixties there was the Inland Surf Association at GHS, a surfer club that booked the Allman Joys for three of their dances at the American Legion Hall—but the general feel of the area tilted more toward danceable mainstream Top Forty rock songs with a large helping of rhythm and blues and soul music. A band playing a frat party could do no wrong if their set list included "Wooly Bully" by Sam the Sham and the Pharaohs, "Louie Louie," and "Wild Thing"; soul hits such as "Midnight Hour," "Knock on Wood," "Land of 1,000 Dances," "Walkin' the Dog," "I Got the Feelin'," and "I Feel Good"; and Jimmy Reed tunes such as "Bright Lights, Big City," "Baby, What You Want Me to Do," and "Honest I Do." Virtually any song by Creedence Clearwater Revival went over well, catchy and danceable songs that conjured visions of riverboats and swamps and running through the jungle, written by John Fogerty, a California native who had never been to the South. Creedence rocked.

The scene: it's 11:22 p.m. on a hot Friday night, and Styrophoam Soule are playing an extended version of "Born on the Bayou" to a drunken group of sweaty Alpha Gamma Rho frat brothers and their dates as two couples are doing the Gator on the floor, a dance unique to Florida, while other partiers form a circle and shout encouragement, clapping and whooping. Add to the atmosphere the combined scent of sweat, cigarette smoke, spilled beer, Hai Karate aftershave, and Brut cologne, and you have an example of a typical weekend frat gig for a Gainesville band in the late sixties.

Southern soul music, especially the Stax recordings out of Memphis—much more raw and sexual than the Motown records—combined with the party-time sounds of these dance favorites, was part of a local player's musical knowledge and helped forge a musical identity that was hard to quantify but included a sort of indescribable white funkiness in the better players around town.

Singing certain pop songs was probably the biggest challenge of a cover band. There were plenty of guitarists around town, but great singers were as rare in Gainesville as anywhere. Many of the songs listed at the top of this chapter were performed live by bands, but you needed good singers if you were going to try songs by the Guess Who or Three Dog Night without being laughed off the stage.

Current songs by the Rolling Stones, such as "Brown Sugar," were always a popular choice as were songs from their earliest albums, such as their versions of Jimmy Reed's "Honest I Do" and Arthur Alexander's "You Better Move On." If to this mainstream pop and rock music, you add a touch of Miami soul music such as Betty Wright's "Clean Up Woman" and a few up-tempo country music and traditional bluegrass tunes such as a danceable version of "Wildwood Flower" or even "Dixie"—this was the South, after all—you have the basic musical marinade of Gainesville, Florida.

It was a deep, rich blend that favored certain quantities of pop, black, and country music, and this fusion of styles made the Gainesville musician more versatile than those who grew up in less musically varied areas of the state.

LEARNING TO FLY

How a musician or a band expressed the musical fluency gained from constantly learning new cover songs was up to them, but learning lots of songs was always the first step. But how did a player get "good"? There were differing approaches. The most obvious one was repeatedly listening to the recording of the song while focusing your attention on what the instrument you played was playing, then playing along with the record until your part matched it. The formal name for this process is "ear training" and is an essential aspect of any music school curriculum. Back then it was simply called learning the song. An Ocala band named the Incidentals was famous for their note-perfect covers of songs by the Beatles, the Zombies, the Who, the Rascals, and the Rolling Stones. They learned by playing the records through their speaker system and slowly backing down the volume of the original song as they played along until eventually band and record matched.

The learning-by-copying process was the most economic and practical approach to gaining fluency on your instrument. A more traditional approach was through music lessons. Gainesville's music stores routinely hired local musicians to work behind the counter and as music instructors.

Charlie Bush was one such guitar teacher, fluent in both jazz and classical technique, whose vast musical knowledge and ribald and expansive personality made him a popular teacher. In the early sixties his Jazz Corner music column in the *Florida Alligator* was the first published pop music journalism in Gainesville, with technical discussions of jazz, jazz album reviews, and artist profiles. He taught both privately and for Santa Fe Community College's community education program and played in his own group. "He was renowned for his sense of humor," recalled Cathy DeWitt. "When deciding whether to take on a new student, he would 'test' them by asking if he could hold their guitar. When they gave it to him, he would then balance it by the tip of its neck on his index finger. The level of their subsequent terror might influence whether he taught them or not. . . . He was truly one of a kind."

Mike Campbell briefly taught guitar lessons, as Nancy Luca recalled: "It was when I was fourteen or fifteen that my friend announced in the high school's restroom, 'My boyfriend's teaching guitar lessons. Know anyone who wants guitar lessons?' and her boyfriend was Mike Campbell. It was ten bucks an hour, and my parents would drive me across town over to NE 16th Avenue. I took guitar there, and so did a couple of my friends. He would teach all of us the same songs. He would show us 'Get Back' by the Beatles, then 'Whole Lotta Shakin''

Goin' On,' and the big song he showed me was 'Cannonball Rag.'"
Luca had her stage debut at fourteen onstage with Mudcrutch at the
Rat, playing a note-perfect rendition of the guitar solo to "Jailhouse
Rock."

Don Felder taught guitar lessons at Lipham Music or Marvin Kay's,
depending on which store he was working for at the time, and a teenage Tom Petty learned basic piano chords from him at the time both
musicians were working at Lipham's. "[Felder] would sit down with
me when business was slow and show me the chords on the piano,
and that's *exactly* how I learned to play it. I didn't have a piano at
home, but I bought a cheap organ. I took the organ home and I would
practice."

While Felder was teaching music, he was also learning as much as
possible, by memorizing guitar solos note-for-note from records, by
studying Mel Bay Jazz guitar books, and by developing a musical relationship with Paul Hillis, a musician who in 1971 opened Hillis Music
Studios at 18½ West University Avenue in the center of downtown.

Paul Hillis was a recent graduate of the Berklee College of Music
in Boston and a jazz guitarist who had switched to piano and taught
on several instruments. He made Felder a deal: in exchange for every
hour Don taught his music students, Hillis would give Felder an hour
of instruction in jazz theory and composition. As Felder put it, "In
less than six months I learned what Berklee College of Music had
taught him in two and a half years. I soaked up every scrap of information." Hillis played piano around town and was the local Mr. Jazz
who put together casual jazz ensembles for upscale clientele at private parties and Woman's Club luncheons and other society events.

Gainesville musicians in general shared their musical knowledge.
A player wanted to be known as the best on their instrument, but
this was often demonstrated through showing the other players how
it was done, a combination of bragging and sharing all at once. One
such player was guitarist Robert Crawford, looked up to by younger
players for two reasons: he was an early adapter of the long-haired
look and was an excellent rock and roll player. Crawford taught guitar lessons at Lipham's and was known for his generosity in sharing

Don Felder working at Marvin Kay's Music Center, 1967. Photograph by author.

musical knowledge. "Robert was kind of esteemed because he could really play," recalls Jeff Jourard. "He was in the Sundowners and could play any solo on any record. I had heard that Robert knew the trick to playing 'She's Not There' by the Zombies. I specifically sought him out to see if he would show me, and he did—turned it into a mini-lesson and showed me exactly how to do it, how to make the shapes, how to strum it. He was totally generous with the 'secrets.' I liked him and appreciated his help greatly, but at that age I didn't know how to express gratitude, so I probably just said something like 'cool' and left it at that."

Benmont Tench received more traditional schooling, with piano lessons starting at an early age. In the words of his father, Circuit

Court Judge Benmont Tench Jr., "I started him with my piano teacher. At that point, I was working on a little Beethoven sonata . . . I came home one afternoon, and I heard it just being ripped off. I wondered who in the hell was playing the piano. It was my six-year-old son." Benmont studied with UF music professor Dr. Russell Danberg and a series of other instructors through much of his teen years.

Before his family's move to Gainesville in 1968, drummer Stan Lynch took music lessons in Miami from Sonny Mange, a well-known local jazz drummer who Lynch recalls "made me buy 'No Matter What Shape Your Stomach's In' by the T-Bones and learn the beat, and I remember playing that beat till my head popped off." In Gainesville Stan took lessons from Gene Bardo, who was "the quintessential percussion guy. He played marimba; he had one in his living room and played beautiful single stroke rolls. His hands could do things that were magic on the drums. He told me, 'There's only one way to learn the drums; you've got to learn the twenty-six rudiments.'"

Lynch learned the rudiments on a practice pad for a full year and had to earn and receive his National Association of Rudimental Drummers certificate before he was permitted to play a full drum kit. "If you wanted to be in the school band, you had to work your way up to snare drummer. And I got thrown out of Concert Band because I was trying to be funny, and I wasn't. And the bandleader thought I was an asshole, and he told my dad the classic line: 'He'll never make it as a musician: he lacks the discipline.' So Dad was terribly disappointed yet let me keep taking my drum lessons with Gene Bardo even though I'd flunked out of school band."

HOW DO YOU DO IT?

Being a good musician was a personal goal; being in a good band was a collective goal. One source of inspiration for a band was watching a great band in action and striving for their level of excellence. Despite the many national acts that came through Gainesville, it was the top local and regional bands that really brought the idea home: "If they can do it, I can do it." Several Florida bands fell into this category, such as Celebration, a local band that had a high level of musicianship combined with an appealing mixture of original and cover songs.

Through the mid- to late sixties, the number-one show band in Florida was the Tropics. Based in Tampa, they performed in Gainesville many times, impressing musicians and audience alike for their musicianship, vocal skills, collective stage presence, and manic energy, as well as an extensive set list that included entire sets of James Brown or Beatles songs. After winning the International Battle of the Bands in 1966 and the prize of a recording contract with Columbia Records, the group recorded a single, the Zombies-inspired "Time" with jazz producer Teo Macero.

The Tropics had a great reputation as a live act, but as Tropic's bassist Charlie Souza discovered, Gainesville had a great reputation of its own . . . as a party town. "The Tropics played all over the South: at Ole Miss in Oxford, LSU in Baton Rouge, Tulane in New Orleans, but . . . the Gators were the wildest bunch. The whole scene was much less reserved than the other campuses we played. I think it had to do with the drinking! They were pretty soused—that seems to be the thing to do in Gainesville. There were a lot of places to play, a lot of parties, and people needed bands. Everybody wanted a band. Other bands would show up from different gigs at the fraternity houses to hear us play, and that was cool."

Bands did come to watch and learn, catching a few minutes of the Tropics during their own band breaks. Fraternity Row was just that, a row of over a dozen fraternities adjacent to one another on the college campus. On weekends during football season, working bands from around the state converged in the area, checking each other out during the fifteen-minute breaks between sets, comparing gear and set lists and enjoying the camaraderie that being in a band always brings. You belonged.

Another band highly respected among local players was the Gainesville band Riff. They played exceedingly authentic renditions of popular tunes, rehearsing daily in one of the warehouse spaces of an industrial park in the northeast part of town, where several other bands also rented space. Keyboardist and saxophonist Trantham Whitley was the musical director of the group. In his words, "The approach was my insistence that it sound as close as possible to the original, and it was rehearsing the same thing over and over again, just the maniacal feeling that it's got to sound right, it's got to be good, it's got to be closer, that's not good enough, let's do it again, start it over, let's take it from the top. I would listen to the record endlessly, and I knew all the parts and would just bang on these guys to make it sound right. We rehearsed every night that we weren't playing. We played frats and concerts. It was fun, and I had a blast, but I remember almost getting beat up in Jacksonville because of my hair, and Herbie [Bohannon] saved us. And the same in Daytona Beach. Because of my hair."

Singer Herbie Bohannon of Riff was one of these Gainesville musicians who had longish hair, but whose relationship to the hippie counterculture was questionable or nonexistent; Bohannon had long hair simply because he was in a band, and in his case there was no chance of him getting hassled because of it. Bohannon didn't back away from the inevitable confrontations that came with having long hair in the South.

"I personally witnessed Herbie taking care of 'business' on several occasions," remembers one friend. "One of the best was when he punched out a frat guy trying to impress his sorority girlfriend by dissing the 'pussy, long-haired, hippie freaks' in the Krystal Burger around 2 a.m., the late hangout after hours. Riff was there winding down after a frat job in their onstage clothes, and Herbie wore a frilly-fronted satin shirt, with long sleeves. Herbie grabbed the guy by his Adam's apple and pushed him up the wall, leaving the guy's feet hanging about a foot above the floor, gave the guy a big squeeze, then let go . . . the guy crumpled to the floor! We all beat it, just in case the local gendarmes showed up."

Honor was a serious aspect of southern culture, and not everyone with long hair turned the other cheek.

HERE, THERE, AND EVERYWHERE

A Gainesville musician was exposed to varied examples of professional musical excellence right there in their very own town. In addition to all the acts that played at Celebration '70, the university brought to town the Temptations; the Chambers Brothers; the Association; Spirit; Blood, Sweat, and Tears; and the Guess Who ("American Woman," "These Eyes," "Undun"). Stan Lynch attended their show: "I remember that they sang really, really great. They were the first band I ever saw that didn't jam. They played the hits *exactly* like they played the records. It was earth shattering to realize that these guys were not using any studio trickery when they made their records."

Atlanta Rhythm Section was another example of a band whose live performances exhibited the highest level of playing. Consisting of accomplished studio musicians from Doraville, Georgia, the band included J. R. Cobb on guitar, cowriter of the Classics IV million-sellers "Stormy," "Spooky," and "Traces." Their live shows were almost indistinguishable from the sound of their recordings, and their southern roots were even more encouraging to local players. Another popular live act that played outdoor shows around the university campus was Eric Quincy Tate from Atlanta, whose drummer, Donnie McCormick, set his cymbals high and played an actual chicken coop as part of the act.

The national tours of major rock acts often included a stop at the Jacksonville Coliseum, seventy miles to the northeast, ninety minutes away by car. In the first few years of the seventies, concerts at the Coliseum included the Allman Brothers Band; Creedence Clearwater Revival; Derek and the Dominos; Emerson, Lake, and Palmer; Grand Funk Railroad; Jethro Tull; Ten Years After; Three Dog Night; Deep Purple; Alice Cooper; Elvis Presley; and Fleetwood Mac.

At the start of the seventies, it was still easy to get around without owning a car, with ridesharing boards at the college, hitchhiking as an accepted transportation mode, and I-75. Take it south to Tampa and the Curtis Hixon Hall to hear Led Zeppelin or Santana, or go north

to Atlanta to catch the Cosmic Carnival at Atlanta Braves Stadium—
a one-day rock festival on June 13, 1970, with Traffic, Ike and Tina
Turner, Frank Zappa, Albert King, the Allman Brothers Band, and
Mountain. By evening, as soon as the spotlight zeroed in on Duane
Allman for his first guitar solo of the set, hundreds in the audience
spontaneously stormed the baseball field and ran to the front of the
stage. Southern musicians now had a genuine guitar hero to emulate.

TAKIN' CARE OF BUSINESS

With all these great bands for inspiration, more bands formed, and
more places to play opened, as Gainesville's musical culture deep-
ened. The year 1970 began with the opening of the Cin City lounge at
the corner of SW 13th Street and 16th Avenue, a multilevel club, with
a DJ providing musical entertainment. Cin City soon switched to live
entertainment and booked local bands. In the early seventies you and
your date could dance as Mudcrutch played Jerry Lee Lewis's 1958 hit
"High School Confidential" or Chuck Berry's "Jaguar and Thunder-
bird," and you both slammed back ten-cent Black Russians. The Alibi
Lounge on the west side of town and the Lamplighter across from
Lipham Music also offered live music, especially Top Forty bands
that kept customers dancing and drinking beer. With free drinks for
unaccompanied females on Ladies Night, weekly drink specials that
allowed you and a date to get highly intoxicated for about a dollar,
and a young sexually active population living adjacent to one another
in cheap apartment complexes nearby, the area was called Sin City
for all the right reasons. A year later the Keg opened at the other
end of 16th Avenue at Main Street, in a converted convenience store.
Dub's at the north end of the city continued to offer a free keg of beer
on Tuesdays, and the perennially popular Thursday night miniskirt
contest.

Playing original songs in a bar setting was problematic because
people liked to dance to familiar songs. "The Lamplighter Lounge let
us play the first set of original songs as long as we did cover songs
the rest of the night," recalls Frosted Glass bassist Mark Pinske. The

band name was chosen because the club owner thought it fit the bar setting. Mudcrutch's set list also included originals, and when playing at Dub's, the band would announce the next song being "by Santana" before playing one of Petty's latest compositions. If you played a cover song that brought people to the dance floor and quickly followed it with one of your originals, you found yourself in the novel position of watching people dance to a song you had written. This experience encouraged additional songwriting and was an important transitional step from being in a cover band to being in a band that played all original material, bands like the ones whose songs you covered.

Styrophoam Soule was a busy and long-running local band that served as a sort of boot camp for many local players. With brothers Randy and Lonnie Morris as the only constant in an ever-changing lineup and with their father, Roy Morris, managing and booking the act, the band was run as a sort of family business from the start, and Morris's business connections and promotional savvy kept the band constantly working. The group was outfitted with a complete set of blue sparkle tuck-and-roll padded Kustom instrument amplifiers and Kustom organ and matching uniforms that changed with the times. Styrophoam Soule worked nonstop in Florida and neighboring states for six years.

When the band broke up in 1974, it had been a musical training ground for more than fifty Gainesville musicians. Among the many was drummer Stan Lynch, who joined in 1970 soon after he found himself gazing longingly at a set of drums at Lipham Music he could not afford. Styrophoam Soule was looking for a new drummer, and at that moment Lynch heard the sound of opportunity knocking. "The kit that was so great were called Ludwig Thermo-Gloss. They were blond maple. John Bonham had the same drum set, and Ringo played that kit on the Beatles' rooftop concert, and I had to have them. Buster probably gave me next to nothing for my old kit and sold me the Ludwigs for list price, but he sold them on credit. Buster was more than happy to give you credit and get the gear off the shelf. He asked if I had a job, and I fudged it; I said, 'Yes, I'm going to be working with the Styrophoam Soule.' I'd already made some connection with Randy Morris; I think someone in the band asked me to join, and they were *working*, and it was a salaried gig. It was two days a week; you made two hundred dollars a week. Actually you made three hundred dollars a week, but they deducted the rental of the lights, the truck payment, and the B3 organ payment. Sometimes you made one hundred and fifty dollars, but it was still a lot of money. I made my payments and bought the kit. And the day I paid it off, I quit the band."

Soon after Lynch left Styrophoam Soule he joined a band called Road Turkey, consisting of Lynch, guitarist Steve Soar, and me on bass and vocals. We rehearsed in a warehouse space in an industrial area north of town, where we learned a blend of fifties rock and roll classics, rock album cuts, Top Forty hits we could play as a three-piece, and several originals we would plant in the middle of our performance

Styrophoam Soule, 1971. Drummer Stan Lynch is third from left. Permission of Lonnie Morris.

Road Turkey, 1972: (*left to right*) Steve Soar, Marty Jourard, Stan Lynch. Photograph by author.

set. If you saw Road Turkey band opening for Mudcrutch at the Florida Museum Terrace in late '71, you would have heard songs by early Rolling Stones, Cream, Free, Creedence Clearwater Revival, Jimmy Reed, and fifties rock and roll by Little Richard. Because our guitarist was good, we also played some Led Zeppelin and Yardbirds songs. Road Turkey was one of the many bands that played around Gainesville, including Mudcrutch, Frosted Glass, Riff, Hogtown Creek, Gingerbread, Mr. Moose, Sam, Purlee, RGF, Styrophoam Soule, Unicorn Horn, Celebration, and Flight.

THE QUALITY APPROACH

"Technique is proof of seriousness," said the poet Wallace Stevens, and every Gainesville musician wanted to be taken seriously. Excellence was all around, and there were enough examples of well-played music for you to know exactly where you stood in the realm of technical skill. Several of today's most respected rock instrumentalists have musical roots in Gainesville, including Stephen Stills, Bernie Leadon, Don Felder, Mike Campbell, Stan Lynch, and Benmont Tench. In addition to their roles as members of bands, each of these musicians has a vast number of recording credits in a wide variety of styles and genres. Stephen Stills's teenage years spent in Gainesville were musically influential through his folk music group the Accidental Trio in high school and his work as a member of the Continentals with Don Felder, as well as in his role in the school marching band, recalling in a 2008 interview that "in playing drums and being right behind the low brass, a lot of those parts seep into your system when you're in the drum line; the low brass is all around you. So later, I turned into a heck of a bass player."

Stills recalled his brief membership in the Continentals in an interview for *Sounding Out*, a 1972 BBC television show profiling the artist: "I played rhythm guitar for a band called the Continentals when I was in high school, and I got to sing two songs, and they were both blues songs, and all the rest was Dick Dale rock and roll, and we played fraternity parties at the University of Florida, and we played bars, where I would lie about my age, which was virtually impossible because at fifteen I looked like I was maybe eleven, and we just kicked around the music."

Why have so many consummate rock musicians come from a single small town? The environment of Gainesville at the time provides a partial answer. Lipham Music catered to a wide variety of musicians of various genres, and a weekend visit to the store could easily bring you within earshot of skilled bluegrass and country music players on banjo, pedal steel, and mandolin. Shot Jackson, co-inventor along with Buddy Emmons of the Sho-Bud pedal steel guitar, would occasionally visit Lipham's and perform. For a rock guitarist still working out how to play basic rock riffs, it was both humbling and inspiring to overhear some older country musician trying out a new Gibson Mastertone banjo playing "Foggy Mountain Breakdown" at breakneck speed. If technique was proof of seriousness, some of the country musicians in midland Florida were quite serious indeed, as bluegrass music required tremendous technical facility on your instrument.

There were other unanticipated examples of musical excellence in Gainesville, perhaps the most unlikely source being a marching band—more specifically, the Florida A&M marching band, who appeared annually in the University of Florida Homecoming Parade. This all-black marching band from Tallahassee was famed for their choreography, precise musicianship, and, in the intervals between song numbers, the funkiest drum cadences of any marching band in the state if not the entire country. The Florida A&M band once included Julian "Cannonball" Adderley and his brother Nat, both graduates of the college. If there was such a thing as a superstar marching band, they were it. No band wanted to follow the Florida A&M band, so they were usually the final musical act in the parade.

Don Felder's guitar skills eventually improved so much that they earned him the nickname of "Fingers," and Bernie Leadon, already an accomplished player when he arrived in Gainesville in '64, left town more experienced as a pop and bluegrass musician and as a songwriter, through his work with Felder in the Maundy Quintet and with local bluegrass players. Mike Campbell arrived in Gainesville as a technically gifted guitarist and continued to refine his technique through his years with Mudcrutch. Benmont Tench combined the technical skill born of years of piano study with a keen understanding and appreciation of rock, blues, and pop music to eventually become one of the busiest keyboard players in the recording business. Stan Lynch's tasteful approach to the drums coupled with thousands of hours onstage and in the studio have resulted in many recording credits that include Bob Dylan, Aretha Franklin, Jackson Browne, Stevie Nicks, the Eurythmics, and so on. The collective discographies of Stills, Leadon, Felder, Lynch, and Tench are a staggering list to behold.

WORKING AT PLAYING

There is no substitute for experience, and along with other musicians, Felder, Leadon, Tench, Lynch, and Campbell put in thousands of hours of playing in performance or practice. When musicians reach a level of skill that allows them to enjoy the sound of their own playing, they play even more, creating a self-sustaining feedback loop of success. "I would ride my bike past Felder's house," musician Trantham Whitley recalls, "and he would be practicing every afternoon, in his bedroom. I would go by there, and there he is, practicing guitar. Felder was always practicing."

Playing cover songs in a club, five sets a night, six nights a week for six weeks, helped add to the hours of playing, and the amount of work available to a band helped bring many musicians closer to the ten thousand hours some social scientists claim are necessary to become an expert in your chosen field.

The laid-back feel of Gainesville was deceptive. Don Felder says: "I think there was a lot of one-upmanship going on in Gainesville. Everybody wanted to have the best band; everybody wanted to be the best guitar player; so [for example] if I heard your brother playing a Jimi Hendrix song at Marvin Kay's, I would go learn it, so I could play it just as well if not better than he could! Duane Allman was the same way. I used to idolize Duane and his playing . . . we were in Battle of the Bands against him, and we hung out a lot. It was always about looking for something new and inventive, and not to be one up on somebody—I guess that's the wrong description of it. It's just to be the best guy in town: the fastest gun in the West, that kind of attitude. So everybody like myself, instead of doing our homework, we'd go in our bedroom and close the door and not plug in the guitar but sit there and play B. B. King licks or anything we could work up or learn, or play slide, or whatever it was, to just improve our chops."

THE WILD, WILD SOUTH

A cover band playing nightly for long hours in a bar was the norm in college towns across the country, and Gainesville was no exception. What set Gainesville apart for bands in the early seventies was the growth of musical concert venues both indoor and outdoor, where the main attraction was not drinking and hooking up but the music and the band. What made this happen was interaction between music-loving entrepreneurs and the university, and city authorities that permitted these types of business ventures to go forth. Gainesville was by now teeming with musical talent, a massive youth population, and an abundance of indoor and outdoor public spaces suitable for musical performances. For a music promoter with ideas and organizational skills, the city was a place filled with opportunity and possibility. And so entrepreneurs with an interest in rock music began to arrive.

ROSE COMMUNITY PRODUCTIONS

Ft. Lauderdale is a traditional party town destination for college kids on spring break, and in the spring of 1968, a Brooklyn college student named Bruce Nearon drove with his college buddies down to the Florida beach town. He recalls, "On our way back my buddy said, 'Hey, let's stop in Gainesville. My fraternity has a house there; we can stay there and not pay for a motel.' The Sigma Phi Epsilon house was beautiful, and my fraternity house in Brooklyn was a slum. I saw that, and I said, 'That's it—I'm transferring here.' It was just beautiful. I fell in love with Gainesville, the trees, the weather, the campus."

Nearon transferred to the University of Florida in April of 1969 and focused on renovating the abandoned Rose Theater (414 NW 5th Ave.) as a music venue, with the intent of raising money to help the black community. With this goal in mind, Nearon formed the non-profit Rose Community Center and began meeting people, including Michael Gannon, a popular university professor and liberal Catholic priest, and other key administration figures. "I meet Father Gannon,

ROSE COMMUNITY CENTER
presents

MUDCRUTCH

with

LYNYRD SKYNYRD

SATURDAY NITE, AUGUST 21,1971 9:00 pm
UNIVERSITY AUDITORIUM ADMISSION $1.00

One of many Rose Community concerts, August 21, 1971. Permission of Jeff Goldstein.

get him on board; he's a reference. I go to another office, Eleanor Roberts, who was in charge of all public functions in the university, and she took a liking to me, and she said, 'OK, fine—you can have your function,' a free concert in the University Auditorium. I told her we also want to do a concert on the Plaza of the Americas on Saturday for free as well, and she said, 'OK,' so it's all approved. So now I'm handing out posters in the Plaza, and who walks up to me but Dr. Jack Faricy, who is the chairman of the Public Functions authority, which has ultimate say on concerts at the U of F. So I was connected. I'm in."

With an abundance of energy, his own nonprofit organization, and a charter from the university to create a similar entity as a student organization, Nearon could now present musical events at the university, utilizing university production equipment free of charge—the stage, lighting, and sound equipment he needed.

A musical impresario was born. In late 1970 Rose Community Productions presented Celebration and Image at the University Auditorium; over the next four years he and partner Charles Ramirez presented more than a hundred concerts and music events.

A TALE OF TWO FESTIVALS

Inspired by outdoor music festivals such as those held at Newport, Monterey, and Woodstock, two musical gatherings in midland Florida took place a week apart in May of 1971: the Gainesville Music Festival and Dusserah. The story of how each festival came to be and how each was received illustrates the conflicting social forces at this time in the region and in American culture. Bruce Nearon's informal approach to creating the Gainesville Music Festival illustrates the manner in which ideas came to fruition in a city with a vibrant counterculture and an inherent sense of community.

"There used to be a bicycle store on 13th Street called the Psycle Shop," Nearon recalls, "a hippie hangout place. I put my concert posters up and got my bicycle fixed. I probably had a bucket there to collect donations for the Halloween Ball. And as I was saying, 'I want to do this rock festival just like Woodstock,' some guy under a VW bus—Charlie Ford—sticks his head out and said, 'Hey, I have a place you can do it. Come out to our farm, and I'll introduce you to Peggi Young,' and I said, 'We want to do this rock festival out here,' and she said, 'OK sure, you can do it.' She was the president of the farm. It was a corporation; it was 240 acres.

"I hired the Alachua County sheriffs to protect the bands from the Levy County sheriffs. I hired Alachua County deputies off-duty, and they had their police cars there; they were our security guards. So when we went to Levy County Sheriff Pat Hartley to get a permit for the music festival, at the courthouse, in the sheriff's office, he has this shotgun hanging on the wall behind him, and we're sitting there, and he's looking at me, a skinny Yankee with long hair. He takes the shotgun off the wall—he didn't point it at us, he's just holding it there, looking right at me. He said, 'Bruce, why do you want to do this to your sheriff? Why do you want to bring all the hippies in Florida to our county? Why? Why do you want to do that?' He's intimidating me. And he's looking at us, and he's dead serious. And he says, 'There's just one thing I need to know, son. How many cattle cars do we need to haul the narcotics violators away?' and he breaks into a laugh and everyone starts laughing. And he says, 'OK, you boys, I already spoke to the deputy sheriff at Alachua County. You boys can hold your festival; it's OK with us. Pay the twenty-five-dollar fee; if you have any problems, let me know.'

"It was 3.5 miles southwest of Archer on the Levy County line, in Levy County. We rented the place, but I never paid them because I never had any money. The festival cost thirteen thousand dollars, and mostly everyone got in for free. The ticket gates broke down. We couldn't control it—there were too many people. It was great. Nobody got arrested, no overdoses, nobody got hurt. We cleaned the place up afterwards. It was cool, but I didn't make any money." The Gainesville Music Festival was held in May 1971, and performers included Power, RGF, Celebration, Mudcrutch, Lynyrd Skynyrd, Shoe Shine Boy, and ten other acts.

But something happened there to upset the uneasy truce between the hippies and the residents of Levy County in the days that followed. There was a vast cultural divide between the hippies' tribe-like communal gathering and the rural residents of midland Florida. As co-organizer Charles Ramirez recalls, "Early in the morning, on the first day of the GMF, we were setting up stuff on stage, which was in a little depression in a big field with the area in front and back rising higher—like a natural amphitheater. On the hill overlooking the backstage was Levy County Sheriff Pat Hartley and his chief deputy, Bubba, in their patrol cars. We were worried because we knew that during the show, there would be plenty of pot smoking going on— both on stage and in the audience—and we didn't want the sheriff to arrest anyone. So we had an idea. We sent someone to the store to buy as much loose tobacco as they could, along with as many different kinds of rolling papers as possible. Papers in all kinds of colors, flavors, even American flag designs. After the supplies arrived, we all sat on the stage and started rolling. Pat and Bubba got out their binoculars and then headed down the hill to see what we were doing. Of course, we gave them both some of our cigarettes and explained that we planned to give them to the fans and bands. Pat understood exactly what our strategy was—that they could not assume that something that looked like a joint was actually marijuana. He had a good laugh and didn't bother anyone smoking anything during the entire show!"

The next festival didn't fare as well. As the Dusserah festival held the following week clearly demonstrated, the interaction between the hippies and the local citizens of Levy County had led to mutual bad will.

Three local music promoters conceived of Dusserah (Arabic for "music fair"), a "music festival without drugs" to include the Amboy Dukes, Moby Grape, Iron Butterfly, Tom Paxton, New York Rock Ensemble, Lynyrd Skynyrd, Mudcrutch, and Game. Billed as the largest music festival in the South since the second Atlanta Pop Festival the previous summer, the thousand-acre site near Williston included two lakes, four springs, and parking for 125,000 cars. Camping was allowed leading up to the two-day event, with thirty-six hours of music beginning on Saturday. At six dollars' admission, the promoters hoped for a projected two-hundred-thousand-dollar profit that, along with a larger contribution promised from the state, would fund a "rehab farm" through the Corner Drug Store, Gainesville's volunteer drug clinic. They also hoped to raise enough money to buy the property from the Chicago owner, who was unaware of the festival.

The locals did not want another music festival, however, and a day before the festival, the owner of the land withdrew permission to use it, and so the site of the Gainesville Music Festival of the previous weekend was quickly chosen as the alternative. Locals tried to prevent the festival through a last-minute injunction by sheriff and residents, and when it was denied, one hundred law-enforcement officials, including sheriffs from Alachua, Marion, and Levy County, the Florida Highway Patrol, members of the Marine Patrol, and ten plainclothes police, all led by Sheriff Pat Hartley, raided the festival for drug use on Sunday afternoon. Eight people were arrested, with officers wielding clubs and tear gas on those who resisted or tried to run away. "Some of the police were in riot gear," reads an *Alligator* news article, "and several Levy deputy sheriffs were mounted on horses."

In the ensuing war of words that followed, one of the Dusserah promoters accused Levy County Sheriff Pat Hartley of wrongly describing the situation as a "riot" and added that "if anybody provoked any of the violence that went on, Hartley and his men did." Sheriff Hartley, having observed drug use and drug sales firsthand, declared that he was determined to either "do my job or turn in my badge," and festival co-promoter Bill Cate said he could find "no redeeming value in sending in armored trucks, with M-60s mounted on top, to stop kids from doing drugs. If that's the way they think they have to approach this generation of young people, this society is in for some real problems." A year later, Nearon was still hosting clean-up parties at the site.

GOOD TIMES, BAD TIMES

American society *was* in for some real problems, and in the South, the conservative and intolerant good ol' boys now had one more social group to verbally and physically attack besides blacks: hippies, adding to their racism an energetic disdain toward the counterculture's fashions, antiwar beliefs, sexual freedom, and dope smoking.

Because of the school integration decision of the Supreme Court, known as *Brown v. The Board of Education,* Gainesville's all-black Lincoln High School was permanently closed during the 1969–70 school year, and the students were transferred to Gainesville High School, causing racial conflicts that resulted in rioting and injuries.

Along with these racial conflicts at the high school were college student protests in and around the university that included sit-ins, civil rights marches, and antiwar demonstrations. Far from being a sleepy southern college town, Gainesville was a turbulent city, and a series of antiwar protests led to riots in May of 1972 that included hundreds of arrests and beatings and the use of tear gas to disperse the large crowds that blocked the college administration building.

STONED SOUL PICNIC

1972-1973

"Heart of Gold" » Neil Young

"Let's Stay Together" » Al Green

"Lean on Me" » Bill Withers

"Slippin' into Darkness" » War

"I Can See Clearly Now" » Johnny Nash

"I Saw the Light" » Todd Rundgren

"American Pie" » Don McLean

"You Are the Sunshine of My Life," "Superstition" » Stevie Wonder

"Diamond Girl" » Seals and Crofts

"Crocodile Rock," "Rocket Man" » Elton John

"School's Out" » Alice Cooper

"Smoke on the Water" » Deep Purple

"Long Train Running" » Doobie Brothers

Gainesville was the "hippie city." That's what the truckers would call it on the CB when they were goin' on by: "Yeah, I'm passin' that hippie city."
Nancy Luca

As the 1970s began to unfold, Gainesville was blossoming into a musical playground and an environment increasingly designed to satisfy the hedonistic urges of the large youth population. With a student body of twenty-seven thousand and a growing number of counter-culture folk—"hippies," "freaks," and "stoners" were just some of the descriptions employed—Gainesville was a city ready to throw a party on a moment's notice, on campus and around town.

The natural abundance of flora and fauna in midland Florida added to the totality of the Gainesville experience, and the weather and climate were inseparable components. Unless you constantly stayed indoors in an air-conditioned room, the natural world was impossible to avoid—the abundant sun and heat, the sudden intense thunderstorms, the all-encompassing humidity and rain of summer, the sounds of bullfrogs and cicadas and crickets and the occasional roar of a bull gator asserting his territory, the broad-branched live oak trees hung with Spanish moss, and the lakes, springs, and spring-fed rivers that were an inherent part of the north Florida landscape. Gainesville had long, hot, rainy summers. Grass grew so fast that as soon as a lawn was mowed, you could detect new growth where you had begun an hour before. Spring brought forth the sweet scent of magnolias and gardenias, and summer occasionally featured those few seconds of sharp mineral scent as the raindrops hit hot concrete; these sights, scents, and sounds were all part of the annual cycle of nature. Along with the songbirds and scented blossoms were an abundance of insects in large sizes and cockroaches and mosquitoes. "Jungle" is just barely too strong a descriptive word.

Water was part of everyday life. Glen Springs, located in the northwest section of the city, was Gainesville's go-to community swimming facility for nearly forty years. Nearby were Magnesia Springs, Poe Springs, Ginnie Springs, and the Ichetucknee River, all with water clear and pure enough to drink. Seventy miles due east was Crescent Beach, a popular weekend and summer destination for students, surfers, hippies, and student surfer hippies.

One local tradition among the psychologically adventurous was to take a hit of LSD very early in the morning and time your drive to the beach so the effects were coming on just as you arrived and saw the sun rise over the Atlantic, a beautiful sight even when straight. Many aspects of north Florida make it geographically a sort of paradise, and a Florida beach at dawn is one example.

Alligators were an oddly common sight at times around Gainesville—Lake Alice and Biven's Arm Lake were havens for the reptiles, protected under the Endangered Species Act and evidently thriving as a result. They would occasionally hide in the water hyacinths near shore and eat dogs that strayed too near the lake. During the rainy summers, rising lake levels sometimes encouraged alligators to wander into unlikely places, including yards, and they were occasionally seen walking down the middle of the street, only to be captured and returned to their native waters.

The hormone-driven youth of Gainesville were not oblivious to the season's cycles—especially when spring had sprung. Visual stimulus abounded. Attractive, tanned students walked and biked around campus wearing as little as possible. There was a lot to want and to pursue. You could almost see the pheromones hovering in the air.

Flora and fauna were in abundance around north-central Florida, including healthy and carefully cultivated examples of flora of the genus *Cannabis*, otherwise known as Gainesville Green.

ONE TOKE OVER THE LINE

The economic principle of supply and demand, combined with the region's abundant sun, rainfall, and fertile soil, created a booming local economy in the growing and selling of marijuana. Gainesville Green was the generic name for a large and varied crop of locally raised marijuana known for its potency and commonsense pricing, based on the fact that it was not imported. *High Times* magazine routinely quoted the current price of Gainesville Green alongside global strains such as Colombian Gold, Jamaican, and Thai Stick. In surrounding rural areas large crops of marijuana were grown in fields, abandoned farmlands, and near swamps, with the plants sometimes reaching heights of eighteen feet.

Prior to the growth of local production, the most commonly available pot was low-grade marijuana from Mexico, universally referred to as "dirt weed," the equivalent of cheap beer, exported in the form of entire marijuana plants dried and collectively pressed into kilo blocks, including the unwanted stalks, stems, and seeds, all of which had to be removed before smoking. Cleaning dirt weed consisted of breaking it up with your fingers and spilling it onto a record album cover held at a slant, repeatedly pushing the mixture in an upward direction with the edge of a pack of rolling papers and allowing gravity to separate out the seeds and stems—or so I am told. Double album covers were an even better choice.

Marijuana and music were inseparable during this time, and clouds of smoke hovered over outdoor musical events, with relatively minimal interference from law officials in comparison to other Florida cities. Gainesville soon became a primary or secondary destination for recreational drugs brought into the state. Drug dealers who drove west on Archer Road could reach Cedar Key in about an hour, a popular import site for the leafy exports of Mexico, Colombia, and Jamaica. When cocaine became increasingly popular, Gainesville was a convenient market stop for northbound dealers bringing a few kilos up from Miami on its way to the East Coast.

Smoking pot was as much a cultural statement as it was a recreational choice; it separated the user from mainstream America and the redneck population that surrounded you. Being illegal in all fifty states, marijuana was a risky drug of choice. A one-year prison sentence for possession of a single joint was possible.

Around town in the early seventies, a lid was by definition fifteen dollars of marijuana, and an ounce cost twenty dollars or less. Gainesville Green was always fresh and often sold in bud form in Mason jars or in heat-sealed plastic packaging to preserve both shape and fragrance. Other variants included Micanopy Madness and Fruity Gonzo, and there were unsubstantiated rumors of a particularly potent strain known as Elvis Presley—one hit, and you're in the movies.

Certain counterculture students majoring in botany at the University of Florida experimented with the cloning of hybrid marijuana strains of increased potency, and just like that, a new marketing niche was born: premium domestic marijuana. A UF biochemistry major manufactured methaqualone powder and packaged it in Knox gelatin caps, competing in both price and quality with pharmaceutical Quaaludes. Psilocybe Cubensis mushrooms were known to grow locally on cow manure after a rainstorm, and locals became adept at identification.

Despite the casual smoking on campus at outdoor concerts held at the Plaza of the Americas, discretion was the key to staying out of jail, and "Are you holding?" was a subtle way of asking if someone had a stash without being specific.

Although marijuana use increased among the counterculture set, alcohol was still Gainesville's most popular recreational drug, and drunk driving was a common and occasionally deadly occurrence. Marijuana was relatively benign in comparison to alcohol. Alcohol consumption sometimes led to physical aggression and driving fatalities, whereas marijuana overindulgence usually consisted of sitting on your sofa with headphones on, listening to the Grateful Dead's *American Beauty* album while eating Screaming Yellow Zonkers, a popular popcorn snack. Cheech and Chong's stoner comedy albums were very popular.

EASY DOES IT

Other aspects of Gainesville made it a place where living was easy. Getting around town was not a challenge; the core of the city was about twenty blocks wide, with University Avenue the main east-west route, and Main Street, West 6th Street, and West 13th Street the north-south arteries. The Volkswagen was where it was at in both the Bug and Bus models, an inexpensive auto that could transport five passengers twenty-five miles on a thirty-five-cent gallon of gasoline. As late as 1972, the sticker price for a new VW Bug was $1,999.

But you really didn't need a car to get around Gainesville, and university students living in dorms were not allowed to have one on campus. You could get around town by walking, or riding a used bike bought from Streit's Bicycle Shop or the Psycle Shop. Hitchhiking was the most common mode of transport for those lacking access to wheels.

The low cost of food, housing, and utilities made Gainesville an inexpensive city in which to live. Apartments at the Place, just north of campus, rented at seventy dollars a month; Kentucky Fried Chicken meals were a buck; a full breakfast at Mac's Waffle Shop was forty-nine cents; and a dime was a decent tip. Various ABC Liquor Lounges around town offered forty-eight-cent drinks at the bar. And there was always the free meals served by the local Hare Krishna sect at the Plaza of the Americas.

Competition for student business among the many bars and clubs led to drink prices approaching zero, with Dub's offering a free keg of beer on Tuesdays, and the Keg offered nickel beer starting at 4:30 p.m., with the price going up a nickel every fifteen minutes—"Come in at 4:30 and drink as fast as you can!" urged a 1974 ad. Live music, beer, and college students were a match made in heaven.

Among the many bars in town were two that featured topless dancers along with live music, a situation that appealed to customers and the bands that played there.

WILD NIGHTS

Trader's South at 2212 SW 13th Street was owned and operated by Tom Henderson and his wife, Gloria. Trader's sold beer and offered table dances for two dollars. Clientele from both the college set and the rural population kept Trader's packed on weekends.

For much of my senior year and the summer months after graduation, I was the bassist and vocalist in the house band that played Trader's South three nights a week, Wednesday, Friday, and Saturday. You entered the flat-roofed building from the parking lot through a side door into a low-ceilinged dark and smoke-filled rectangular room; to the right was a stage and tables with tops the size of large pizzas (just big enough for a topless dancer in heels to stand upon), and an area to the left had more seating, pool tables, and pinball machines. At 9 p.m. with the colored lights blinking and dancers at the ready, Gloria Henderson would hand a band member a quarter to program three songs on the jukebox; always "Fire and Water" by Wilson Pickett and two of your choice. This never varied, and both sides of the quarter were marked with an X in red nail polish for future retrieval when the jukebox service operator came around. Starting at 9:30 the band played their first forty-five-minute set and ended around 1 a.m. The

Trader's South. Photograph by author.

songs had to be three or four minutes long at the most—no long so-los, as the dancers were paid by the dance, so the shorter a song, the better—and the band was routinely told to turn down, as all bands are, but it was a gig with intangible benefits that had lured many a lo-cal musician into pursuing music full-time. Imagine you are a senior in high school, and this is your part-time job. I was a goner.

Despite the titillating nature of the club, Trader's South was your basic family-run business, with the disarming presence of Tom's wife collecting the admission charge at the door, his daughter serving drinks, and his son occasionally sitting in with the band on saxo-phone, at the "suggestion" of Tom.

Through the years many local bands acted as the house band at this thriving business frequented by a diverse clientele. "Some topless places are really crude," Henderson says in a feature newspaper article profiling the club and dancers, "but we run this place clean. There's no bottomless, no strippers, no hustling. We got live music on weekends, and people come here just to have good entertainment."

The Wednesday night topless dance contest prize was fifty dollars, for a dancer the equivalent of twenty-five individual tabletop dances, and competition for the money was always intense, to the delight of band and audience alike.

Across town at Dub's, perhaps in response to the recent passing of the Equal Rights Amendment in January of 1972 as well as the growing ranks of the feminist movement, Dub Thomas discontinued the ever-popular topless dancers. Attracting female customers to the club and therefore attracting even more males to the club was most likely the primary reason, or perhaps the liberal politics of the university student body led to the decision. Whatever the cause, for local bands who played there, it was a sad day indeed.

THEM CHANGES

Mudcrutch continued to perform at university gigs, in the bars and clubs around the area, and as far north as Grant's Lounge in Macon, where they left a demo tape at Capricorn Records that was rejected as sounding "too English." The band played at a country music bar in Lake City, at Katy O'Malley's in Tallahassee, and at the High Springs Tobacco Festival.

In the summer of '72, however, Mudcrutch could generally be heard at Dub's, as Petty continued to develop his songwriting, with the band slipping originals in the set along with their usual mix of late fifties rock, country songs, and danceable Top Forty favorites. "We'd book six weeks at a time," drummer Randall Marsh recalls, "five sets a night, six nights a week. It felt like my second home; we were in and out of there quite a bit."

During one such night at Dub's, Mudcrutch guitarist Tom Leadon altered the course of his musical path while attempting to defend the honor of the band.

In his own words: "We were at Dub's, and he had told us that he wanted to lay us off after the next week, and he told me in a nice way, but he was up during the miniskirt contest, saying, 'I'm gonna expand the room, and get bigger and better bands in here.' All he was trying to do was promote his expansion and drum up business, but I was hearing it like he was putting us down, saying he was going to get bigger and better bands. I was just thinking, 'OK, I'm going to go out of here next week and try and book us around the university' like we usually did, and I was the booking agent. And here he is, in front of all these university kids putting us down. And so the next week I told him not to say it, and he said he'd say whatever he wanted, and I was hotheaded and told him if he said that, I was going to turn the P.A. system off. And that was really the wrong thing to say."

As Randall Marsh remembers it, the band agreed. "We were playing one night, and Dub got up there and grabbed the microphone and said, 'We're gonna expand this club; we're gonna fix it up and make it nice, and get bigger and better bands,' and we kind of laughed, because hey, we're in Dub's, what the fuck, but Tom Leadon took offense, and on break he went back in Dub's office, which looked like a Mafia sanctuary, and he told Dub, 'Don't you ever get up in front of an audience and say you're gonna get bigger and better bands and embarrass our band like that,' and Dub said, 'Well, yeah, I won't, but you're fired. Get the fuck out of my club,' so Leadon had to come tell us that we were fired, and we said, 'You did *what*?' And even with tight bands you don't do that, so we fired Leadon."

With Leadon fired for sticking up for the group, Mudcrutch was now a trio—drums, bass, guitar—and needed another member, whom they eventually met at the annual Halloween Masquerade Ball.

THE HALLOWEEN BALLS

People have been dressing up in costumes on Halloween and partying since Halloween and parties had been invented, but the coming together in Gainesville of live music, Halloween costumes, and a communal gathering began happening on a large scale beginning in late 1970, when Bruce Nearon and his Rose Community partner Charlie Ramirez were approached by two university students who told Nearon about "this Halloween Ball, that they couldn't get permission to put it on, and I said, 'No problem—put the paperwork in.' It was at the Plaza of the Americas."

With a charter for Rose Community from the university allowing him to move forward, what happened in the coming days is an example of Gainesville's attitude toward outdoor festival-like events and the combination of charm and hustle provided by Nearon and his partners: "The university had staging. I knew where it was, but they said the Ladies' Glee Club was using it, but we drove up there with a bunch of trucks and some construction-worker hippies, and we took it, hauled it to the Plaza of the Americas and started construction. We erected towers on each side of the stage for the university's public address system, and we had Super Trouper spotlights from the university. We built a fence with sound towers on each side, and towers in the audience for the spotlights. We knew a lot of hippies who worked on construction projects, and they'd bring trucks to put the Super Troupers up on the towers. Charles Ramirez was my partner in this. He was my stage manager, and I was the promoter."

The theme for the First Annual Halloween Ball Masquerade was "Can You Pass the Acid Test?" Two thousand attendees at an event that *began* at midnight and continued until four in the morning—the majority in costume and enjoying the effects of psychedelics and marijuana—hallucinated and danced to the loud hard rock music of RGF.

Despite protests from the school administration, a second event was approved the following year in the same location, with a more elaborate production financed by Rose Community through donations collected in buckets placed around town on the counters of local merchants.

These free outdoor public concerts with bands playing original music, financed through donations of cash and with production assistance from a sympathetic local business (Ryals Plumbing provided staging equipment and transportation), embodied the collective spirit between music and the city.

With full access to university facilities and the money to pay for advertising and other expenses, the Second Annual Halloween Ball was a bigger success, with music by Mudcrutch and Goose Creek Symphony, the latter group popular for their version of Janis Joplin's hit "Mercedes Benz." A review of this show appeared several weeks later in the Atlanta counterculture paper *Great Speckled Bird*, and the following excerpts provide a look at how Gainesville's cultural environs were viewed by outsiders from a much larger southern city: "As we drove around looking for the site, a light drizzle was falling and it looked like the party might not happen. After finding the huge grassy site and parking, however, we saw that the tech people were setting up the PA with supreme confidence. 'The rain's always over by 11:30,' one local freak reported to us. The brother was right. By 10:30 the rain had stopped, but there were very few people around and it was looking like the weather was keeping the people away.

"But as midnight approached people began arriving, including revelers costumed as Disney characters, two guys working together dressed as a ten-foot lit joint, and a coven of witches being followed by a priest trying, unsuccessfully, to subdue them."

"There was tons of dope and no pigs," the article continues. "This free atmosphere continued throughout the night. The music didn't start on schedule and by 12:30 people were getting restless. Around 1:00 a.m. the real music started. Mudcrutch, a local Gainesville band, was first to play. They are a really fine, national quality band. They play a wide variety of music, and we wish they would tour or record so more people could hear them." As Petty and company opened with "Johnny B. Goode," "more and more people filtered into the open area until it was completely filled. There could have easily been ten thousand people there. There was so much dope that the smoke hung over the crowd like a gray iron plate. The whole crowd transmitted a freaky, electric, totally involved feeling that was impossible to pin down, and just as impossible to avoid. It was an orgy that (for the most part) was without sex."

THREE STRIKES, YOU'RE OUT

By the third year, it sounded too good to be true—a free party where you could do whatever you wanted!—and it was. Referred to in retrospect as the Evil Ball, the 1972 Halloween Masquerade Ball embodied many aspects of the Gainesville cultural landscape, featuring sex, drugs, rock and roll, university authorities, and music-friendly plumbers.

The university authorities were not in favor of this third annual event, but it was through the actions of Rose Community's Jeff Goldstein that the ball occurred, and he explains how business was done in 1972: "A few days before we planned to present the Third Annual Halloween Masquerade Ball, Bruce and I met with the powers that be. They always said, 'No, you can't do it,' no matter what we wanted, so that's what we expected. We told them our plan and asked permission to get the University's stage and begin setting up. They told us the stage was booked by some other organization. Bruce and I looked at each other and said, 'Oh well . . . ' and walked out. I had an appointment to announce the show on the radio that night, which I did. We called our buddy Danny Ryals and had him deliver a load of scaffolding for the towers in the Plaza and then bring the trucks with the bubbas to the University's warehouses to pick up the stage and take it to the Plaza. Then we called the sound and light guy, Chuck Wheatly, and told him to grab his guys and all the gear and bring it to the Plaza. Two hours after them telling us 'no,' we were setting everything up. No one stopped us, and no one asked what we were doing. When finally approached by someone from the University administration the next day, I told them, 'We have the stage set up, the show is announced, the bands are ready to play. Ten thousand students are

ROSE COMMUNITY CENTER
Presents The Third Annual

HALLOWEEN
MASQUERADE BALL

MUDCRUTCH
ROAD TURKEY
MIDNIGHT MACHETE
JOHN JONES

SAT. OCT. 28, 1972   9:00 p.m.
PLAZA of the AMERICAS

The Third Annual Halloween Masquerade Ball, 1972. Permission of Jeff Goldstein.

going to show up by 10:00 p.m. for the show! Are you really going to not let us do it?'"

The show went ahead as planned. Mudcrutch and Road Turkey were the featured acts at the 1972 Halloween Ball, along with support acts and the last-minute addition of guitarist Danny Roberts, the former bassist of Power. Roberts performed along with a drummer as the opening act and was accompanied by his sister on vocals. "I played a set," Roberts recalls, "and when I finished, I took my little Epiphone amp to the back of the stage so that Mudcrutch could finish setting up and play as a trio of TP, Mike Campbell, and Randall Marsh. Tom and Mike said they enjoyed what I had done and asked if I'd be interested in joining their band."

As the night rolled on, the vibes in the crowd became increasingly maniacal. Maybe it was the pentagram on the poster advertising the event, or extensive use of a new recreational drug called Quaaludes that made the crowd loose and ornery; or perhaps it was enhanced by the recent release of *A Clockwork Orange*, a Stanley Kubrick film featuring the violent antics of young thugs named Droogs, whose bizarre outfits of bowler hats, a false eyelash, and codpieces were emulated by many Halloween revelers that night, including a trio of Droogs who jumped on stage and refused to leave, one brandishing a ten-inch stiletto, causing the stage crew to vanish abruptly. Finally the Droogs left the stage, which was soon overrun by audience members in an impromptu costume contest and who refused to leave, so the band refused to play until the stage was cleared. By the time order was partially restored and the event's final act, Road Turkey, began playing, university officials swarmed the stage and began unplugging microphones and pulling power cables. Eleanor Roberts, head of Public Functions, was so intent on stopping the music, she grabbed the drumsticks from the band's seventeen-year-old drummer, Stan Lynch, prompting a graphic, unprintable suggestion from Lynch. After this Halloween Ball the event was no longer permitted on the UF campus. But at this third ball, Mudcrutch had found a new guitarist, and Danny Roberts soon joined the band.

With Rose Community banned from any concert involvement, several years passed before the event returned to the Plaza of the Americas, and the next two events were held off campus. "We did one out at Santa Fe Community College," says Ramirez, "but they didn't like us either, and one at the Archer farm where we had previously held the Gainesville Music Festival. Somebody got their car stuck on the dirt road to the farm, and instead of trying to get it out of the way, they just parked their car there, so cars started backing up behind that one, and a lot of people just partied by the side of the road all the way back to Archer."

OUT OF THE BARS

The Halloween Balls were one of hundreds of music events presented over the next few years by a team of friends and promoters consisting of Bruce Nearon, Charlie Ramirez, and Jeff Goldstein, a recent arrival from Miami and later president of Student Government Productions. Jeff was known locally as Madhatter when he appeared as the emcee at many Halloween Balls in top hat, bowtie, and a cane made from a dried marijuana plant stalk. Together they produced shows under the names Rose Community, the Rose, and Ye Pirates Crew, presenting many local and national music acts at Halloween Balls, at the Plaza of the Americas, and in the University Auditorium and other venues, including the Archer site of two outdoor music festivals and the new Santa Fe Community College campus west of town.

These three entrepreneurs, one from Brooklyn, one from Miami, and one from Gainesville, worked within the administrative constraints of the university to gain access to university facilities and produced music concerts that allowed bands to perform original music for a paying audience in a concert setting, a new form of presentation for many local musicians.

This situation was highly encouraging for bands with higher aspirations than playing cover tunes. Bar and club owners generally did not want bands playing original material, insisting instead that the band play songs that brought customers directly to the dance floor and then back to the bar for a refreshing beer or three. The drinking age in Florida had been lowered to eighteen in the summer of 1973, but even then it kept many bands with minors out of the bars and lounges because of a player's youth, limiting gigs for younger bands to private parties, teen centers, and high school dances, although some club owners were not particularly interested in determining the age of each band member. Gainesville had plenty of these young musicians.

Among the cover bands whose sole purpose was to learn and perform Top Forty tunes in bars and lounges were others bands working hard on their own music and image. Included in the latter group were Mudcrutch, RGF, Road Turkey, Dark Star, Dreyfus, Frosted Glass, Purlee, Power, and Jacksonville bands Lynyrd Skynyrd and Cowboy, both of whom lived for a period in Gainesville. Goldstein recalls Lynyrd Skynyrd "driving all the way from Jacksonville in their little beat-up white van, setting up in the University Auditorium, and playing a kick-ass set, for sixty dollars." Shows such as these presented by Rose Community in Gainesville provided an outlet for bands eager to present themselves as an act with original material at concerts open to all ages. For a band to be hired by Rose Community, they needed at least half their set to be original songs. Events such as these gave Gainesville musicians an opportunity to develop as musical artists and performers on a concert stage, vastly different from the small stages and the constraints of a bar or frat party's song repertoire. You had a chance to show your stuff, if you had any.

Mudcrutch drummer Randall Marsh agrees: "Gainesville was so different than other colleges, a blend—a liberal college, small-town hippie thing. Bands playing at the university—they would pay you, build a stage, put up the sound system. Petty was writing original material. At some of these gigs, we'd play to two thousand people at the Plaza. How many local bands could play original stuff to two thousand people?"

Rather than having to spend money on radio advertising or print ads, the majority of these shows were promoted by Goldstein and his two partners through posters, a cost-effective and labor-intensive method of generating publicity. "You would take 200–300 flyers and put them along your arm and have a roll of tape on your other wrist, and we each had a route that we took, and we plastered the entire university and the entire town with those posters. That's how we got the fans into those shows; we didn't advertise on the radio, although we did for some of the paid shows. It was all done through the posters, and they created word-of-mouth. People would take the posters off telephone poles, off the walls, take them home, and talk to their friends about it."

LISTEN TO THE MUSIC

Gainesville was now teeming with bands and places to play and major acts coming to town. Bar and club owners and the social directors of fraternities routinely sought live music, along with entrepreneurs such as Rose Community who were working within the university and also separately. The university was the major concert promoter in Gainesville, and Student Government Productions utilized an internally generated budget that allowed them to book major acts at the larger concert facilities of Florida Field and the Florida Gym. Over the course of a couple years, SGP presented Isaac Hayes, Stephen Stills, Jeff Beck, Ted Nugent, the Beach Boys, Seals and Crofts, the Doobie Brothers, Todd Rundgren, Stevie Wonder, and Elton John. The university's Inter Fraternity Council (IFC) provided their seasonal Frolics events, funded by fraternity membership fees. Acts brought to town through the years by the IFC included Wilson Pickett, Janis Joplin, Dion, the Carpenters, Rare Earth, and John Mayall.

Around the city were various bars and lounges that hired bands, from converted convenience stores such as the Keg, to the Bench and Bar, Bilbo and Gandalf's, and the Longbranch Saloon, as well as three music bars recently bought by the Big Daddy's chain: Cin City, the Lamplighter, and the Alibi Lounge.

The weekly schedule at the Lamplighter (1 NW 10th Ave.) is demonstrative of Gainesville's party environment and the competition among music venues to attract the college set: Local band Homer played throughout the week; Monday drinks were thirty-five to fifty cents; Tuesday drinks were fifteen cents for members of a selected frat and sorority; Wednesday had free hot dogs and twenty-five-cent beer; Thursday featured two free drinks for unescorted ladies; and Fridays and Saturdays brought happy hours. Basically, listening to live music and getting drunk in Gainesville was cheap and convenient. Fake IDs were easy to come by, but doormen at the bars learned the trick of asking for your zodiac birth sign, knowing the date range that corresponded with each sign. If you didn't know your birth sign, you probably had a fake ID.

Live music was presented in unlikely places around Gainesville, including several shows at the outdoor Suburbia Drive-In Theatre (2715 NW 13th St.) and in the back of cafeterias: Dr. John's in the College Inn across from campus and the Back Door at the Sweden House, a smorgasbord cafeteria rumored to have gone out of business when the Gator football team discovered the restaurant's all-you-can-eat specials and demonstrated the financial consequences of honoring such a policy.

Although certain bars such as Dub's and Trader's South hired "house bands" for months at a time, most clubs constantly rotated bands in and out to ensure variety; this club circuit was a thriving music scene separate from the university's music bookings. It was the many university-sponsored music events combined with the thriving club and bar scene that accounted for Gainesville's increasingly pumped-up music culture.

Despite this abundance of live music, in early 1973 a feature article in the *Florida Alligator* complained of a dearth of big-name acts coming to town compared to previous years. To find out why, they interviewed the student body president, the head of Student Functions, and Miles Wilkin, the new business manager for Student Government Productions (an organization with a budget of forty-four thousand dollars for the school year). Wilkin explained the challenges in negotiating with major talent agencies unwilling to deal with what he called a series of "student-of-the-week" SGP chairmen, some of questionable competence. "The agents didn't know who was in charge of

SGP, so they had no faith in us. We couldn't establish a good rapport. Plus, we had no redeeming features like a coliseum, to interest them," adding that the university didn't employ a full-time staff member whose sole job is to book acts as did other universities throughout the state. Another criticism was announcing band concerts prematurely, as in It's a Beautiful Day for fall quarter, and Neil Young for winter, without a firm booking on the groups. Wilkin explains the process in the simplest terms. "In booking a group, you first find out when they're available and coordinate these availabilities with facility possibilities. Then you place an offer for a set dollar amount. The group then accepts the offer, refuses it, or sends it back for revision. When the contract is approved by Public Functions, and the group signs it, then the act is booked, not before," Wilkin said. Acts that had been booked at Florida Field and failed to perform for reasons that included weather, illness, or poor sales included Leon Russell, Jefferson Airplane, and the Rascals, all no-shows.

With the football stadium as the largest live-music venue in Gainesville—an outdoor facility in a city where rain was common and hard to predict—rain insurance was a prohibitive expense, and major music acts booked at the facility were generally less interested in playing Gainesville when asked to agree to a rain check, agreeing to return at a future date if the initial date was rained out. The university had been trying to raise money for a coliseum through concert profits as early as the 1968 concert at Florida Field featuring the Beach Boys, Buffalo Springfield, and Strawberry Alarm Clock, but five years had passed with no plans or funding for a large covered facility.

ON THE AIR

Adding to this vast potpourri of live music was the sound of radio, dominated by Top Forty AM stations, continuing as the main source of music for the young listener. From "American Pie" by Don McLean to Bill Withers's "Lean on Me," these songs were part of a steady stream of AM radio hits that became the "soundtrack of your life," songs that bring nostalgic feelings when heard, in some cases through the beauty of their emotional expression and in other cases because they had been shoved down your throat through endless heavy rotation on the station playlists.

The saturation of playlists was not because of the personal taste of a program director but rather through conscious application of an airplay formula. By the early seventies AM radio had been under the guiding thumb of radio program consultants for several years, and playlists were tightly controlled. Joe Folsom (GHS '70), a DJ at both WUWU and WGGG at the start of the seventies, before moving on to the national markets as JoJo Kincaid, describes the birth and domination of this radio airplay policy: "It was very tight. At that time, about '69 or so, a wave swept through radio. It was called the Drake era. What Bill Drake did was come in with a new approach to programming Top Forty stations, because up until that point, particularly in the mid- to late sixties, there were these really gabby DJs, and they would actually stop the music. A song would play, and they'd just talk and gab. Drake's approach was keep things going. No dead air; do not talk over dead air; one record after the other; keep your talk to about ten to fifteen seconds—that's it. With that approach came a tight playlist and heavily managed rotations.

"The songs were broken into about four or five categories. We had the power records, the ones that spun around the most, the popular hits—that was the A category. B category was up-and-coming stuff that was getting actively hot; it was new, or songs that had been in high rotation and were being slowed down. We had another category of recurrents, and another category of brand new music. We were expected to follow those rotations properly and not cheat, not play ahead. Because every song was on a three-by-five card, in a metal flip-up holder with category separators. Each song had a grid on it, date and time, and we had to find the right square and put a check mark in there of when it was played. And the music director and the program director would go through this stuff, and if we were cheating we'd get caught. The bottom line was, I didn't have much of a choice as to what I played and how often I played it."

A new FM station in Gainesville found an audience using a different approach. WGVL-FM began broadcasting in May 1970 as a country station before switching in 1971 to progressive rock or "underground music," as it was then called, and twenty-seven-year-old station owner Irving Uram gave the staff relatively free rein on song choices. WGVL played album cuts from popular artists as well as more experimental musical groups such as Pink Floyd or Frank Zappa, and in doing so opened up a fresh source of musical variety vastly different from the Top Forty fare of mainstream radio programming, available free to anyone with an FM receiver. A strong stereophonic FM radio signal sounded very good indeed through the big stereo amps and bookshelf speakers popular in the seventies.

By 1972 WGVL was broadcasting twenty-four hours daily and had begun to dominate the adult male 18–49 demographic, often beating out WRUF-AM and WGGG-AM, the two Top Forty stations in the market. Montana (Bill Thacker), Sebastian, Bishop, and Barbara were among the eminent hipsters who brought the music to the people, and in the sanctimonious verbiage of the time, one print ad for the radio station reads: "It works. Because we believe in it. We at WGVL-FM would like to extend a sincere thanks to all of our brothers and sisters in Gainesville who have helped to make our approach to radio a success. We live and breathe musical communication and we're glad you get off on it as much as we do."

In 1975 WGVL declared itself the Quadship and broadcast in "quadraphonic" format, in theory four discrete channels of sound, left and right front and left and right rear, requiring a quad receiver and four speakers to achieve quadraphonic sound, a short-lived concept that was briefly popular in the early seventies. WGVL employed a signal processor that made rear speakers sound slightly different than the front, so they in fact were not broadcasting in true "quad," but no one cared; the station played songs nobody ever heard on AM radio, and the station's free-form programming appealed to the stoner willing to listen to entire sides of *Dark Side of the Moon*, the new album by Sand, or bands such as Soft Machine, the Nice, and Emerson, Lake, and Palmer. The station would announce when they were about to play an album in its entirety with no interruptions, allowing time for listeners to cue up a blank tape in their cassette deck and record the album at home, a precursor to today's ubiquitous free music environment. WGVL's programming continued until 1982 before changing formats.

LET'S MAKE A RECORD

Few Gainesville bands had the resources and access to recording facilities to make a record and achieve the holiest of holies, radio airplay, but several bands did make the leap to vinyl, including the Rare Breed ("I Talked to the Sun," "In the Night," and as backing band for soul singer Gene Middleton on several locally produced singles), the Certain Amount (covering the Zombies' "Is This the Dream?"), and the Maundy Quintet ("2's Better Than 3," "I'm Not Alone"). In the summer of '72 Road Turkey contributed to a compilation album, *So It Goes*, for the Emory University Almanac in Atlanta. The trio drove to Atlanta and recorded their song "Out on the Shreds," and the album was released in early '73 to mild acclaim.

Mudcrutch received financial backing to record a 45 single from a friend who owned a pepper farm, and in the summer of 1973, the band drove down to Criteria Studios in Miami and recorded two originals by Petty. "It was a long drive," Randall Marsh recalls. "We did it so quick, went in there. I remember Petty out there all by himself singing the lead vocal—he was looking kind of vulnerable. We did the whole thing in just a few hours, came back, and we'd be calling the radio station in town, acting like we were fans. We'd call in, 'Hey man, we like that Mudcrutch song. Why aren't you playin' it?'" Released on their own label, Pepper Records, the two originals "Up in Mississippi" and "Cause Is Understood" are the first recordings with Tom Petty and Mike Campbell playing together.

Musical and social camaraderie naturally happened among this community of local players and led to the occasional stoned soul picnic on a summer afternoon.

Summer 1973, Gainesville, Florida, with various members of Mudcrutch, Road Turkey, Power, and friends and family. Permission of William "Red" Slater.

SOUTHERN MAN

The sounds of Gainesville musicians in live performance continued as always, but their musical talents were now available on the radio and on vinyl. Since leaving Gainesville in early '64, Stephen Stills had recorded three albums with Buffalo Springfield, three with Crosby, Stills, and Nash (sometimes Young), two solo albums, and two with his new band Manassas, who performed at Florida Field in '72. Stills also played as a sideman, including guitar on Bill Withers's hit "Ain't No Sunshine."

The Eagles' second album, *Desperado*, included several songs by member Bernie Leadon, including "Witchy Woman," a song he co-wrote with Don Henley that reached number nine on the charts and was the band's follow-up single to "Take It Easy." Leadon had left Gainesville in the summer of '67 and was now in a band with five hit singles, including "Witchy Woman," "Take It Easy," "Peaceful Easy Feeling," "Tequila Sunrise," and "Desperado."

Don Felder had been playing in a new group called Gingerbread with two former members of the Incidentals, John Winter on organ, flute, and sax and drummer Mike Barnett, along with ex-Jades bassist Chuck Newcomb, who grew up in nearby Lawtey, Florida. Gingerbread played their own blend of blues, jazz, and rock and were very popular in Gainesville, but similarly to Mudcrutch, the band found themselves repeatedly playing the same small venues in the area, eventually becoming overexposed through agreeing to play for free at virtually any charity benefit concert, and there were plenty. Gingerbread moved to upstate New York; the band changed their name to Flow, and in 1970 released an album on Creed Taylor's new jazz label, CTI, that was musically exciting but under-produced and had a low-budget album cover. The band soon drifted apart, and a restless Don Felder moved to Boston, where he found steady session work at a recording studio. After repeated suggestions by Bernie Leadon to move to the West Coast, in the summer of 1972, Felder and his wife drove from Boston to Los Angeles, where Leadon introduced Don to manager David Geffen and management partner Elliot Roberts, who arranged for Felder to play guitar on an upcoming tour for singer/ songwriter David Blue. In the words of lyricist Carole Bayer Sager, that's what friends are for.

Felder's first gig was the opening night of a new Sunset Strip club called the Roxy Theater. Soon the duo act began opening for the Eagles, under the proud gaze of Bernie Leadon watching from the wings. By the fall of '73, the group was opening for Crosby and Nash. Five years previously, Felder had watched Nash perform as a member of the Hollies at the Florida Gym; now he was in a band opening for Nash and ex-Byrd David Crosby. Felder had played cover versions of songs by both groups in earlier bands, and now it was evident he was getting closer and closer to the sources of this music.

One night Felder agreed to cover for Crosby and Nash's ailing guitarist, David Lindley, and after successfully playing the show, was asked to join the band. Felder was now in both opening act and headliner. As the tour continued, on October 31, 1973, at the Spectrum in Denver Steve Stills joined the group for a few songs, briefly reuniting the two former members of the Continentals, and Felder was, at least for a few minutes, the guitarist in Crosby, Stills, and Nash.

If success occurs when preparation meets opportunity, Don Felder was prepared for opportunity. It came a few months later when he got a phone call from the Eagles' Glenn Frey. Would Don be interested in adding some guitar parts on two Eagles tracks for the band's upcoming third album? Not surprisingly, Felder said yes.

THE LIVING ROOM SESSIONS

Meanwhile, back in Gainesville Mudcrutch was beginning to experience the hollow victory of being the biggest act in the region yet not being able to move beyond the circuit of clubs, university gigs, topless bars, and outdoor concerts. Realizing that they needed a record deal on a major label with a real record company, the band arranged a recording session for a demo tape that took place in the living room of keyboard player Benmont Tench's parents' home, a large carpeted space where the group set up their gear. Local sound engineer Rick Reed recorded the group in the fall of '73, shortly after Benmont's twentieth birthday. These sessions proved to be the initial step that gradually allowed the band to escape the local club and concert circuit.

"The Mudcrutch sessions were the only rock and roll multiple-microphone recording I had done," recalls Reed. "Everything else had been just two microphones on tall stands in an auditorium, recording concert bands or choral performances. Sandy Stringfellow hung out with these guys and also worked at my audio store, and when he suggested the idea of recording a live demo tape, Tom and the band agreed.

"I had a big single cable known as a 'snake' that I reeled into the living room, with a terminal box at the end and inputs for sixteen microphones. We put microphones on the Tench grand piano and the guitar amps. Keith McAllister was helping me understand how he would mic them for a concert; then he and I sat in the truck out in the driveway and tried to get a decent mix as the band played. After the first few takes the band would come out to the truck, and we'd make a few adjustments. We recorded a few hours a day for two days that way, and we left everything set up in the living room after the first day, so the second day we just had to plug the 'snake' back into the truck and start recording again.

"Then the band came up to my house, and we did the editing with everyone's input in one afternoon, and I created a master tape with leader tape between each cut—there were eight songs—then I made reel-to-reel copies on seven-inch reels for them to take out to wherever. I do remember one thing about Tom: he was no-nonsense, which really stood out at the time. During the playback and editing, he seemed to be real tuned-in to making it happen in an organized, efficient way. It was all business. My next memory is Tom calling me after they'd gotten the record deal and saying he needed to come out to the house to retrieve all the outtakes from the sessions.

"The last time I saw Mudcrutch was the farewell concert at the University Auditorium. I was invited by Keith to sit with him down in front. I had to leave after the second song because it was so loud my ears were just bleeding at that point."

With Bernie Leadon in the Eagles, with Don Felder about to contribute guitar to a couple songs on the Eagles' upcoming third album, and with Mudcrutch's demo tape making the rounds of the West Coast record labels, the music world was about to get a healthy dose of rock and roll energy from Gainesville's more ambitious rock and rollers.

SOMETHING IN THE AIR

1974

"The Joker" » Steve Miller
"Band on the Run" » Paul McCartney and Wings
"Benny and the Jets" » Elton John
"Until You Come Back to Me (That's What I'm Gonna Do)" » Aretha Franklin
"Takin' Care of Business" » Bachman-Turner Overdrive
"Radar Love" » Golden Earring
"Hello, It's Me" » Todd Rundgren
"Hollywood Swinging" » Kool and the Gang
"Spiders and Snakes," "Wildwood Weed" » Jim Stafford

As the seventies continued to unfold, there was something in the air besides the cloud of marijuana smoke that appeared over so many Gainesville musical events: there were big changes going on in the worlds of politics, culture, and pop music.

Ten years had passed since the Beatles' 1964 appearance on the *Ed Sullivan Show*, during which time Americans absorbed the musical influences of England's "British Invasion" and responded with our own American rock and roll. Now the pop music scene was in a sort of lull as the country struggled with multiple challenges.

GENERAL WACKINESS

Popular music tends to both shape and reflect the culture wherein it lives, and in the mid-seventies the music and culture of the United

States of America was in an odd place. The Vietnam War had finally ended, but now there was a new political scandal known as Watergate that led to a Senate committee preparing for impeachment proceedings against President Richard Nixon. In August 1974 Nixon resigned from office, the first U.S. president to do so, replaced by Vice President Gerald Ford, who immediately pardoned Nixon from any possible criminal prosecution.

Even with Nixon gone, all was not well: the stock market was in a slump; inflation was at 11.5 percent; and an OPEC oil embargo resulted in gas rationing, with stations across the country posting a green flag if fuel was available and a red flag if they had run out. The national speed limit was lowered to 55 miles per hour, and "Feelings" by Morris Albert was a worldwide hit, a song whose lyrical and musical content epitomized the worst aspects of seventies soft rock.

Culturally it appeared to be a time of general wackiness as well. South Carolina evangelist Jim Bakker and his wife, Tammy Faye, founded the PTL (Praise the Lord) television ministry, soon to become a multimillion-dollar religious empire. Streaking became a popular fad, with people running naked in public as a sort of pointless prank. Ray Stevens's latest novelty song was "The Streak," and it streaked straight to the top of the charts.

THE MUSIC GOES ROUND AND ROUND

Generally speaking these were soft and gentle times for popular music, possibly as an escape from the cultural malaise of the period. The top of the pop singles charts was constantly awash in such sonic lemonade as Roberta Flack's "Killing Me Softly with His Song," Paul Anka's "(You're) Having My Baby" (voted Worst Song of All Time in a poll conducted in 2006 by CNN.com), John Denver's "Sunshine on My Shoulders" and "Annie's Song," and Terry Jacks's "Seasons in the Sun," a record that sold more than fourteen million copies worldwide. On the brighter side of pop music there was the intriguing "Rock On" by David Essex, Bad Company's hard rocker "Can't Get Enough," the supercharged pop of "Waterloo" by Abba, "Band on the Run" by Paul

McCartney and Wings, and the Rolling Stones' "It's Only Rock and Roll (But I Like It)." Glitter Rock showed its heavily made-up face but arrived more as a fashion statement than a specific music style, where sound and vision merged in such gender-ambiguous artists as David Bowie, Lou Reed, Elton John, Todd Rundgren, Roxy Music, and the New York Dolls, who in full makeup really did look like dolls.

Meanwhile, something else was transpiring on the dance floors of clubs in Miami and New York City, with Kool and the Gang's rhythm and blues chart topper "Hollywood Swinging" featuring a rhythmic pulse and arrangement that hinted at a musical style soon to come.

The South had plenty of music to offer in 1974. Jacksonville's Lynyrd Skynyrd, a band you could have heard for fifty cents in the University Auditorium a few years back, had released a second album that included the hit single "Sweet Home Alabama," a song that rose to number eight on the charts and sold a million. Jim Stafford, a singer/songwriter from Winter Haven, released three Top Twenty singles in a row, "Spiders and Snakes," "Wildwood Weed," and "My Girl Bill." Gram Parsons's second solo album *Grievous Angel* was released posthumously and included performances by Emmylou Harris and Bernie Leadon. Parsons grew up in Winter Haven and is considered by many musicians and music critics to be the father of country-rock through his solo work and his role in the Byrds and the Flying Burrito Brothers. The Allman Brothers Band, despite the tragic deaths of founding members Duane Allman and bassist Berry Oakley, were now bigger than ever and had recently performed an outdoor concert along with the Grateful Dead to six hundred thousand people at the Summer Jam at Watkins Glen, New York. In the song "The South's Gonna Do It," Charlie Daniels name checks several southern acts, including Lynyrd Skynyrd, Wet Willie, ZZ Top, and the Marshall Tucker Band.

Musically, Florida had a lot going on, and in Gainesville the music venues continued to proliferate. On the university campus were at least eight sites that presented live music, including Florida Field, the Florida Gym, University Auditorium, Rathskeller, and various outdoor venues, such as the Museum and Arts Building, the Plaza of the Americas, Graham Pond, and the north lawn, south terrace, and Grand Ballroom of the Reitz Student Union.

If you lived on campus or just off campus in the student ghetto north of the school, at various times a few minutes' walk south could take you to the University Auditorium to hear Todd Rundgren's band Utopia, and a few blocks north you could hear Freddie King at the Longbranch Saloon, either show for three dollars and fifty cents. Down at the Rathskeller you could catch a set by Dion, a rock and roll singer whose career hits included "A Teenager in Love," "Runaround Sue," "Ruby," and "Abraham, Martin, and John." Venturing south of town to a supper club named the Beef and Bottle, you could catch a new comedian named Steve Martin, who told jokes in a white suit while playing banjo with a toy arrow apparently stuck through his head.

Housing was still inexpensive, and there was an abundance of rental houses where bands lived and rehearsed. The communal living culture was alive and well, and six people in a house could live inexpensively. Road Turkey rehearsed in a house on the east side, next to the Coca-Cola bottling plant; Celebration lived and rehearsed in a house near the Sin City section of town at 16th Avenue and 13th Street. Four blocks north, where a railroad bridge crossed 13th Street, was a five-acre wooded property known as the Stone Castle. David "Lefty" Wright, drummer for the Druids and Brothers Grymm and the Better Half, lived in the house built of stone there, and tenants of another house, nearer to the street, included for a time Tom Petty and the band Cowboy. Mudcrutch would set up outside and play, quickly attracting an audience from passing traffic, and Cowboy played a similar concert there with similar results. The property is now the site of Wildflower Apartments.

There were more live music venues than ever in the town. Regional bands that played included Eric Quincy Tate, Atlanta Rhythm Section, Hydra, Goose Creek Symphony, Cowboy, and Boot, formerly the Split Ends, a popular band from Port Richey, with Bruce Knox on lead guitar, and a drummer who, during his inevitable solo, played drumsticks with built-in microphones plugged into a tape-delay device, resulting in a cavalcade of sound. It was real gone, and Gainesville was alive with the sounds of music.

HEY, LET'S GO

But no matter how hip Gainesville was, a small town is a small town. Having played every venue in the region available to an unsigned musical act, Mudcrutch had now reached a turning point. Petty has said of Mudcrutch, "The whole point of the band had been to make a record." With the release of their single "Up in Mississippi," the band had indeed made a record and received regional airplay and a higher performance fee, but that was about it. Mudcrutch's demo tapes were now making the rounds of the record labels in Los Angeles, or so the band thought. Most likely the tapes were in a large pile in the mailroom along with those of numerous other bands all seeking the same thing, a record contract with a major record label. Unsolicited tapes were generally ignored at major record companies.

The band decided to take matters into their own hands by going to Los Angeles and delivering the tapes in person. In late 1973 Tom Petty, guitarist Danny Roberts, and the band's stage manager, Keith McAllister, headed west on I-10 in Roberts's 1969 VW camper van. Soon after arriving in Los Angeles, the three began making the rounds of record companies.

The first stop was Playboy Records, where an executive of the label took them into his office and explained, "Hey guys, it's not done this way; you just don't walk in." Petty recounted his reply: "'Well, we're here, and there's a tape deck, so why not put it on and listen?' He played not quite thirty seconds, then stopped the tape and said, 'I've heard enough; get out of my office.'" Thus ended the first day.

The next day they dropped in at Capitol Records, whose staff member liked the tape and offered to record a demo of the band; Petty pointed out that Mudcrutch had already made a demo, and the guy had just heard it. However, this was a step in the right direction, and they moved on.

Next stop was MGM Records, whose representative listened to the tape and was more encouraging, immediately offering the band a singles deal, agreeing to record and release one song, and if it did well, then discuss the next step. "No," Petty countered, "we're looking for an album deal." Still, the band had now received an offer from a major label to record and release a single.

Their final stop was London Records, the label the Rolling Stones were on in America. The label representative listened to the entire tape, Petty recounts, "and he starts clapping his hands and jumping around going, 'This is fantastic. You've got a deal! I want to hear the band right away. I want to make a record. This is great!'" When Petty explained that the band was in Gainesville, Florida, the response was, "Well, go get them!"

So just like that, Mudcrutch was offered a record deal with a major label, all on the basis of a live recording of the band. Of course, every bar and concert gig the band had played, every personnel lineup Mudcrutch had been through, and every song the band had played, written, thrown away, or rewritten had brought them to this point. They were ready to make an album. On London Records.

THIS MAGIC MOMENT

The trio drove back to Gainesville, where band, wives, girlfriends, crew, and dogs prepared for the move to Los Angeles. But there was one final detail to attend to. "I do remember having to talk to Ben's father, who was a big-time judge and was intimidating," Petty recalled. "And I had to talk him into letting his son quit college. And I made a pretty good case." Petty's talking points must have been compelling, as Judge Tench agreed.

During a band rehearsal, the phone rang. Not recognizing the voice, Petty figured it was someone calling about a car they were selling in order to raise money for the trip. As he began describing the

Tommy Ohmage and the Fantabulous Tornados, West Side Park, early 1974. Photograph courtesy of author.

car—"Well, it's not that good, but it's only a hundred bucks"—the voice at the other end said, "No, no, this is Denny Cordell, and I'm calling for Mudcrutch."

Denny Cordell was a legendary figure in the music business who as a record producer in the sixties was responsible for hit singles by Procol Harum ("Whiter Shade of Pale"), the Moody Blues ("Go Now"), and in later years for albums by Joe Cocker. Cordell was also co-owner with Leon Russell of Shelter Records, a record company with offices in Los Angeles and Tulsa. Cordell had heard Mudcrutch's demo tape and told Petty it was the best thing he'd heard in years and suggested the band drop by Tulsa on the way to Los Angeles to meet and check out Shelter's recording facilities.

Cordell was hoping to convince them that Shelter Records was a better choice than London Records, or as he later described it, "head 'em off at the pass." The band agreed to visit on their way to Los Angeles and set about raising money for the trip with several local farewell concerts.

One such concert, held outdoors at Westside Park, was a one-shot musical extravaganza billed as Tommy Ohmage and the Fantabulous Tornados, with a lineup that included all the members of Mudcrutch and Road Turkey with additional musicians and backup singers. Tommy Ohmage was delivered to the stage in a Lincoln Continental, dressed tastelessly in clashing paisley clothing and an Elvis tank top. The band played an assortment of rock and roll and rhythm and blues oldies. The audience seemed to like it, and they danced.

On April Fool's Day 1974 Mudcrutch began the trek west. After a series of automotive mishaps, the band arrived in Tulsa, and as Mudcrutch guitarist Danny Roberts recalls, "Denny Cordell took us to breakfast and told us he wanted to sign us on April 6th, 1974, after we had spent about forty-eight hours in the Church [recording] Studio."

With an advance of five thousand dollars cash from Cordell, the band arrived in L.A., rented two houses, and began recording at the Shelter studio at the record company's office, a two-story house off Sunset Boulevard.

It had taken just ten years and a few months for Petty to make the journey from watching the Beatles on TV to begin working on an album with his own band on a major record label.

HIPPIE ATTORNEY

There was something about Gainesville that stimulated the creative thinking of certain new arrivals. One such arrival was Jeffrey Meldon, who gradually became an active part of Gainesville's growing music community. In the early seventies, Jeffrey Meldon was one of several liberal activists who collectively called themselves the Candle People and whose interaction with Gainesville's music scene stemmed from their desire to contribute to the local counterculture through community involvement and organization.

Or something along those lines, as idealism ran high in those days.

They needed to start somewhere, as Meldon explains: "On the other side of Lincoln High School, there was a riding stable with about two hundred acres of woods and a rundown cabin; we rented it and called it the Candle Farm. We'd buy giant blocks of wax from the Gulf Oil Company, buy crayons at Toyland, and we'd make hippie candles, over a fire. Then we'd go to the college campus and sit outside the girls' dorms and flirt with the girls, put our candles on a picnic blanket, and sell them."

The group formed the Hogtown Food Co-op and an alternative school called the Windsor Learning Community. Then Meldon and company began getting involved with musicians and bands.

Jeffrey Meldon's interest in music began at a young age through spending time in his father and uncle's jazz club: "My father and his brother went into the jazz nightclub business in 1950 and opened a club in downtown Cleveland called the Loop Lounge, the largest jazz club between New York and Chicago at the time. It could seat about four hundred people and was one of the top jazz clubs in the country.

"That was my first exposure to music; every significant player in jazz played at this club. Charlie Parker played there for a week in 1954. My dad thought he was the hottest." At Ohio State Meldon became social director of his fraternity and hired bands for parties, including Booker T. and the M.G.'s and Doug Clark and the Hot Nuts.

In addition to working with Rose Community in helping produce the Mudcrutch Farm festivals, Meldon had recently passed the Florida bar exams and was now practicing law. If you were busted for marijuana possession, Meldon was the attorney to call, the Hippie Lawyer. "I got my law license in November of 1971; at that point Mudcrutch was still trying to get dates, play places, so I started working with Mudcrutch in my law office. They'd come in every week or so, and we'd talk about where they could play. I got them a gig at the Holiday Inn in Lake City, Florida, which they hated because they had to play cover songs, and that's the last thing they wanted to do. I was their booking agent for some gigs, and I was a lawyer, so they came to me for some advice. They had a young guy, Keith, who was their roadie, but Tom Petty and Tom Leadon were the guys that talked to me. So I went down to Miami to meet with Albert Teabagy; at the time he was working with a big Florida promoter. I went with some

Mudcrutch tapes to try to get them some gigs. I almost had them on, but the agencies booking the lead acts always wanted their own acts to open for the headliners; they nixed the deal. So we worked together for a few more months, but my law practice was building, and Petty didn't want to play Top Forty. I knew they were going to have to go somewhere else to make it big."

ROTARY RECONNECTION

A year later, Meldon's childhood friend Dick Rudolph relocated to Gainesville along with his pregnant wife, Minnie Riperton, a vocalist with a five-octave range who had sung in town years ago as a member of Rotary Connection and who would eventually become well known for a song she cowrote with her husband in Gainesville.

"'Lovin' You' was written (or at least inspired by the birth of Maya Rudolph) at Pirate's Cove restaurant on Biven Arm's Lake," Meldon recalls. "I was having dinner out there with Dick, Minnie, and an old 'Gator' working for Epic Records, Larry Ellis. Minnie had written 'Lovin' You,' and it was the start of her getting signed with Epic. My wife and Minnie and Dick were all interested in developing music in Gainesville and started trying to create a venue. There was an old barn in the black neighborhood that once was a juke joint called the Cotton Club, a major black music venue in the forties or fifties, but it needed too much work, so we passed. Just around then they got a call from L.A. and a contract and moved there in '73 and made a record with Epic Records."

Minnie Riperton's "Lovin' You" topped the U.S. singles chart in 1975, reached number two in the United Kingdom, and sold millions. This was the second song conceived in Gainesville that went to number one, the other being 1955's "Heartbreak Hotel."

IT'S SO EASY

In pursuing his desire to open a music venue, Meldon eventually settled on the Florida Theater at 233 W. University Avenue, a vacant twenties-era two-story brick building near the center of town with seating for more than a thousand. With his interest in music and a natural talent for the world of business and local politics, Meldon saw in the vacant building the same thing Bill Killeen had seen eight years ago in a vacant warehouse two blocks to the west: opportunity. "Around the end of 1973, the Jacksonville owners were interested in leasing the property. Across the street from it was a clothing store called the Young American Shop. The owner, Jim Forsman, had heard about my interest in starting a music forum, so he proposed that we go fifty-fifty on the project, and we cut a deal to do it. We went to Citizens Bank and somehow got a loan for fifty thousand dollars to renovate the theater. We needed to serve alcohol to make money, so we went to Jack McGriff [owner of the Gator Sport Shop], who was very influential in Tallahassee. He somehow got us a liquor license for the music hall for free. So we had the license."

Locate a suitable building, find a partner, arrange a fifty-thousand-dollar bank loan, score a free liquor license, and turn a movie theater into an eight-hundred-seat concert venue. Done. There were benefits to starting a business in a small southern town if you knew how.

But how do you convince national acts to play a small college town in north-central Florida? Meldon approached various booking agencies and explained the benefits of playing the Great Southern Music Hall. "I got the names of all the agencies, CMA, William Morris, and started calling them up and said, 'We have a place that holds eight hundred people; we can do two shows a night, Friday and Saturday, but if it's a hot act, we'll do it any other night.' We wanted to get the acts at a good price; we would take them when they were between shows in Miami or Orlando or Tampa or Jacksonville and traveling to a weekend booking, and we'd take them on a Sunday or a Thursday or whatever. We could get them for a lot less if we could get them on an open day of their tour; that's how we got our acts."

Opening night, April 6, 1974, featured the Earl Scruggs Revue. The venue had excellent sound and was within easy walking distance if you lived near downtown. "Eventually we began to expand. There was a wine bar underneath the raked seating near the back—we had a solo artist there—and above on University Avenue we opened the Downtown Deli, a full delicatessen from lunch till after dinner. On the left side we opened the Backstage Bar; it held about a hundred people. The bar would have bands playing during the week. The Backstage Bar was our idea of having live music during the week."

The Great Southern Music Hall presented fifteen shows in their first year and became a significant concert venue, presenting the top performers of the day in the heart of a small college town. And who played there? Pull up a chair. Meldon consults his list. "Bo Diddley, Jerry Lee Lewis, Patti LaBelle, Jean Luc Ponty, Dave Brubeck, Pat Travers, Jimmy Buffett, Cowboy, Wet Willie, Molly Hatchett, Rossington Collins Band, Leo Kottke, Dan Fogelberg, Richie Havens, Jesse Colin Young, Bob Seger, Steppenwolf, Mahogany Rush, the Outlaws.

"Country Joe and the Fish, Alvin Lee, Savoy Brown, Rick Derringer, Bonnie Raitt, Doug Kershaw, Vassar Clements, Stanley Clarke, Todd Rundgren, Randy Newman, John Prine, Gamble Rogers, It's a Beautiful Day, Jerry Jeff Walker, Muddy Waters, Jimmy Spheeris, Cheech and Chong, Elvin Bishop, Kraftwerk, Waylon Jennings, Al Kooper, Seals and Crofts, Melissa Manchester, Ray Charles—for two nights . . . Ray liked his champagne!—B. B. King, Steve Martin, Count Basie, Roger McGuinn, Howlin' Wolf.

"Grover Washington, Jimmy Cliff, Peter Tosh, Hot Tuna, Quicksilver Messenger Service, the Chambers Brothers, Martin Mull, Poco, Robin Trower, the Runaways, Joan Jett, Spirit, Taj Mahal, Iron Butterfly, Blue Oyster Cult, Souther-Hillman-Furay, the Band, José Feliciano, Tim Weisberg, Leon Redbone, Sea Level, Pat Metheny, John Hartford, Billy Cobham, George Duke, Dave Bromberg, John Hammond, Johnny Winter, Al Jarreau, Gregg Allman, Head East, Johnny Shines, Herbie Mann, Chick Corea's Return to Forever (with Stanley Clarke), Weather Report, Minnie Riperton, America, and Eric Burdon."

Not included in this list are the many local bands that opened for these artists and those playing in the two smaller performance areas.

Unlikely scenes transpired on occasion, as recalled by local player Roger Schliefstein: "I met Frank Zappa at the Backstage Bar. I was jamming on harp with some guys in the Wine Cellar, and he was chain smoking and drinking water with his bodyguard, Baldheaded John. I asked Frank if he'd like to sit in with us in the Wine Cellar. He said, 'Sure, why not?' I hustled frantically back to the wine cellar to find the band, and we all agreed. I went back to the bar just in time to see some drunk UF student say, 'Fuck you, Frank Zappa!' and he poured a mug of beer all over Frank's beautiful white suit. Baldheaded John picked up this little S.O.B. and literally threw him so hard through the front double doors that the kid landed clear into the right lane of University Ave. Needless to say Frank and John left the bar, and we never jammed. Frank was still trying to keep his beer-soaked cigarette alive."

SONG OF THE SOUTH

Gainesville bands with the desire and connections to play gigs beyond the local club circuit, and whose members were not blessed with a steady job, could find bookings throughout the Southeast. Along with the long hours spent driving and playing four sets a night were moments of high adventure. Dave Grohl (Nirvana, Foo Fighters) describes this feeling when he explains, "When you're young, you're not afraid of what comes next. You're excited by it." Gregg Allman also recalls being young and having "so much want-to." This was also the case for the Gainesville musicians who ventured beyond the city limits in search of other places to play. All roads led out of Gainesville, and US 441 and I-75 beckoned.

Bands booked out-of-town gigs in a variety of ways: through contacts such as friends from high school now in college on the entertainment board of the school or fraternity; through regional booking agencies such as the Armstrong Agency, Bee Jay, Prestige, and Blade Productions; and just as often by word-of-mouth from other bands regarding clubs or bookers. This loose collective of bars, clubs, fraternities, and other music venues spread as far north and south as you were willing to drive—north to Jacksonville, Tallahassee, Atlanta, Macon, Athens, Tuscaloosa; south to Ocala, Orlando, Tampa,

Road Turkey in front of the College Inn, 1974: (*left to right*) Carl Patti, Stan Lynch, Marty Jourard, Steve Soar. Photograph by author.

and even sometimes as far south as Miami. Tracing the path of Road Turkey—now a four-piece band with Stan Lynch, Carl Patti, Steve Soar, and me—offers an example of mid-seventies band touring.

In February 1974 Road Turkey played an outdoor show at the university's North Union Lawn. The next month the band spent eleven days in Cocoa Beach, first at the Pillow Talk Lounge in the Satellite Motel, an aging relic from the fifties, playing from 9 p.m. to 1 a.m. the first few nights and 9 p.m. to 3:30 a.m. the next three. The following week the band found a better gig down the road at George's Steaks, a club that presented two bands nightly from 9 p.m. to 7 a.m. The Flaming Danger Brothers performed the first shift on Monday but were fired, so Road Turkey played from 9 p.m. to 1 a.m. for four nights, until New Days Ahead headlined Friday and Saturday, shifting Road Turkey to the 2 a.m. to 7 a.m. slot. Customers of this beach bar during the graveyard shift in the mid-seventies included insomniacs, transvestites, drug dealers, prostitutes, night-shift workers not ready to go home yet, and other people of the night.

In June the band played on the North Union Lawn, in August a three-day gig at Our Place, a jock bar in Tuscaloosa, Alabama. Neither band, nor patrons, nor bar owner were happy about the booking. Whatever they wanted, it wasn't us. Venturing from Gainesville to other southern towns was an eye-opening experience. Not every town had a large hippie population; long hair was uncommon; and the eclectic nature of a Gainesville band's set list was not always welcomed with open ears. "Do y'all play any songs we've heard before?" was one of the more polite comments.

By September Road Turkey hit the road, five in a van, towing a U-Haul trailer rented from Tubby's '66 service station "for two days," kept for weeks, and returned late at night. No one at the gas station seemed to notice or care.

The band was booked by the Armstrong Agency out of Macon, Georgia, for four nights at Uncle Sam's, a large club with two stages just outside the city, built and owned by Capricorn Records president Phil Walden as a sort of personal hangout and concert facility for acts on his record label. Road Turkey alternated sets with Eric Quincy Tate on separate stages, and the band stayed at the Courtesy Court across the highway for ten dollars a night.

While setting up gear the first night playing the club, we noticed a Triumph "chopper" motorcycle parked inside the club's liquor stockroom, heavily chromed and customized, with Maltese Cross rearview mirrors and extended front forks. The motorcycle was Gregg's, the bartender explained, but they wouldn't let Gregg drive home the previous night. Taking the prudent course, a policeman drove Allman home personally in his police cruiser. The bartender put it this way: "We don't want fifteen million down the drain." In Macon they looked out for their own.

A visit to Macon's H&H Restaurant revealed the reverence in which the Allman Brothers Band was held in the town, with the walls of the soul food restaurant adorned with photographs of the band in earlier years, and a painting of Duane Allman playing guitar in heaven, complete with angel wings and a halo, sitting on a cloud. At the H&H, for two dollars and five cents you could eat fried chicken with butterbeans, collard greens, and macaroni and cheese, washed down with a Mason jar of iced tea and finished off with a slice of sweet potato pie.

From Macon the band drove to Atlanta and stayed at a friend's house, as potential gigs fell through, finally playing one night at Alex Cooley's Electric Ballroom for one hundred dollars, opening for Mother's Finest.

In October the band played four nights at the Whippin' Post in Tampa and were rehired for New Year's Eve weekend for one hundred and fifty dollars a night. Later in the month Gerry Greenhouse filled in for ailing drummer Stan Lynch, and the band played an apartment complex in Atlanta for one hundred and seventy dollars and an abortive series of nights in Athens, Georgia, at the Hedges, where local favorites Dixie Grease were asked to play alternate sets using our equipment after the owner decided he just didn't like Road Turkey. That he was describing our booking agent as "that hook-nose Jew in Atlanta" directly to two Jews in the band made it a bit more amusing.

Venturing outside the bubble of "hippie city" Gainesville into the mainstream Deep South was often a reality check for bands that wrongfully assumed the easygoing atmosphere of their hometown was shared by other cities. Generally speaking, it wasn't.

Thanksgiving weekend back in Gainesville, the band played the Granfalloon, a music club previously the King's Food Host restaurant, then back to Atlanta later in the year at Hot 'Lana, playing alternate sets with Mazer. A party for the Vero Beach Fireman's Association in central Florida was followed by one final run in Tampa at the Whippin' Post for New Year's Eve week, with Benmont Tench driving down to hang out and jam. Musicians did that sort of thing.

At this level, working bands very much toured on the cheap,

sometimes sleeping four or five to a motel room or just as often on someone's living-room floor in a sleeping bag. But you were young and playing music and getting paid and occasionally laid and seeing more of the great big world beyond your hometown. And adventure or near-disaster lay just beyond the next rise in the road.

LAUGH, LAUGH

The Gainesville band scene had its own unique sense of humor. How else to explain band names such as Mudcrutch? Road Turkey? Fat Chance? Tight Shoes? Froggy and the Magic Twangers? Or the Master Gators, a hastily assembled group of musicians that played a Gators' basketball game halftime show and received a big laugh when their name was announced over the loudspeaker. Band names such as Mr. Poundit and the Master Race, RGF, Fresh Meat, Flash and the Cosmic Blades, Uncle Funnel, Good Things to Eat, and Mr. Moose seemed to indicate a certain playfulness because, despite inevitable conflicts between band members, and between bands and club owners, despite the inevitable drunken cries of bar patrons demanding "Free Bird," playing in a band had genuine moments of high comedy.

FLY LIKE AN EAGLE

Meanwhile, way out west in Los Angeles, Mudcrutch were recording tracks for Shelter Records, and Don Felder was officially a member of the Eagles, soon after the band listened to his guitar work on two tracks, "Good Day in Hell" and "Already Gone." At twenty-seven years old Felder was a veteran of playing and recording music, a consummate guitarist with an intense drive and work ethic that was beginning to pay off. Ten years previously, Bernie Leadon had asked Buster Lipham the name of the best guitarist in town; ten years later record producer Bill Szymczyk asked the Eagles if they knew of "any good incendiary guitar players" who might bring the group's sound closer in style to the big guitar-driven sounds of Led Zeppelin and the Who. In both cases the answer to the question was Don Felder.

The first day in the studio, Bernie greeted his bandmate from the Maundy Quintet days, and Felder wondered later if Leadon had mixed feelings about his arrival and Glenn Frey's stated intent of steering the band away from country and toward rock. To put it in Felder's own words, "Glenn wanted to speed things up and Bernie wanted to slow things down." *On the Border* was released in March of 1974 and within two months had achieved gold record status, the Eagles' fastest-selling album yet, with "The Best of My Love" reaching number one and selling more than a million. Now, two Gainesville boys were in a chart-topping band.

By the end of the year, the Eagles began work on a new album, *One of These Nights*, with Felder arranging the title track's intro and bass guitar part as well as playing "incendiary" guitar. Bernie Leadon, however, was increasingly downhearted with the direction the Eagles were taking and with his diminishing role as a songwriter and founding member. Change was in the air.

DISCO INFERNO

1975–1976

"One of These Nights," "Take It to the Limit" » Eagles

"Get Down Tonight" » KC and the Sunshine Band

"Fame" » David Bowie

"Shining Star" » Earth, Wind, and Fire

"How Long" » Ace

"Let Your Love Flow" » Bellamy Brothers

"I'm on Fire" » Dwight Twilley

"Pick up the Pieces" » Average White Band

"You Should Be Dancing" » Bee Gees

"Rock'n Me" » Steve Miller

"Tonight's the Night (Gonna Be Alright)" » Rod Stewart

"Disco Inferno" » The Trammps

"Depot Street" » Mudcrutch

During the mid-seventies a new rhythmic pulse flowed through the heart of popular music, born in the dance clubs of New York City and gradually becoming a major trend in American culture. Built around the steady pulse of a bass drum on all four beats of a measure—boom, boom, boom, boom—this indication of where the beat was—you couldn't miss it—was described by some critics as "music even white people could dance to." Around this beat grew a music genre known collectively as disco, the abbreviation of *discothèque*—Parisian nightclubs that offered dancing to records (*disques*) played loudly.

The rise of disco music and the culture that accompanied it grew from a need for self-expression that was not being represented in the current rock music and fashion. Music that expressed the feelings of white straight males had been around since the beginning of rock and roll, but mainstream pop music that expressed aspects of the black, gay, and female experience had not yet entered the cultural mainstream; to a certain extent disco helped fill this vacuum.

Disco began in the early seventies, grew in cultural prominence through 1977, then peaked and faded away in the final two years of the decade. Although identifying the first disco song is as problematic as identifying the first rock and roll song, one likely candidate is 1972's "Soul Makossa" by Cameroon saxophonist Manu Dibango, a record discovered in an import store by a DJ who recognized its appeal and began playing it incessantly at a New York City dance club.

"Soul Makossa" has all the prime characteristics of disco: the repetitive bass drum pattern, bass-heavy production, orchestral interludes, moderate tempo, and a six-minute length geared for the dance floor rather than radio airplay. The song's underground success led to massive airplay on WBLS, the top black radio station in the city.

Popularity tends to support itself, so more records came along geared to appeal to these trendy dance clubs frequented by gays of all sexes and races and the straight women and men who enjoyed the racy demimonde atmosphere. Chests were bared, often by both sexes, and the human body was celebrated as dancers shook their booties while clad in body-hugging Spandex. A disco culture of music and style began to unfold on a scale comparable to the British Invasion of music and fashion of the previous decade.

"Rock the Boat," the 1974 hit by the Hues Corporation, was an early disco song that reached number one on the pop music chart, starting with extensive play in dance clubs. Certain records were zooming up the charts based on true grassroots appeal rather than through record label promotion, and "Rock the Boat" had inspired another number-one song, "Rock Your Baby," sung by George McCrae over a backing track originally intended as a rough demo recording created in about twenty minutes by two members of KC and the Sunshine Band. "Rock Your Baby" sold eleven million units, and its catchy rhythm track, itself derived from "Rock the Boat," inspired the rhythmic pulse of ABBA's "Dancing Queen" and John Lennon's "Whatever Gets You Through the Night," also number-one hits. The chart-topping disco sounds continued with "Love Train" by the O'Jays and Billy Preston's "Will It Go Round in Circles."

The writing was on the wall as disco's production values and emphasis on the repetitive beat became increasingly popular. Mainstream artists rode the rhythm all the way to the top, including the Eagles with "One of These Nights" (1975). Yes, two former members of Gainesville's Maundy Quintet were now in a band with a number-one disco song, providing cowriters Henley and Frey with another peaceful easy feeling. Further disco-based hits included Elton John and Kiki Dee's "Don't Go Breaking My Heart" (1976), Barry Manilow's "Copacabana" (1978), Rod Stewart's "Do Ya Think I'm Sexy?" (1978), the Rolling Stones' "Miss You" (1978), and Blondie's "Heart of Glass" (1979).

To put this musical trend in perspective: for one week in April 1964, the Beatles held the first five positions in the singles chart. For one week in July 1979, the first *six* positions in the singles chart were disco songs. The soundtrack album to the movie *Saturday Night Fever* sold fifteen million units and stayed on top of the U.S. album charts for twenty-four weeks in 1978. Disco was big, bigger, the biggest style around.

Disco was loathed at least as much as it was loved, primarily by the large cadre of working rock musicians whose livelihoods were being severely diminished by the increasing dominance of disco records for dancing rather than live music at the clubs, bars, and taverns where they had been playing all these years. Rock musicians saw the change in the current hit singles chart and watched as the dance floors of their local clubs bulged with men in polyester Nik-Nik shirts and satin bellbottoms who danced with women in silver-sequined tube tops and platform high heels as "You Can Ring My Bell" pounded out of a massive sound system—all at the very clubs where these musicians once played five nights a week.

But a backlash was already in effect from other sources, people with different tastes and angry young guys who wanted to rock out to acts like Foreigner and Bob Seger and Lynyrd Skynyrd. A grassroots "Disco Sucks!" movement led up to a Disco Demolition Night promotional event held between the two games of a baseball doubleheader in the summer of 1979 at Chicago's Comiskey Park. Most of the fifty thousand attendees were there to see the promotional event rather than the game, and when a crate containing thousands of disco records was blown up with dynamite, a riot occurred as fans charged the field.

The musical tide was rapidly turning. Two months after Disco Demolition Night the top song on the *Billboard* singles chart was "My Sharona" by the Knack, a four-piece rock band whose onstage sixties British band image was a direct homage of the Fab Four.

If you were in search of a fifteen-year music cycle, there it was.

So disco came, and disco eventually went, but its popularity had a major effect on several aspects of the music business that would play out for some time.

TURN THE BEAT AROUND

During disco's dominance on the record charts, the attention of the record industry had shifted away from rock bands and toward songs and music acts created by teams of writers, arrangers, producers, and hired studio musicians playing written arrangements. These were not bands as we know them, and although the singer on these recordings was often presented as the artist, the true creative force behind these recordings was the behind-the-scenes team that produced the song from top to bottom, including a recording engineer who made sure there were plenty of those deep bass frequencies for the giant subwoofers of the massive club sound systems. If anything good came out of disco, it was an improvement in recording drums and bass. For this we give thanks.

These songwriting and production teams could create hits from such lyrics as "sweat/sweat/sweat until you get wet," "do the hustle," or the refrain "you can ring my bell (ding dong ding)" chanted over repetitive rhythm-track backing. There were of course a few notable songs, such as Gloria Gaynor's "I Will Survive," which became a sort of anthem, and Yvonne Elliman's "If I Can't Have You" had a certain cool. Musical ensembles for these productions began with a rhythm section of drums, bass, guitar, and keyboard, then added layers of Latin percussion sounds and electronic drums such as the Synare and string and horn arrangements as overdubs (a good example being "Love's Theme" by the Love Unlimited Orchestra).

As a result of this trend, many rock bands felt they were on the edge of extinction. A typical four- or five-piece bar band could not reproduce the sound of a disco hit built from such a complex musical arrangement and instrumentation. Playing "The Hustle" by Van McCoy in a cover band required a new set of sounds not available from drums, bass, and guitar. The Bee Gees' "Night Fever" featured a falsetto vocal over a ten-piece band. Disco culture had more to do with individual songs and less to do with the artists. There were a few disco acts that qualified as actual bands, such as KC and the Sunshine Band and Kool and the Gang, but in other cases these disco "groups" had been assembled by a manager or impresario, a good example being the Village People, a cartoon-like band with each member playing a role—the cop, the construction worker, the cowboy—whose succession of hits included "Macho Man"(number twenty-five), "YMCA" (number two), and "In the Navy" (number three).

Sensing the economic advantage of catering to this trend, Gainesville clubs began introducing "Disco Night" along with the usual live music nights, and a few clubs began alternating a live band with disco records played through massive sound systems.

The loud music and lighting effects were reminiscent of the light shows at sixties rock venues such as the Fillmore West. In both decades the idea was to create a disorienting alternative experience, but now the recreational drugs had moved beyond psychedelics and marijuana and into cocaine, amyl nitrate "popper" ampoules, and methaqualone, a powerful central-nervous-system depressant marketed under the name Quaalude, a pill that made you feel drunk without drinking, the white tablets referred to in clubs as "disco biscuits." Disco was becoming a self-contained culture with its own fashion styles, recreational drugs, and music.

In Gainesville, as in other cities, the local trend veered away from the rock and roll band as a music source for dancing and toward disco music played by a DJ. The Cin City Lounge, a bar and music venue with a live music policy over the years, hopped on the wagon. Audio engineer Jim Nygaard took the sound system belonging to David Carr and installed it at Cin City: "The regional manager of Big Daddy's was Steve Boberski, and Steve told us that Big Daddy's was going to sell off the Cin City Lounge because it wasn't turning any money. The band Homer had decided to let a friend book them instead of Carr, so we had the four Century speakers and the Phase Linear 700 Amplifier that we had bought for Homer. David had heard me talk about the 'Phono Bars' (*disco* wasn't a word yet) that I had seen in Europe. He begged Boberski to let us just take the door and do a 'Phono Bar' at the Cin City Lounge. Since they were going to sell it anyway, Boberski found no problem with this 'no investment' gamble. In two weeks we had Cin City earning more money, per square foot, than any Big Daddy's property. Joe Flanagan later hired me to come to Miami, join his staff, and build discos at twenty-five of the Big Daddy properties." After the initial cost of the sound system was recovered, the only entertainment expense was to pay a DJ to select and play the records.

Dub Thomas, a man constantly abreast of cultural trends from the topless go-go dancers of the sixties to his miniskirt contests, hopped aboard the trend by mid-1975.

Stan Bush, a singer and guitarist in several local bands, recalled this shift in the music scene: "We had been playing all over the South for decent money, but when the disco thing came along, we had to start playing for a lot less money. A lot of the clubs stopped having live music, and the ones that did paid less money. We had to learn some of those songs, Average White Band, KC and the Sunshine Band, etc., and we were rockers (and very white), so that funky stuff

Dub's Disco Party Night, circa 1975. Reprinted from the *Independent Florida Alligator*.

definitely wasn't our forte. By the mid-seventies the club scene was pretty bleak."

GOING SOUTH OUT WEST

In February of 1975, Shelter Records released Mudcrutch's first single, "Depot Street." Producer Denny Cordell was an early fan of reggae music—the license plate on his Ferrari Daytona spelled RAAS—and Petty's song leans in that direction, with a Caribbean rhythm feel unlike any song the band had ever played. "Depot Street" didn't really leave the station though, and the song's failure to chart was one indication of a band in transition. Denny Cordell began encouraging Petty's songwriting over the efforts of other band members. Internal frictions increased, and with Petty wanting to switch over to guitar, he asked former Tropics bass player Charlie Souza to join the band on bass. Souza came to Los Angeles, but by the time he'd arrived, the label had dropped Mudcrutch while retaining Tom Petty as a solo artist. Petty immediately went to Mike Campbell and said, "Don't leave," and the two musical partners began recording Petty's songs using top session players such as Jim Gordon, Donald "Duck" Dunn, John Sebastian, and Al Kooper.

Petty, however, wanted to be in a band making albums, not a solo artist backed by session players, no matter how good. Writing and recording continued.

HERE COME THE GATORS

Meanwhile, back in Gainesville, the music scene rolled on. Despite disco's impact on club play, live music from national acts continued, with the Great Southern Music Hall presenting a variety of major country, blues, jazz, and rock acts, and with student activity organizations at the university presenting Johnny Cash, Stephen Stills, Bob Dylan's Rolling Thunder Revue, Leon Russell, Billy Cobham, and Roger McGuinn. Road Turkey had broken up, and Stan Lynch drove his VW bus to Los Angeles, adding another Gator to the ranks of expatriate Gainesville musicians now in the City of Angels, including former RGF members Mike Hitchcock and Jeff Jourard, who were in a new version of RGF that featured Chris DeMarco, a singer the band met in Boston the previous winter. Chris DeMarco and RGF played a few gigs in Los Angeles, then fell apart after a fistfight between Chris and guitarist Thomas Patti.

The migration of the dozen or so Gainesville players to the West Coast was gradual and took place over several years but with one common denominator: constant support and encouragement from those who had made the move themselves. Rather than viewing fellow musicians from Gainesville as more competition, they were seen as familiar faces in a new town. Southern California was another world, and it was good to see players from back home with similar musical roots. There was an unspoken bond amongst Gainesville musicians that seemed an extension of band camaraderie.

As the youngest player in the group, Lynch needed encouragement to make the move. "I'd already done a dry run a few years previous when I drove with my sister Jody out to L.A. to attend school. We drove almost straight through," he recalls. "I drop her off, and she says, 'Get out of here.' Mike Hitchcock [former RGF drummer] took pity on me that day, took me out for breakfast, and said, 'What are you gonna do?' I said, 'Well, go home,' and he replied, 'I thought you came out here to live.' And I told him I'd love to, and he put the seed in my mind and told me about Musicians Contact Service and showed me L.A. I think I spent one day there, and he drove me to LAX airport, and I flew home. So I had this one little primer through Hitchcock's eye of L.A."

Lynch finally arrived in early 1975 and soon joined Slip of the Wrist, a rock band with blues roots, recently arrived from Texas and led by singer and guitarist Gary Myrick. In Lynch's words, "I'd been out there about a month. I signed up with Musicians Contact Service and got a call from Myrick. We rehearsed in Pasadena at the Pasadena Athletic Club, an old building from the twenties. Van Halen rehearsed in the next room over. It was a very formative time for me on the drums. They wanted simplicity, and I mean simplicity. I learned the value of repetition from those Texas boys. They beat it into me." At nineteen years old Lynch was the youngest of the Gainesville musicians relocated to Los Angeles, a list that now included Tom Petty, Mike Campbell, Benmont Tench, Randall Marsh, Danny Roberts, Mike Hitchcock, Jeff Jourard, Ron Blair, Trantham Whitley, and Tom Leadon. All were in pursuit of the same thing: success.

The act of moving from Gainesville to Los Angeles with the intent to pursue a music career rather than staying in the South was the great divide. Not every musician had the ability or willingness to take such a leap of faith, as it indeed was. But some did. Petty and Campbell continued recording together in Los Angeles in search of a sound and, in the back of Petty's mind, also a great band to play his songs; Lynch was drumming in Slip of the Wrist and playing gigs around Southern California. Tom Leadon was out there too, invited by his older brother Bernie. "I moved out to L.A. at the end of 1972, a few days before New Year's, living with my brother out in Topanga Canyon. The first thing I did was form a band with Michael Georgiades and [bassist] Mark Andes from Spirit and Jo Jo Gunne and Firefall, but we never played anywhere, made a bunch of demos of original songs. These were the only guys I knew. Michael made a record with my brother, and he was and still is one of Bernie's closest friends.

"I did a few gigs with Don Felder. We had a house together in Topanga Canyon, but weren't in a band together. I played lead guitar for Linda Ronstadt in September and October of 1973. She had a tour and needed a guitarist. My brother had played guitar with her previously; he recommended me, and I auditioned. We went on the road back east, mostly larger clubs."

The tour ended, and Leadon was now a member of a large collective known as musicians at liberty—that is, out of work. But in Los Angeles you tended to meet a lot of people in the music business. "There were long, long periods when I didn't work. There were a lot of times that it was really slow. Then I got a job with a band at the Scotch and Sirloin on the corner of Pico and Sepulveda, five nights a week gig, a country-rock jam band. And that's where I met Johnny Rivers, and he hired me for his band. They needed a bass player, and I became a bass player for two or three years with Johnny Rivers, touring around the country, and Bernie introduced me to John Hartmann, who had his own Hartmann/Goodman management company that managed America and Poco. They had another act, a trio called Silver, and they were looking for a bass player and drummer. So Harry Stinson and myself tried out, and we were hired and auditioned for Clive Davis, and they already had the song 'Wham Bam Shang a Lang' recorded, but no one in the band had played on it; they just sang on it. It had been a song that John Batdorf had already cut in an act called Batdorf and Rodney; they took Rodney's voice off and added the three of them singing on this record. They just had studio people, Dean Parks on guitar, Jim Gordon, Scott Edwards on bass; they didn't mention that on the record—they wanted people to think we were on it. It came down to our manager said, 'You can do this or go back to work with Johnny Rivers,' so I said OK. But we played on the rest of the album, and it was well received."

"Wham Bam Shang a Lang" hit the Top Twenty, peaking at number sixteen, and sold a remarkable seven hundred thousand copies, but none of the subsequent songs were hits. The band got in a disagreement with Clive Davis on who would produce the second album, another tale of the business side of the music business, as Leadon explains: "The band wanted to use Bill Halverson, the engineer of the first Crosby, Stills, and Nash album. Clive had another guy in mind, and we weren't in a position to argue with Clive. We were on the outs with Clive, and we left or they dropped us and didn't get another deal and that was that. We were one-hit wonders."

TAKE IT TO THE LIMIT

By now Don Felder and Bernie Leadon had recorded their second album as members of the Eagles, a band with a large dose of Gainesville. The band's fourth album, *One of These Nights,* was released in

June of 1975 and rose to the top of the charts, the first Eagles album with a majority of songs written by the band members.

Within months the Eagles became the top-selling rock band in America. The three singles "One of These Nights," "Lyin' Eyes," and "Take It to the Limit" reached number one, number two, and number four, respectively. Of the nine album tracks, five included either Leadon or Felder as writer or cowriters, and the credits on "Hollywood Waltz" include Felder and the two Leadon brothers, Bernie and Tom.

Having a song on an Eagles album is a good thing, and Tom describes how it went down: "When I first lived with my brother in Topanga, that spring there were acacia trees blooming bright yellow all over Topanga Canyon, and I was with him in his truck when he mentioned that would be a cool thing to write about—something about the acacias are blooming—and I wrote a song that was in three-quarter time. When I later saw my brother, I played it for him, and he liked it. A couple years later they were in Miami working on the *One of These Nights* album, and I was playing down at the Scotch and Sirloin with a band when I got a message to call him. So I went to the pay phone and called, and he asked me from Miami how that song went, and I sang it to him over the phone. And he said he was going to show it to Glenn and Don, and they might want to rewrite a lot of the words, and I said, 'Tell them to do it however they want.' They did and then recorded it, and that's how I cowrote that song with them. That was a really interesting way to cowrite a song. I didn't ask to hear it or give approval because I knew that if I put any kind of delay on it, or any kind of stipulation, they might decide, 'Well, we won't do this.' They made it into a Hollywood, Southern California, thing to fit the concept of the album, kind of philosophically about life in L.A."

One of These Nights sold four million copies and was nominated for Album of the Year.

Writing a successful song is a great way to make money. "It helped a lot, and was a real education in the music business; I learned about publishing and how people can rip off your publishing, and I didn't get all the money I was supposed to get, but I did get a lot of it." Leadon pauses for a minute and reflects. "Music is a great thing, as you know."

LEAVING THE NEST

The Eagles were selling millions . . . but somehow it just wasn't enough. Aside from the inevitable personality clashes inherent in the band, the group was also caught up in the musical struggle between Bernie Leadon's country and bluegrass roots and Glenn Frey's intention to toughen up the band sound with high-energy rock, something they had achieved in large part through Felder's guitar work. Ongoing tensions led Leadon and Frey into a final disagreement; when Leadon suggested Frey "chill out" and illustrated the suggestion by pouring a beer over Frey's head, the end was near. In late December of 1975, band manager Irving Azoff announced the departure of Leadon from the band and the arrival of replacement Joe Walsh.

The Eagles now had two great rock guitarists in the band, and Leadon went off and recorded the album *Natural Progressions* with his friend Michael Georgiades.

BRING IT ON HOME TO ME

At the beginning of 1976, I drove from Gainesville to Los Angeles to attend the University of Southern California, with an underlying intent to become involved in the same music scene that brought every other Gainesville musician to the West Coast. The only people I knew in Los Angeles were Gainesville musicians, and the day after I arrived, I observed a Tom Petty recording session—more specifically, John Sebastian adding harmonica to Petty's "Louisiana Rain." Sebastian had brought along a shopping bag of his harmonicas, several in each key, explaining that each was pitched slightly differently. This was one of many recording sessions booked at night by producer Denny Cordell at various studios around Los Angeles with the intent of completing a Tom Petty solo album.

Benmont Tench, at liberty after Mudcrutch broke up, had joined the Nasti City Soul Revue, a multiracial soul music band in Altadena, but had since quit and was now working on his own material as part of a project he and drummer Stan Lynch had concocted after a random meeting of the two ex-pat Gainesville musicians. "My first place in L.A. was a garage in Culver City," Lynch recalls. "I lived there for a few months until I ran into Trantham [Whitley, former Riff keyboard player], who told me he was moving his piano out of Doug D'Amico's garage [former RGF singer] and that maybe Doug would let me live there. Sixty bucks a month, no bathroom, kitchen, or heat.

"That's where I ran into Ron Blair [former RGF bassist] next door and ran into Mike Campbell and Benmont Tench a month later. Campbell lived down the hill, and Ben was visiting. I was walking up the hill because my VW bus had broken down, and Benmont picked me up and hung out in the garage with me. We conspired to start a band called Drunks."

Tench had wrangled free time at a recording studio through his friend Tim Kramer, an engineer at Village Recorders, and quickly assembled a roster of Gainesville players for his songs, including Campbell, Lynch, Randall Marsh, Jeff Jourard, and Ron Blair.

Drummer Mike Hitchcock explains the arrival in Los Angeles of Ron Blair: "I wanted to be in a band with Jeff and Ron, who at that time was in Macon, Georgia. Ron's sister Janice was married to Gregg Allman, and Gregg was thinking about putting Ron in the band; Ron was real close to playing bass in the Allman Brothers Band. And then Gregg and Jan had marital problems, and Ron basically told Gregg to fuck off because he was real supportive of his sister. So I asked Ron to come out to L.A. Then Trantham Whitley came out, and we formed the Empire Band with Ron Blair on bass. Jeff Jourard was in the band for a while, but we weren't making any money, so he went out on the road with a cover band called Shadybrook."

It was this mixture of transplanted Gainesville musicians that Tom Petty heard when he dropped by the studio at Ben's request. In Petty's own words, "I walk in and I'm sitting in the control room listening to this band playing. I was like, wow, I gotta steal this band. That's my first thought is, this should be *my* band. So they came in on the break and I started my pitch."

What was his pitch? "Well, my pitch was, 'I've got a record deal, and so you know you could go all the way around the search for record labels, just come with me.' And they all knew me and I think that they quickly decided to go in with me."

Petty gradually eased various members into his recording sessions, first Stan on drums and then Benmont on keyboards. By the middle of the year, a Tom Petty and the Heartbreakers album began to take shape under the watchful eye of producer Denny Cordell, with many songs recorded and rerecorded, many new songs, and many remixes occurring as standards rose and ability increased. As work continued, Petty later recalled, "I was so excited. I thought we've got our band, it was kind of like you've got something really good and nobody else knows it, but you know they're gonna know it."

Cordell's role during this critical period was to help the band create a coherent image and presentation. Various names were considered, including Tom Petty and the King Bees, Tom Petty and the Pickups, and, on March 19, for a single performance at a recreation center in Van Nuys, Tom Petty and Nightro.

PEACEFUL EASY FEELING

As Tom Petty and the Heartbreakers were coming together, Don Felder had already moved to Malibu, far from the humble Gainesville neighborhood of his youth. *The Eagles: Their Greatest Hits (1971–1975)* was released in February 1976 and sold a million the first week, quickly earning the very first RIAA platinum album award. Although the album was released as an interim project while the group worked on a new one, total sales to date are more than forty-two million copies, making it the third best-selling album of all time.

One afternoon while enjoying his ocean view and no doubt the general situation, Felder sat on his sofa and idly strummed an acoustic twelve-string, eventually refining his musical idea into a carefully crafted guitar arrangement. Using a Teac four-track reel-to-reel recorder, Felder first recorded his Rhythm Ace drum machine playing a cha-cha beat, then added acoustic and electric guitar and bass, then an idea for two solo guitars. Don Henley listened to a cassette mix of this song and more than a dozen others Felder had submitted for consideration and declared this rhythmically complex instrumental the best, giving it a working title of "Mexican Bolero," and along with Glenn Frey wrote lyrics that transformed Felder's music demo into "Hotel California," the title track of the next Eagles album and its first single.

The debut album from Tom Petty and the Heartbreakers was released on November 9, 1976. Initial sales in the United States were slow, but the album became a breakout hit in England. With Petty smirking from the album cover, wearing a black motorcycle jacket and an ammunition belt slung across one shoulder, initial reviewers decided this was a "punk band," an inaccurate description of both the group and their music. They were an American rock band with deep roots in American music.

A month later, on December 8, 1976, the Eagles' fifth album, *Hotel California,* was released, with the title track cowritten by Don Felder. Within three months of its release, "Hotel California" was a number-one hit single, earning a platinum award for a million sold and in ensuing years has sold more than three million as a digital download.

Gainesville's rock and roll roots had reached deep into the musical soil of its own region of the Deep South, producing a crop of musicians who actively engaged the pop music world with their regionally developed talent. The music that influenced these players while living in Gainesville was a rich and varied blend of blues, Top Forty, country, folk, rhythm and blues, soul, gospel, and early rock and roll, in a combination specific to midland Florida. Gainesville musicians had moved out to the West Coast, encountered the music business head-on, and brought what they had to that big party called rock and roll. As it turns out, they brought a lot.

GOLDEN YEARS

1977–present

"Night in the City" » Joni Mitchell

"Ain't No Sunshine" » Bill Withers

"To a Flame," "Love the One You're With" » Stephen Stills

"American Girl," "Listen to Her Heart," "I Need to Know" » Tom Petty and
the Heartbreakers

"Already Gone," "Hotel California" » The Eagles

"Only the Lonely," "Total Control," "Suddenly Last Summer" » The Motels

"Whisper/Touch" » Code Blue

Between the late sixties and the mid-seventies about two dozen or so Gainesville musicians migrated to Los Angeles, and a surprising number of them found success in the music business as recording artists. Those who had arrived earlier were continuing their initial success, as newer arrivals began to establish themselves. Their paths varied, but they all sought involvement in the music industry and were bringing new energy, experience, and ability to the rock music scene, each of these traits fostered in Gainesville's intense and varied musical culture and the live music opportunities the city had provided them.

CARRY ON

By his own count Stephen Stills attended five high schools during his youth, making it somewhat tenuous to claim him as an exclusively

Gainesville musician. Having said that, Stills's relationship with Gainesville has continued through the decades up to the present day.

Stills's nickname of "Captain Manyhands" is appropriate for this musical prodigy equally adept as a songwriter, singer, arranger, and multi-instrumentalist, playing guitar, bass, percussion, and keyboards. Stills played bass on Joni Mitchell's 1968 "Night in the City" and guitar on Bill Withers's 1971 hit "Ain't No Sunshine." According to recording engineer Bill Halverson, Stills played the acoustic guitar track in "Suite: Judy Blue Eyes" in one take, all seven and a half minutes of it, later overdubbing the bass and percussion. He played organ, bass, piano, and electric guitar on Crosby, Stills, and Nash's song "Marrakesh Express." During recording sessions for a 1977 Crosby, Stills, and Nash album, Stills found his friend Barry Gibb down the hall in a separate studio, working on a song for the soundtrack to *Saturday Night Fever*. At Gibbs's request Stills played timbales on the Bee Gees' "You Should Be Dancing," resulting in the "only platinum single I ever had for a long time."

His career as a singer, songwriter, musician, and bandleader remained in high gear through the seventies: Stills released a solo album, a live solo album, and a compilation solo album; partnered with Neil Young on the Stills-Young album *Long May You Run;* made a Crosby, Stills, Nash album, *CSN,* that sold four million; and as a member of the group received a star on Hollywood Boulevard. Stills showed up one night at the Troubadour in Los Angeles and sat in with the Knack (a band that signaled the beginning of the end of disco in our last chapter). Basically, Stephen Stills played whatever he wanted with whomever he wanted, and has been a welcome participant in many recordings, including those of Al Kooper, Dave Mason, and Ringo Starr.

Stills liked Gainesville, and in 2003 he donated one hundred thousand dollars toward a rehearsal facility for the University of Florida Marching Band, named appropriately enough the Stephen Stills Band Rehearsal Room. During dedication ceremonies in 2008, Stills commented, "I went to the first, second, and third grades here and sold Coca-Colas in the stadium when I was about nine, so I've been part of the Gator Nation since I was about ten years old." The house built by his father in the northwest section of Gainesville came up for sale in that same year, and Stills bought it, where he occasionally stayed in order to attend Gator football games and, as he puts it, chill out. "You eventually pick a place where you are most comfortable, so I always had a little special feeling for Gainesville," he says in a 1993 interview, calling the city "a real nice little town."

Stills remains the only person inducted into the Rock and Roll Hall of Fame twice in one night as a member of two bands—Buffalo Springfield and Crosby, Stills, and Nash. From his 1967 hit record, "For What It's Worth," up through the present day, he continues to create a vast and diverse body of music.

MAKE THAT CONNECTION

During the second half of the seventies, Tom Petty's singular obsession with rock and roll was beginning to pay off. In the months following the release of their eponymous debut album in late 1976, Tom Petty and the Heartbreakers began the new year by playing a couple dozen shows in the United States. The band then flew to England, where they were unexpectedly greeted at the airport by reporters from the music press; apparently the album was a hit in England. As the opening act for Nils Lofgren, they gradually stole the show from the headliner as the tour progressed.

After completing the Nils Lofgren tour in Great Britain, the group continued on to France, Germany, and Holland before returning to England as a headliner. The excitement of performing to enthusiastic audiences across Europe was a thrill; in Petty's words it was "such an exhilarating thing, the biggest mainline shot of adrenaline you could have."

Tom Petty and the Heartbreakers stood out as edgier than such current American chart-toppers as the Eagles, Hall and Oates, ABBA, and Leo Sayer. The energy and attitude of the band appealed to British audiences and journalists already engaged in covering the new punk music and culture. Although musically the Heartbreakers were a straightforward American rock band, their lyrics and rebellious image aligned them with acts such as the Sex Pistols and the Clash much more than with top-selling groups such as Fleetwood Mac, whose album *Rumours* spent twenty-seven weeks topping the U.S. charts, or the Eagles, whose *Hotel California* spent seven weeks at the top. Tom Petty and the Heartbreakers had arrived, and they were making their own distinct sound and image in the current pop musical environment.

Back in the States by the summer, the group began building a domestic fan base through extensive touring, sometimes as headliner and at other times opening for acts such as Kiss, Be Bop Deluxe, The J. Geils Band, Rush, and Meatloaf.

The turning point for the band came in August 1977 in the form of a two-night stand at the Whisky a Go-Go in Los Angeles, where the road-tested band's live performances were met with universal acclaim. Record producer and mentor Denny Cordell described the shows: "The place was absolutely packed, and they came on, and they just *did it*. Everything was perfect. The band *rocked*; every solo was a burner; everybody was in cracking form; they looked phenomenal. And that was the day the tide turned really."

Tom Petty's songwriting and the musical fluency of the Heartbreakers led the group to increasing successes on stage and in the recording studio. The second album, 1978's *You're Gonna Get It!*, reached number twenty-three on the charts and included the two singles "I Need to Know" and "Listen to Her Heart." The album quickly achieved gold-record status and was followed by 1979's *Damn the Torpedoes*, which peaked at number two and earned a platinum-record award and two songs in the Top Fifteen: "Don't Do Me Like That" (number ten) and "Refugee" (number fifteen).

A dispute over album pricing for the band's next release led Petty to declare if the record company raised the list price to $9.98, he would name the album *Eight Ninety-Eight*. The label backed down, and *Hard Promises* was released at the standard album price.

Many more albums, lengthy tours, various legal woes, personnel changes, triumphs, near tragedies, and real tragedies have transpired over the years, including the departure of bassist Ron Blair in 1982, drummer Stan Lynch's exit in 1994, the death of bassist Howie Epstein in 2003 from a drug overdose, and, on a more positive note, the return of Ron Blair on bass twenty years after he had left the band.

A survey of the Tom Petty discography reveals the length and breadth of his songwriting and recorded output: thirteen studio albums and six live albums as Tom Petty and the Heartbreakers, three Tom Petty solo albums, two Mudcrutch albums, two albums as a member of the Traveling Wilburys, a band boxed-set compilation (*Playback*), and more than sixty singles, ten of them reaching the top of the *Billboard* Rock Singles chart. The group's videos, many directed by the band's lighting and set designer, Jim Lenahan, received wide acclaim during the early years of the MTV video revolution. The 2007 documentary film *Runnin' Down a Dream,* directed by Peter Bogdanovich, won a Grammy for best long-form video, and the group's *Greatest Hits* album has sold twelve million, with the group's total sales of more than eighty million records worldwide. Petty has played rock and roll music for more than fifty years, the band for nearly forty. Inducted into the Rock and Roll Hall of Fame in 2002, Tom Petty and the Heartbreakers continue to do what they do best—play rock and roll.

I CAN'T TELL YOU WHY

Don Felder's cowrite of "Hotel California" had brought great critical and financial success to both him and the Eagles, while at the same time his years with the band presented Felder with a real-life example of Henley's lines from that very song, "This could be Heaven / This could be Hell." It seemed to be both.

Along with increased success came increased tension in a band of alpha males, none of them apparently willing or capable of backing down from any stance—artistic, personal, or business. Manager Irving Azoff apparently viewed the band members as mutually antagonistic and kept the constantly bickering multimillionaires apart from one another through separate hotel suites, separate stretch limousines, and separate backstage dressing rooms until show time, each member in their own space. This management strategy led to a seemingly inevitable falling out between Felder and the team of Henley and Frey, whom Felder refers to sarcastically as "the Gods" in his tell-all memoir.

For reasons that remain vague and disputed, Felder was fired from the Eagles in February 2001. Felder filed a fifty-million-dollar lawsuit for wrongful termination, which was followed by countersuits from attorneys for the Eagles. An out-of-court settlement in 2007 for an undisclosed amount probably assured Felder financial security but left him at odds with Henley and Frey, although he remains friendly with former bassist Randy Meisner and longtime friend Bernie Leadon.

Felder moved on, including recording-session work with the Bee Gees and Stevie Nicks, songs in movie soundtracks, hosting a television comedy show, two solo albums, and touring as a solo artist and as guest guitarist with various bands, including Styx and Foreigner. His 2008 best-selling memoir reveals details of his acrimonious split from the Eagles, including his opinion of Henley's and Frey's behavior, details that no doubt continue to harsh the mellow that once existed amongst these talented and highly successful rock musicians.

WE CAN WORK IT OUT

Bernie Leadon also went his own way after his split from the Eagles, starting by recording an album with musical friend Michael Georgiades in 1977. In the mid-eighties Leadon's career continued as a session musician in Nashville, where he recorded an album of bluegrass and gospel favorites with Ever Call Ready, a group that included Chris Hillman and Al Perkins, and played with the Nitty Gritty Dirt Band in the late 1980s. He joined Run C&W in 1993, a novelty group singing Motown hits "bluegrass style" that recorded two albums for MCA Records. In 1998 he rejoined the Eagles for one performance in New York City as part of their induction into the Rock and Roll Hall of Fame. In 2004 Leadon released his second solo album, *Mirror*. Leadon rejoined the Eagles for their *History of the Eagles* tour in 2014. Yes, Bernie Leadon, the band member who poured a beer on Glenn Frey's head decades ago, was now reunited with Frey each evening, performing "Take It Easy" and "Peaceful Easy Feeling" and "Witchy Woman."

The music business is funny that way.

NEW WAVE

Two other Gainesville musicians had moved to Los Angeles and eventually became members of a band signed to a major label, Jeff Jourard and his younger brother (me).

After the demise of RGF, Jeff was determined to join another band and in early 1978 decided to contact the Motels, a group he had seen at a local club. After tracking down lead singer Martha Davis, he found the band had broken up on the very eve of their signing with Capitol Records. Dean Chamberlain, the Motels' original guitarist, went on to form Code Blue, a power trio that included former Mudcrutch drummer Randall Marsh and whose 1980 Warner Brothers Records album contained "Whisper/Touch," a song included in the hit movie *Pretty In Pink*.

Davis was from Berkeley, California, and had been writing songs for years before relocating to Los Angeles. After various auditions, a band formed that eventually included me on synthesizer and saxophone.

The Motels shared a rehearsal space with the Go-Go's at the Masque, a punk rock rehearsal and concert facility that was created by rock promoter Brendan Mullen and located in the basement of an adult movie theater on the corner of Hollywood Boulevard and Cherokee Avenue. With Davis fronting a new Motels lineup, the band played clubs for six months around the city, primarily at Madame Wong's, a Chinese restaurant turned rock club in Chinatown.

The phenomenal story of the Knack playing the L.A. club circuit, getting signed, and recording a debut album for eighteen thousand dollars—an album that stayed at the top of the album chart for five weeks and spawned the hit single "My Sharona"—had led major

The Motels at the Masque, Hollywood, 1979: (*left to right*) Marty Jourard, Brian Glascock, Michael Goodroe, Jeff Jourard, Martha Davis. Permission of Marvin Rinnig.

record companies based in Los Angeles to take a much closer look at local club acts. The Motels were among the many that generated record-label interest, signing to Capitol Records in mid-1979 and in September releasing their debut album, *Motels,* which reached only number 175 on the *Billboard* album chart. The band played forty shows that year in support of the record in Europe and in the United States, and the song "Total Control" became a hit in Australia, where it reached number two, resulting in Australian gold records for both the single and album.

A band is in many ways a marriage, and some marriages break up. Jeff Jourard exited the band after one album, replaced by Davis's boyfriend, Tim McGovern. The second album, *Careful,* produced a Top Twenty hit in France with the single "Danger."

In 1981, soon after the third album, *Apocalypso,* had been rejected by the record company as not commercial enough, McGovern was fired, and the band remade the album as 1982's *All Four One*, resulting in the Top Ten single "Only the Lonely" and their first U.S. gold album award. Two videos directed by Russell Mulcahy, "Only the Lonely" and "Take the L," received extensive play on MTV during the television music channel's first year, and Davis won an American Music Award for her performance of "Only the Lonely."

A new synergy between music and promotional videos led to a period of highly successful cross-marketing between the film and music businesses as movies generated soundtrack albums featuring songs from a multitude of rock and pop artists. This connection resulted in the movie and the soundtrack album promoting one another, as well as an abundance of easily made MTV videos of an artist's performance of the song intercut with scenes from the movie. The teen-oriented movies of the 1980s often used rock songs playing in the background behind the dialogue in key scenes, and movie soundtrack albums were collections of these songs. Phil Collins's "Against All Odds" is an example of a movie's theme song reaching the Top Five and winning a Grammy for Best Pop Vocal Performance (Male) in 1985.

The basic process of having a song placed in a movie began with a screening of a rough cut of the film, and a sample song would be dubbed in where a song was needed. In many cases it was "Sweet Dreams Are Made of This" by Eurythmics, the favored song of the season, and after a few screenings it became increasingly comical to hear this song on a variety of rough cuts.

The Motels contributed songs to three movies, *Moscow on the Hudson, Teachers,* and *Soul Man,* and their fourth album, *Little Robbers,* yielded another Top Ten single with "Suddenly Last Summer" and a second gold album. Tours of Australia, Europe, Japan, and the United States followed over the years. After the release and lackluster sales of 1984's *Shock,* the group worked for a year on a new record but broke up in 1986, and the project was reconceived as a Martha Davis solo album that yielded two songs that charted in Australia. After a break from the music business as the eighties ended, Davis returned to writing and performing and reassembled various versions of the

Motels; the current lineup includes Martha Davis and me as the only original members.

TAKE THE LONG WAY HOME

Gainesville musicians who migrated to the West Coast in the sixties and seventies had joined or formed bands that eventually achieved success, collectively selling hundreds of millions of records. But there are many other ways to be involved in the music business, and several Gainesville musicians who began as members of a band took a different path as they found themselves drawn to other pursuits in the broad world of music. They had been drawn to the relatively open social climate of Gainesville that also attracted many of the region's education seekers, cultural misfits, entrepreneurs, and free thinkers. For creative types the city was a welcoming beacon in the wilderness of a mostly conservative state. The Gainesville area was, and continues to be, full of musical folks who through either choice or chance have found their own path through the far reaches of the music business. After the initial wave of Gainesville players migrated out West, a second wave of musicians and music-oriented entrepreneurs brought even more local talent to the wide world of music. Their contributions are significant despite taking place outside the spotlight, and are explored in the following chapter.

GO YOUR OWN WAY

"Too Many Colors" » Aleka's Attic
"The Touch," "Dare" » Stan Bush
"Valley Girl" » Frank Zappa
"All for You" » Sister Hazel
"Mighty K.C." » For Squirrels
"Thrash Unreal," "Black Me Out" » Against Me!
"Gainesville Rock City," "The Science of Selling Yourself Short" » Less Than Jake
"Drag My Body" » Hot Water Music

The oft-quoted line from Walt Whitman's poem "Song of Myself"—
"I am large / I contain multitudes"—could just as easily apply to the
world of music and the variety of occupations inherent in the music
business. The focus of this book has been musicians in bands, but
among these musicians are those who branched off from or completely out of musical performance or band membership, yet retained
a fierce interest in music. From the mid-sixties to the present day, the
journeys of the following Gainesville musicians, bands, and music
entrepreneurs are examples of creative people finding their own path
through the challenges and triumphs of the music business.

THE TOUCH

Stan Bush's musical journey is one such story. Born in 1953 in Orlando, Stan moved to Gainesville when he was twelve and by his early
teens was playing in cover bands, including Hobart, the Third Degree,

Frosted Glass, and Mr. Moose, who were "kind of a Top Forty band. I think we learned every song off the first Allman Brothers album," the singer recalls. "We played Trader Tom's, fraternity parties, the usual stuff around town. After that I started doing nightclub stuff with Mark Pinske in a band called Squash. We began to play all around the South—the Carolinas, Alabama, Georgia—and then changed the name to Riff; the original band Riff had broken up, and we just grabbed the name. That was how I cut my teeth, playing clubs for years. That's how you get good, by playing all the time."

By the mid-seventies a band named Helix had formed in Boulder, Colorado, whose lineup included Gainesville musicians Marty Stinger, Bob Harris, and Mark Pinske, who invited Bush to join the group on guitar and vocals. Pinske left, and Todd McKinney and Mithran Cabin joined, both musicians who had spent time in Gainesville. "We got signed to Elektra and changed the name to Boulder in 1979. I was in Colorado two and a half years."

Bush recalls, "We did one album for Elektra, and it went plywood. The other guys in the band went on the road with Warren Zevon as his backup band. The manager had a friend who was a mastering engineer and got me into recording at Elektra Records studios nights and weekends, and that's what got me a deal for my first solo album in 1983 with CBS Records. I got dropped after one album and a couple years later signed to Scotti Brothers and did an album for them. They were kind of shady characters; I guess their father was a longshoreman, and these were tough guys, sort of semi-Mafia kind of people."

Sometimes all it takes for a measure of success is the synergy of talent and a lucky break. "Then Lennie Macaluso and I cowrote a song called 'The Touch,' and it was in *Transformers: The Movie,* and it wasn't a huge hit, but all these people that grew up watching that cartoon movie are now forty, and they loved that song. Since then 'The Touch' has been my staple song. It was in Guitar Hero, in *Boogie Nights* with Mark Wahlberg, *Chuck* on NBC, *American Dad* on Fox, the Transformers game, Transformers toys. I had a deal with Hasbro; I'd go to the Transformers conventions and hang out and sell CDs and perform sometimes. When the movie was released, we did a concert

Boulder, 1979: (*left to right*) Todd McKinney, Zeke Zirngiebel, Bob Harris, Stan Bush, Mithran Cabin, Marty Stinger. Permission of Gary Heery.

at Paramount Studios. 'The Touch' was supposed to be in the first film, but at the last minute it was pulled."

Then along came movie soundtracks. "I sang in Jean-Claude Van Damme's first two movies, three songs in each of those. It's funny, because this 'action genre' became my thing; every album has a couple 'go for it / believe in yourself' type songs. It is true: you can do amazing stuff when you put your mind to it."

This philosophy seemed to work, as Stan began providing vocal talent for national television commercials. "I started doing jingles, the voice for Toyota trucks and Coors beers. I was one of maybe six guys that had the big rock voice thing, so I was one of the main guys doing that back in '89 and '90. The 1989 Super Bowl I had six national commercials airing, three were Toyota and three were Coors beer; I did the voiceover for that, and so I got paid double. I really had a good run with stuff."

Bush then returned to the world of rock and roll. "Scotti Brothers licensed a 1987 album of mine called *Stan Bush and Barrage* that included 'The Touch,' and their affiliate label in Germany got behind it on their own, and it went to the wall. I had a photographer come to my house in Van Nuys with my little toddlers, and they put me in magazines with a three- or four-page spread like I was Bon Jovi or something! It was crazy."

And so Stan Bush began to record albums and release them in Germany. "I would write songs with Jim Vallance or Jonathan Cain, and I'd have these master recordings, and I'd have enough to make an album. I'd get twenty-five thousand dollars from some German label for a record. I kept on doing it; they'd bring me over, and I'd perform.

"But it's not really a living, and I went through this period in the late nineties where I thought I'd just totally had it."

Then Bush found another way to make a living with sound. "After that I fell into audio books, books on tape. I've probably read a thousand books in the last ten years. I edit the recordings. They bring in narrators, actors, and then give it to me on a hard drive with mistakes and all, and I just take out the retakes and so forth and make it seamless and put it in CD format. It's the coolest job in the world because I love reading, and I have a Pro Tools setup at home."

As the Fixx observed in their eighties hit, one thing leads to another.

TAKIN' CARE OF BUSINESS

Sister Hazel is a Gainesville rock band named in honor of Gainesville community activist Sister Hazel K. Campbell, who opened a rescue mission and thirty-five-cents-a-meal diner in the mid-seventies. From the very start the band built a self-sustaining career through a vertically integrated business structure that allowed them to leverage the success of their hit single.

With a group sound alternately described as punchy country-rock, blues pop, and rootsy alternative rock, Sister Hazel played extensively throughout the Southeast, eventually leading to a national hit single with "All for You" that brought their debut album, *Somewhere More Familiar*, into the Top Fifty. They gradually and methodically built their huge fan base (known collectively as Hazelnuts), and the intense interaction between band and audience was duly noted early on by the marketing director for Universal Records: "When I first went down to Gainesville and saw Sister Hazel play, there were two thousand people there and the band just stopped [playing] while the audience sang the lyrics [to "All for You"]. Fans relate to the lyrics through a lot of times in their lives. It's hard to find a song that strikes you like that these days."

Guitarist and vocalist Drew Copeland is a true Gainesville native—his grandfather was one of the founders of Copeland Sausage, a well-known local brand, and his father owned the Huggins-Copeland Funeral Home. Copeland recounts how Sister Hazel formed: "Ken Block moved up from Miami when he was six weeks old, and he and I are the two original Gainesville residents of the band. Dub's was happening back then in the early eighties, and Ken played in a bunch of cover bands there like Redline and Scorcher."

The two did not hook up musically until 1991, when "we were tailgating with some friends at a Florida-Tennessee game. Ken picked up a guitar and started playing 'Peaceful Easy Feeling,' and I started singing harmonies with him, and everybody around us was very socially lubricated, but, you know, they say, 'Hey, you guys are great!' so I started doing that right when I finished school at Florida."

There were plenty of local venues for the duo to play around town. "There was a period where it was just me and Ken playing acoustically around Gainesville five nights a week, from Napolitano's to Cafe Calypso to what is now called the Swamp on University Avenue, at the Denny's downtown, and at Rickenbackers."

With the addition of three more members, Sister Hazel began touring as a five-piece band throughout the region with a simple strategy in mind. "When the band formed and we began playing out of town, we did those concentric circles thing where we would hit venues multiple times, and we went from having a few people show up to having a few hundred. We made those circles a bit bigger every time we went out. The first rounds were Gainesville, Jacksonville, Tallahassee, Orlando, Tampa, and then we made it a little broader, to Athens and Columbia, and Atlanta, sometimes into Mississippi, and kept building that following until we kind of earned the Southeast. It was spreading quick about us—I say it's quick, but it was really '93 to '96, three years we kind of beat the pavement that way."

The band released two albums on their own Croakin' Poets label before being picked up by Universal Records, who rereleased the second album soon after learning the band had sold out their own initial pressing of thirty thousand records.

One song in particular was receiving massive response at live shows. "All for You" was written for a competition for placement on a compilation album. "The guy called and said, 'You've got till tomorrow to get it done,' so Ken got two cassette players and recorded the basics for 'All for You' in his apartment, got the song on the record, and then we rerecorded it as a band on a sixteen-track at Mirror Image in Gainesville, and a couple years later when it got picked up by Universal, we went in and tweaked it in the studio up in Memphis."

"All for You" was released in June of 1997 and rose to number eleven in the *Billboard* Hot One Hundred and number one in *Billboard*'s Adult Top Forty chart. The album sold more than a million and received a platinum award. Sister Hazel had arrived nationally.

The band is a self-contained business, as are several Gainesville bands that have learned to go their own way through controlling every aspect of the creative and business sides of music. Having released many albums on their own label since being dropped by Universal in 2003, the group's internet presence and website includes merchandise featuring the band name on T-shirts and caps and even on such items as license plate frames, barbecue grill accessories, and Christmas ornaments. Then there is the Rock Boat, Sister Hazel's annual "floating music festival" co-organized by a travel firm specializing in themed cruises, where bands and fans gather on a chartered cruise ship and enjoy a five-day musical party in the sun. "This year will be the fifteenth year we've done the Rock Boat. The last couple of years we've gone to a private island and one other stop, a cruise with twenty-five or thirty bands, and we plan the music for the entire four nights. Ken and I will do about six shows during that time. He and I both put out solo records, and we'll do solo sets, and then a Ken and Andrew acoustic set and then Sister Hazel." The group has released a dozen albums, and they continue to record, participate in the Rock Boat cruise every summer, and tour throughout the Southeast and overseas.

PLANET OF MY DREAMS

Sometimes opportunity knocks through the side door. After arriving in Gainesville in the early seventies from Arlington, Minnesota, musician Mark Pinske was a member at various times of Homer, Bouquet, Frosted Glass, Hogtown Creek, and other local bands, easily finding work as a bassist in a town filled with guitarists. After graduating from the University of Florida with a degree in electrical engineering, and with a job offer in Los Angeles, Pinske moved there to work for a company that manufactured professional audio-mixing consoles.

In 1980 Mark auditioned as Frank Zappa's audio engineer and thus began his seven-year relationship with the iconoclastic composer and musician. Pinske eventually recorded more than twenty Frank Zappa albums and mixed the live sound and recordings on his concert tours.

Mark remembers the audition. "He auditioned each engineer for about one day in the studio, and then you'd go down to a sound stage. The band was rehearsing for a tour and the sound system was all brand-new Midas mixing consoles, and he had a guy kind of mess them all up and say, 'OK, make it sound good.' Zappa had me put the mix on a cassette while we were doing it. He was going to take the tape in the studio and listen and get back to me in about two weeks."

After two weeks had gone by with no word from Frank, Mark was at work as usual. "The phone rings and he says, 'You ready to go?' He didn't say who he was, he just said, 'Are you ready to go?' So I accepted the gig."

Among the twenty Pinske-engineered Frank Zappa albums is *Ship Arriving Too Late to Save a Drowning Witch*, a 1982 release that included "Valley Girl," featuring Zappa's daughter Moon Unit reciting a comedic monologue in "Valleyspeak," a social dialect born in the San Fernando Valley. The song reached number thirty-two on the charts and was Zappa's only Top Forty single in the United States.

Mark Pinske continued to engineer studio sessions and mix live sound with a variety of artists, including B. B. King, Ray Charles, Weather Report, Bobby Brown, David Lee Roth, and Men at Work and is currently head of sales and marketing at an audio engineering and manufacturing company in Orange, California.

AUDIO INNOVATOR

Music at its most basic level is sound, and creative control of sound became the path for another local musician. Doran Oster moved to Gainesville during the mid-sixties to pursue an electrical engineering degree at the University of Florida and upon graduation in 1971 opened Sabine Strings, a guitar repair and flute manufacturing shop, eventually adding accessories and guitars to the inventory until the store became the largest music and instrument retailer in north central Florida.

Oster was a well-known musical presence around town as a banjo player and singer. In addition to his solo performances, Doran played flute as a member of the 34th Street Laundromat String Band, a group of musicians who in 1973 routinely met at a Gainesville coin laundry to perform Appalachian and old-time folk tunes as their clothes were washed.

Oster combined a strong musical background with his knowledge of industrial design and electrical engineering to create Sabine, Inc., a musical products design and manufacturing company with a large facility in nearby Alachua. Sabine's first electronic product was the

MT-4001 compact metronome, followed by the ST-1000 digital tuner in 1987, which quickly became the best-selling chromatic tuner in the United States. A few years later Sabine introduced the FBX, the first automatic feedback controller. The company continued to expand and release new audio products.

Oster had found a highly successful career path through his interest and skill in both music and audio engineering and eventually sold Sabine to a large company that, in the words of corporate newspeak, "provides voice and visual communication solutions to the world." Another Gainesville musician had found success on his own terms.

GAINESVILLE ROCK CITY

For a few years in the nineties a Gainesville music organization named GAMA gave birth to a series of local music festivals that brought hundreds of musicians and thousands of music fans together at an outdoor concert setting just north of town.

It all began with an idea from college student Codi Lazar, whose interest in music reached beyond his role as drummer in the group Loose Fragments. His look back at the Gainesville scene of the early nineties illustrates the perennial power of nostalgia and the "good old days." What GAMA achieved in the early nineties is strikingly similar to the work of the Rose Community promoters Nearon, Goldstein, and Ramirez in the early through the mid-seventies: get bands out of the clubs and onto a concert stage in a concert setting.

"I was in a band in Gainesville in 1992," Lazar recalls, "and it was really an amazing town for music at that time. Those of us who were there talk really wistfully about what it was like then. You would go around the student ghetto—you just get on your bike and go listen to the band, keg parties with bands, outside, all over town. It felt like everyone was in a band. It was such an extremely vibrant town for music."

In the spring of 1993, Lazar was invited to play drums backing blues artists at the Florida Folk Festival, and he found both the festival and his involvement equally inspiring. "What I had thought was just another music festival by the Suwannee River turned out to be more of an annual convention and networking event for independent folk musicians of Florida. I thought, if it worked for the folk scene, why not for the indie rock crowd?" Lazar consulted with two promoters of previous festivals, Joe Nicholson and Bill Hutchinson, and attended a Special Events Planning Public Panel Discussion at the Thomas Center. "I wanted the festival to be big and substantial, and the pitch was to do a nonprofit festival where the bands were going to play for free, a 'Yay Gainesville!' festival highlighting the great Gainesville music scene, all about the bands—tell them, 'You're not getting paid, but we're not getting paid either,' all nonprofit—that was the big pitch." His partnership with roommate and fellow musician Marshall Lowe led to "a friend that lent us some money; his parents lent us some; we did some fundraisers, a few nights around town where bands would play for free."

Gainesville native Geoffrey May, drummer in Jam Sandwich and a friend of Marshall, became involved, and together they began choosing the final lineup of two dozen bands for the two-day event. "We tried to have this objective committee; it ended up being me and Marshall and Geoffrey, and acts brought their demo tapes, such as Whore Culture, the Tone Unknown, Big White Undies, some of the bigger bands. Also we expanded; some of the other bands selected were from northern Florida—Woodenhorse from Pensacola, Common Threat from Jacksonville, one from Daytona, one from Ocala." Lazar and Marshall then formed the Gainesville Alternative Music Alliance (GAMA), an organization whose sole purpose was to promote independent and alternative music of Gainesville and North Florida.

After more than a year of planning, the first Alachua Music Harvest took place at the Alachua County Fairgrounds January 15–16, 1994, with five thousand in attendance. The event continued in that venue through 1999. Geoffrey May recalls the process of putting on the first show: "We rented a stage setup from Canada. They drove the semi down; we set it up. January 1994, Big White Undies, Green, Soma, Sister Hazel, Less Than Jake. Did that for two years. By the third year, we said, 'Hey, we want to get people to notice it; let's bring in a national act,' even though it kind of went against what we were saying, but we convinced ourselves if we brought in a national act, more people would come to the show and see the local bands. So we brought in Gov't Mule, and Widespread Panic. We went on to do it several consecutive years, growing it to five stages, presenting Herbie Hancock, George Clinton, Blink 182, Matchbox Twenty."

After the first festival Lazar bowed out of future involvement: "I told Marshall just to take it over; he was the director of GAMA. He continued, and it became a three-day festival, and twenty thousand people showed up, and it became a really big deal. People would drive some distance to go to it; there were three stages; there were some headlining acts to bring people in, but it still maintained its focus on promoting local bands." Marshall and the GAMA crew continued on for several years, growing the production into a full-time business. The festival grew to exceed twenty to thirty thousand in attendance and added many national acts such as James Brown, P-Funk, They Might Be Giants, Ben Harper, Widespread Panic, and others and continued through 1999.

Lazar is now an assistant professor of geology at California State University in San Bernardino, but in the early nineties he, Marshall Lowe, and Geoffrey May were three young Gainesville musicians with a desire to support the music scene in a creative manner. Lazar reflects on the experience and on the city where it happened: "Gainesville's story deserves to be told. It's a remarkable place. I don't think Gainesville will ever be an Austin or an Athens, but I think that's kind of part of its charm. At the end of the day, if you're a good band, it doesn't matter where you come from."

Two Gainesville music venues that presented many of the local bands who played the Alachua Music Harvest are worthy of a history beyond the scope of this book: the Hardback Cafe (232 SE 1st St.) and Common Grounds, later the Covered Dish and currently High Dive, co-owned by musician and entrepreneur Moe Rodriguez. Lazar describes the city and the ending of one phase of its apparently continuous music scene: "Gainesville was awesome because of all the house parties, and at Moe Rodriguez's block party the cops came because people rioted, and that's the moment that the Gainesville Police Department started cracking down on all the house parties. In 1998 they instigated a 2 a.m. curfew. That's when the authorities were kicking the parties away."

Pinske with Frank Zappa, Oster with Sabine Music, and Lazar, Lowe, and May with the GAMA and the Alachua Music Harvest are all examples of music lovers finding their own way in the world of music. Another example is a young, talented movie actor who, after starting a band in the Gainesville area, pursued an alternate career as a musician up to the last days of his brief life.

ALEKA'S ATTIC

Micanopy is a small town located ten miles south of Gainesville with a population of six hundred. Its history dates back to the early 1800s as the first white settlement in Alachua County and the oldest inland town in Florida, and the main thoroughfare was originally the path of an old Indian trading trail. With streets and dirt lanes shaded with Spanish-moss-draped live oak trees, Micanopy is a classic example of a sleepy southern town. Artists, hippie types, and musicians began to discover the place in the late sixties, attracted by the isolation, cheap rents, and natural beauty of a small town that time seemed to have forgotten. In the early seventies a commercial building on Main Street was converted to an art gallery and artist studios, and the band RGF rehearsed there for a while. Hippies found the landscape and outlying areas suitable for growing crops of varying legal status, including marijuana, and a potent variety known as Micanopy Madness was a clear indication of the town's growing reputation. Micanopy soon became a sort of annex of the Gainesville hippie counterculture.

River Phoenix had already completed his sixth feature film in 1987, when he purchased a farm property in Micanopy for his parents and siblings, and between film shoots Phoenix often stayed in the area to visit and play and record original music. A musician and a performer since childhood, River and his siblings—Summer, Leaf (Joaquin), and Rain—had played music in earlier years on the streets of Guate-mala to earn money; the Phoenix clan was there through the parents' role as local missionaries for the Children of God, a religious cult the family eventually became disillusioned with and left.

In Gainesville, Phoenix formed the group Aleka's Attic with sister Rain along with bassist Josh McKay and drummer Josh Greenbaum. Aleka's Attic performed for several years around Gainesville in cafes and other intimate venues, including the Acrosstown Repertory The-ater in the old Baird Hardware location at SE 6th Avenue and Main Street.

During a movie shoot Phoenix met Chris Blackwell, head of Island Records, who offered the actor a two-year music development deal that led to recording sessions at Gainesville's Mirror Image Studio by engineer Mark Pinske, who recalled: "I recorded River for three and a half years. All of the master tapes never got released. There was a lot of session work and some moments with him singing and playing in the vocal booth that were filmed in home video cameras that would really move you. It was his escape from his always hard-working film life."

A busy movie schedule interfered with the recording sessions, and Island Records passed on their option to renew the deal. Aleka's Attic continued to record tracks for a future self-release, which never oc-curred, because of the untimely death of the twenty-three-year-old actor in Los Angeles on October 31, 1993. R.E.M. bought the rights to Aleka's Attic's recordings from Island Records in 1997, so the band's material may still be released. Ask Michael Stipe.

WHO ARE YOU?

Perhaps the ultimate example in this book of a musician going his or her own way is the story of the punk band Against Me! and the trans-gender journey of Laura Jane Grace, the group's leader and singer.

Born as Tom Gabel in Fort Benning, Georgia, the son of an army major, she—not a misprint; let the narrative unfold—grew up in var-ious locations including Texas, Ohio, and Italy. Her parents divorced when she was eleven, and Gabel moved with her mother to Naples, Florida.

A fan of punk music and culture, Gabel was arrested at fourteen and in the process was assaulted by a group of Naples policemen; the experience had a profound effect on the young teen's feelings toward authority and helped mold the attitude of the self-proclaimed anarchist punk musician who left high school at seventeen and moved to Gainesville in 1998. As Grace observed in a recent interview, Naples wasn't a friendly place for youth. "If you're living in Florida," she said in an earlier interview, "and you're eighteen and just moved out of your mom's house, Gainesville's the place to go."

Gabel released the cassette recording *Vivida Vis!* in 1998, followed by *7 Song Cassette* two years later. By 2000 Gabel had persuaded guitarist and fellow punk-rocker James Bowman to relocate from Naples, and along with drummer Warren Oakes and bassist Dustin Fritkin, the four musicians formed Against Me! Two years later the band's first album, *Against Me! Is Reinventing Axl Rose,* was released on Gainesville's No Idea Records. After releasing two more independent-label albums, the group signed to Sire Records. The 2007 album *New Wave,* produced by Butch Vig, was their best-selling album to date, voted *Spin* magazine's album of the year, and listed at number nine in *Rolling Stone*'s Top Fifty albums of the year. The record's single "Thrash Unreal" reached number eleven on a *Billboard* singles chart. After Tom Gabel moved to St. Augustine with a wife and child in 2010, the band released *White Crosses* with new drummer George Rebelo, on loan from Hot Water Music, another Gainesville band. The album was their highest charting yet at number thirty-seven.

In 2011, Grace, still identifying herself as Tom Gabel, purchased an abandoned post office building in Elkton, Florida, converting it to a recording studio where she began work on what was to become the 2013 record *Transgender Dysphoria Blues,* in reference to the 2012 gender reassignment of Tom Gabel into Laura Jane Grace, who had struggled with dysphoria her whole life and is now performing under that name, as a woman. She, along with the band, is going her own way.

LESS THAN JAKE

Another example of Gainesville's consistent appeal to those involved in alternative musical styles is the longtime presence of the band Less Than Jake. Drummer Vinnie Fiorello at sixteen years of age moved from New Jersey to Port Charlotte, a city three hours south of Gainesville, where he met guitarist and singer Chris DeMakes when they both attended the same high school during their senior year. In 1991 DeMakes moved to Gainesville and enrolled in the university. Fiorello made the move a few months later to enroll, but he had already checked out the city. "I had come up to Gainesville in 1988 with a friend to visit his older brother who was going to college, and I was eighteen and kind of blown away by it—a lot of music stores and a lot of good vibe, a lot of bands—but what I reflect back on is, Gainesville was a kind of island. It was secluded from a lot of other influences, prior to the Internet and a lot of other things. So what you had was a really fertile ground of creativity, which most universities have, but Gainesville was located in a secluded part of Florida, far from the beach and Disneyland and any big city."

The two found a bassist to form a trio and eventually added saxophone and trombone to create Less Than Jake, a band with the horn-driven rhythmic drive of a traditional Jamaican ska lineup in combination with the fast tempo and distorted guitar sounds of punk bands to create a unique ska-punk hybrid. The band name was inspired by Fiorello's dog Jake, who was treated better than the rest of the household, so everyone in the family was considered "less than Jake."

By mixing super-fast punk rock and ska music, the group created a singular style, "a kind of crazy frontier we were pushing into that hadn't been experimented with before. Gainesville being the place it is, it let us be able to do that experiment in music, but on account of how small it is, Gainesville held us back as well."

The question arises as to how Gainesville, Florida, bred a ska-punk band, two styles of music not generally associated with the Deep South, but the source of Less Than Jake's musical influences is the same as what inspired so many Gainesville teens back in the mid-sixties—England. "You ask how ska came to Gainesville? There is an obvious connection, which is English music. England adopted ska music, but also punk rockers embraced that vibe and put that twist and edge onto it. There was a Third Wave of ska like the Specials and English Beat or early Elvis Costello influences and of course the Clash. In the UK it was embraced by a lot of working class, and the Third Wave came and was edgier and darker. It took the upbeats and added a little distortion guitar to it and sped it up a little bit, and the thematic behind the music, instead of "My Boy Lollipop" [Millie Small, 1964] was "Ghost Town" [the Specials, 1981]."

So Gainesville had its own ska-punk band, a result of the natural migration of musical styles from one part of the world to the other. The band began releasing their own records, first a single, followed by an extended-play single as they built a strong local following. Less Than Jake released their first full-length album, *Pezcore,* in 1995, then signed to Capitol Records and released 1996's *Losing Streak*. Meanwhile Fiorello had formed a record label, Fueled by Ramen, now based in New York and releasing records by punk-inspired rock bands through a distribution deal with Warner Records, along with another record label, Paper + Plastick, selling books, records, and fashion accessories.

After their second Capitol release, 1998's *Hello Rockview*, the record label and the band parted ways, and Less Than Jake's next album, *Borders and Boundaries,* was released on indie label Fat Wreck Chords. It was 2003's *Anthem*, distributed by Warner Brothers and Sire Records, that led to the band's mainstream success, with a single in the Top Forty and extensive live performances on three tours.

The geographic isolation of Gainesville undoubtedly contributed to the band's self-reliant approach. "We started making our own T-shirts, pressing our own records, booking our own shows. Now, twenty-two years later, it's just an extension of all those lessons we were taught. So it makes sense if you follow the timeline of how the band is that we should be doing those things we do. We handle our own web store; we do our own publicity; we're heavily involved in the social media of our band; we record and market our own records." The band records in Gainesville at the Moat House, a studio built in the bassist's house on Depot Avenue, a few blocks from where Fiorello runs the band business from his office in the Baird Hardware Company Warehouse, built in 1890 and the site of many arts-related enterprises over the years.

Ultimately, what brought Fiorello to town was music. "What drew me to Gainesville: it had a fertile punk scene and a specific sound in the punk scene, kind of melodic but gruffy vocals. I liked some of the bands from Gainesville and the scene happening in the moment." Less Than Jake is now part of that scene happening in the moment, and the Gainesville-based band has an active touring schedule that varies but usually includes "one main U.S. tour a year, one European tour every year, festival appearances in the UK and Europe, one-off tours and festivals in the U.S., and every two to three years go back to Australia or go to Japan."

MORE

Many other musicians and music entrepreneurs have contributed to the collective musical output of Gainesville in ensuing years, and other bands rightfully scream out for inclusion. Although selective, this brief glance at the city's music scene through the eighties and nineties provides evidence of Gainesville's ever-present and agile musical culture, and these few examples are indicative of the city's continuous relationship with popular music in its many forms.

A PLACE IN THE SUN

Florida, sir, is not worth buying. It is a land of swamps, of quagmires,
of alligators and mosquitoes! A man, sir, would not immigrate into Florida.
No, sir! No man would immigrate into Florida, no, not from hell itself!
Sen. John Randolph (1773–1883), debating the purchase of Florida from Spain in 1819

We have now traced the relationship between rock and roll and Gainesville, Florida, from the mid-fifties to the present day. So exactly how
did this small American city manage to fly under the cultural radar
while steadily encouraging the careers of such a large number of successful rock and pop musicians and songwriters? If we consider just
two rock bands with Gainesville musicians, the Eagles and Tom Petty
and the Heartbreakers, the total of records sold is in the hundreds
of millions. Add albums by Sister Hazel, the Motels, Stan Bush, Less
Than Jake, Against Me!, and Hot Water Music, and the total is—well,
even bigger, with every sign of more music to come.

TELL ME WHY

The rapid growth of the local music scene that began in Gainesville
in the mid-sixties is directly traceable to the success of the Beatles, a
yet-to-be-surpassed example of what a rock and roll band could be, a
self-contained musical ensemble whose artistic interactions brought
out the best talents of every member. The Beatles' music certainly
had an impact, but of equal importance to the specific songs was
the attitude of artistic freedom and growth the band embodied. The

Beatles showed us that you could write a song about practically anything—holding hands, taking LSD, a yellow submarine, being tired, sleeping, rain, doing it in the road, eating a savoy truffle, a London street ("Penny Lane"), the back yard of a children's home ("Strawberry Fields Forever"), a birthday, a blackbird. You could take a song idea and experiment with different styles, different time signatures, using a variety of musical instruments and musical approaches. No one could predict what the next Beatles single would sound like, and hearing "Lady Madonna" or "Come Together" for the first time could be a mind-altering moment for a musician, as it certainly was for the writer.

At its best, this synergy among a group of musicians is what set the band model apart from a solo musical performer. A band was a musical ensemble and a social unit, bringing interactive aspects of the musical process into play. A band could be a powerful musical force.

The band culture developed in Gainesville naturally, through how easy it was to start or join a band, learn to play music, and earn money playing, all while still in high school. You were a teenager with a novel job—a working musician playing dance music, a time-honored role that has existed through the centuries. A band such as the Maundy Quintet playing "Time Won't Let Me" by the Outsiders at a fraternity party in 1966 was providing the same service as that of a dance orchestra in 1902 playing a ragtime schottische at a country club social event, the only real difference being the musical style and undoubtedly the decibel level. Both music ensembles were playing for the dancing pleasure of a paying audience.

There will always be a demand for live dance music, and playing the popular songs of the day is a common first step for many musicians who eventually become songwriters and performers of their own compositions and therefore part of the next generation of musical artists.

LOCATION, LOCATION, LOCATION

Musically, Gainesville's proximity to the borders of Georgia and Alabama has influenced the city's musical identity more so than the lower regions of Florida. Of course, rock and roll is a product of the South. With the notable exceptions of Chuck Berry from the Midwest and Buddy Holly from western Texas, a majority of the early pioneers of rock and roll were from the South, including Elvis Presley, Bo Diddley, Little Richard, Fats Domino, Jerry Lee Lewis, Carl Perkins, and Gene Vincent—musical artists from Mississippi, Texas, Georgia, Louisiana, Virginia, and Tennessee. A region of the country named by geophysicists the Coastal Plains includes the birthplaces of most of these pioneers of rock and roll.

BEING SOUTHERN

If we choose to view Gainesville through the cold and dispassionate eye of a social scientist, we begin by noting that it is a mid-size city located in the Deep South, more specifically midland Florida. The main population centers of Florida are Miami, Tampa/St. Petersburg, Orlando, and Jacksonville; Gainesville is not among them, ranking seventeenth in population.

The South is more than a geographic region of the United States—it is a cultural mindset and reference point. Although each state is unique by definition, the southernmost state of Florida is often viewed as "more unique" than most, with the longest continuous coastline in the continental United States, as the only state bordering the Gulf of Mexico and the Atlantic Ocean, the only state with every point within sixty miles of saltwater, and, despite the dire predictions of Senator John Randolph in 1819, now the fourth most populous state.

It is generally agreed that the South embodies "otherness" in the United States more so than any other region, such as New England or the West Coast, an identity that sprang from the antebellum plantations of the South and the slavery and the social environment it created and sustained until the Civil War. In *The Mind of the South* W. J. Cash attempts to sum up the archetypal southern characteristics and concludes the typical southerner was an individualist, unconcerned with status and wealth as the final arbiter of social standing, a pleasure-seeker whose world-construction was bound to be mainly a product of fantasy, with a tendency toward romanticism, quick to start a fight over perceived slights or insults, with honor being an integral aspect of southern culture. Cash writes, "in that void of pointless leisure that was his, the poor white turned his energies almost wholly to elaborating the old backcountry pattern of amusement and distinction—became (though it is shocking to say it) one of the most complete romantics and one of the most complete hedonists ever recorded."

It can be argued that "romantic hedonism" is a fancy term describing the mindset of another archetype, the rock and roll musician, who transformed the well-known hendiatris "wine, women, and song" into "sex, drugs, and rock and roll." If we assume that the sole purpose of music is to provide pleasure, the hedonism of the southerner would include music and the rebellious attitude it took to be a rock and roller.

UNIVERSITY OF FLORIDA

A major source of Gainesville's rock and roll music culture can be directly traced to the University of Florida and all that it brought to the region. It was the foresight of Gainesville's civic leaders more than a hundred years ago that brought the university to a small Florida town known primarily as the largest shipper of Sea Island cotton in the South and—through its truck farming, phosphate, tung oil, and turpentine industries—as a regional agricultural trading center and railway transportation hub.

The presence and consistent growth of the university eventually made Gainesville into a vibrant college town teeming with students who—when not attending classes and studying—were actively looking for fun in the sun, and music was commonly part of that fun.

Businesses sprung up in support, including every place that presented live music, music and record stores, and FM and AM radio stations. Recreational drugs were readily available, and a vast underground economy was generated through the growing and selling of local marijuana that may in fact continue to this day. Even as late as the eighties, truckers often referred to Gainesville as "the hippie city" on their citizen-band radios as they drove past on I-75.

On a more intellectual note, the university's steady growth transformed the city into a regional center of learning and continued to attract faculty from around the world, including those who brought families with musically oriented kids who found themselves freshly arrived in a city that practically dared them to start or join a band. Among the children of university faculty members were future members of the Eagles, Tom Petty and the Heartbreakers, the Motels, and Sister Hazel. The presence of the university made Gainesville a cosmopolitan city of the South.

QUAINT

The charm of any city is difficult to quantify or enumerate and is often the sum of qualities both visible and hidden. Gainesville's subtle charm attracted new residents through the years, such as Major John W. Tench of Newnan, Georgia, in 1877, the great-grandfather of Benmont Tench III, keyboard player in Tom Petty and the Heartbreakers; Stephen Stills's father, who, while driving through Florida in the fifties, as Stills later noted, declared the city was "the prettiest place he ever saw"; music entrepreneur Bruce Nearon, who noted how much nicer the Gainesville chapter of his fraternity was compared to the one in New York; Bill Killeen, while visiting from Tallahassee in the mid-sixties to sell his college humor magazine, *Charlatan,* who quickly determined that Gainesville had "a bigger and hipper student body than Florida State University," leading him to move from one college town to another; and Against Me!'s leader, Laura Jane Grace, who headed straight for Gainesville from Naples, Florida, as soon as she dropped out of high school, describing the college town in a later interview as the place to go "if you're eighteen and just moved out of your mom's house."

Minnie Riperton relocated to Gainesville in the early seventies, while pregnant with her daughter Maya Rudolph, having remembered the city from when she had performed there in previous years with the band Rotary Connection. People came to visit Gainesville and stayed, or visited and eventually returned, pulled in by the city's low-key charm. Rock and roll pioneer Bo Diddley moved to nearby Hawthorne, Florida, in the late seventies and spent the last thirteen years of his life in Archer, Florida, fifteen miles southwest of Gainesville, until his death in 2008, often visiting Lipham Music and becoming friends with Buster Lipham. Gainesville wasn't a booming metropolis, and it wasn't on the coast, yet it consistently attracted artists and artistic people who found a comfortable place to live that allowed them to experiment and focus on the craft of their art and the art of their craft.

Opening a business seemed a lot easier in Gainesville than in other cities, as in the example of Jeffrey Meldon's obtaining a free liquor license for the Great Southern Music Hall through a well-connected local official. The city government was relatively progressive, as along with the dozens of churches in town, there were two steadily patronized topless bars, one at the north side of town, one at the south. The Subterranean Circus hippie boutique opened in 1967, selling drug paraphernalia from their opening day and remaining in business for more than twenty years. Entrepreneurs of all sorts were attracted to the possibilities of the city.

POP MUSIC

If we examine the songs of bands with Gainesville musicians as members, it seems evident that the city's musical identity was informed to the greatest extent by pop music and the influence of Top Forty songs. In the sixties and seventies a cover band's job was to play the hits, the familiar songs. For a working Gainesville musician in a cover band, pop singles were programmed into your head at the very start, from the radio and from your focused study of how these songs were constructed in order to play them properly. Gainesville was a pop music city that celebrated *songs* rather than instrumental virtuosity. The pop songs everyone heard on the AM radio of the sixties and seventies provided the musical common ground for these cover bands, who were constantly learning newer songs, dropping songs that were no longer popular, and reviving older favorites. With all these bands playing many of the same songs, a musical community built around a common goal, and the pursuit of similar musical skills made the Gainesville musician a member of a large group of peers. The main issue was quality, being good. There were plenty of examples of good players in town, and by watching and listening to a top regional band such as the Tropics, Mouse and the Boys, the Nation Rocking Shadows, or Ron and the Starfires, you knew what good looked like and what good sounded like. These players were the midland Florida rock stars of their time and place, universally respected examples of excellence. This exposure to hearing a well-crafted pop song played with skill was a strong presence in the Gainesville musical community.

I CAN SEE CLEARLY NOW

One result of playing in a cover band for years was the eventual recognition of reoccurring musical patterns, starting with the ubiquitous twelve-bar blues form, the most common chord progression in popular music, applicable to blues, early rock and roll, pop, rock, and jazz, followed by the almost equally ubiquitous I-vi-IV-V progression, from "Blue Moon" to "Every Breath You Take" to "I Will Always Love You." A working musician in a cover band had to become adept at the musical sounds and rhythmic styles of the moment, and there was always some new sound or a new guitar riff to master, be it the fuzz-tone guitar psychedelia of the Strawberry Alarm Clock or Iron Butterfly, Creedence Clearwater Revival's iconic chugging rhythm, the syncopated "chicken scratch" style of James Brown's guitarist

Jimmy Nolen, or the laid-back groove of a Jimmy Reed song. A guitar player in a busy cover band also needed to learn catchy guitar "hooks" such as those in the Rolling Stones' "Satisfaction" and "Jumpin' Jack Flash," in Free's "All Right Now," and Deep Purple's iconic riff from 1972, "Smoke on the Water." For some of these musicians in cover bands intimately familiar with the forms of popular rock music, songwriting was the inevitable next step. The two songs of the Maundy Quintet's 1967 single are an example of Bernie Leadon's early mastery of the pop song form and Don Felder's playing and arranging skills.

Actually, some bands never stopped playing oldies. There is essentially no difference between Tom Petty's 1971 performances of "Cry to Me," as a member of Mudcrutch when they played at Dub's, and Tom Petty and the Heartbreaker's version of the song at coliseum concerts in 2014. A good song is a good song.

FUNKY GAINESVILLE

The French composer Maurice Ravel (1875–1937), whose famous composition "Bolero" has been featured in film, television, video games, and anime, was an early admirer of American blues and jazz, and his composing and orchestration skills were of such craft and perfection that Stravinsky referred to Ravel as "the most perfect of Swiss watchmakers." However, in the only music lecture he ever gave, Ravel stated, "we should always remember that sensitiveness and emotion constitute the real content of a work of art."

The true content of music *is* emotional expression, and music embodies the feelings of all races and expresses universally held emotions. Gainesville has some native African-American rhythm and blues, gospel, blues, and funk in its musical roots, a trait not evident in the music of every southern college town.

Bands that played black music with feeling and understanding got plenty of work in Gainesville. An unexpected example of the far-reaching musical influence of black musical culture is through Don Felder's explanation of his guitar solo on an Eagles song: "My strong influences were from the African-American community, so my playing on 'One of These Nights'—that's basically an alto sax solo. We didn't have a sax player in the Eagles, so I wrote something that sounded like what a sax should play." Felder's musical involvement with John Winter, the sax and organ player in Gingerbread (later Flow), influenced and guided Felder's approach. "He played soprano sax like Miles Davis. He was selective about his notes and very melodic. I learned my phrasing from John Winter." Winter listened to John Coltrane, Jimmy Smith, and many other black jazz musicians. Felder's unlikely musical source when conceiving a guitar solo is one example of Gainesville's diverse musical environment. Everything a musician heard eventually came out through their instrument.

Blues, rock and roll, and jazz—three genres of music that were born and raised in America—would not exist without the contributions of African-Americans, who were brought to this country against their will as free labor to raise and harvest the crops indigenous to the South. For several months following the end of the Civil War, the 3rd United States Colored Troops regiment was stationed in Gainesville, and their continued presence attracted freed slaves and more African-Americans to come to the city, including a large number of black migrant workers hired to pick cotton. At one point, blacks outnumbered white persons in the city. This core fact may explain a key aspect of Gainesville's musical roots dating back one hundred and fifty years. The African roots of music had been there since the end of the Civil War.

SMALL WORLD

Another aspect that worked in Gainesville's favor was its relative isolation, a city located in a region of Florida unrelated to the tourist trade, partly because of its being almost precisely between the two coastlines. This isolation led to a core of players interacting for longer periods of time in comparison to those in larger cities that might offer a broader choice of players and musical genres, and it helped create a do-it-yourself culture in Gainesville that remains in place today through such bands as Less Than Jake and Sister Hazel. In the seventies Mudcrutch's desire to play for large gatherings of their hippie friends rather than the typical patrons of bars and clubs led to their creating festivals at the Mudcrutch Farm. In the nineties Codi Lazar, Marshall Lowe, and Geoffrey May formed the GAMA to promote Gainesville bands and were instrumental in producing the Alachua Harvest Festivals that featured many local bands playing at a series of outdoor shows.

Gainesville's acceptance and encouragement of large-scale rock music events continues. An annual music festival known simply as the Fest features punk and alternative music. Held in Gainesville over a weekend every fall since 2002, it was created by music entrepreneur Tony Weinbender with support from No Idea Records, a local record company founded in 1994 and a large force in the current Gainesville music scene. The Fest is now in its fifteenth year, attracting more than twenty thousand attendees and nearly four hundred bands, and has grown bigger with each event.

PUT UP OR SHUT UP

Two traits inherent in the Gainesville band culture are a general lack of artifice, also known as "posing," so common in rock and roll, and a do-it-yourself approach that remains vital when living in a city geographically isolated from the larger urban centers.

For a musician, Gainesville was too small of a scene to "cool guy" your way through. There was no social infrastructure to climb and be socially superior to another musician—only talent allowed you that privilege, and your performance said it all, for better or worse. Also, being cool in terms of fashion was virtually impossible in a subtropical climate. Jeans, shorts, sneakers, flip-flops, and T-shirts were the basic garb. No one showed up in a costume on stage except lounge acts and "show bands." You could either play or you couldn't, and a certain amount of southern pride figured into it. Once you had heard

Duane Allman play, either on record or live, the facts of the matter were clear: this is what virtuoso musicianship sounded like. Those Gainesville musicians who relocated to Los Angeles were surprised to encounter numerous musical posers, musicians with the finest music gear, the proper hairstyle, the perfect wardrobe, and the "rock star" attitude—everything but musical ability and musical experience. The City of Angels was heavily populated with these musical posers and remains so today. It was a shock to meet musicians in Los Angeles and, after talking to them awhile, realize that despite your small-town roots, as a Gainesville player you had more onstage experience than most of them. A lot more.

Generally speaking, a Gainesville musician who arrived in Los Angeles easily had at least a thousand hours of onstage experience. At twenty hours a week, this had taken a year or two in a player's life, working the club circuit steadily. Few players in Southern California could say the same. There wasn't a lot else to do in Gainesville, and as it turned out, you had become pretty damn good as a live musician through playing all those cover songs in the frats and bars.

Gainesville created its own thriving musical culture, put on free concerts for the fun of it, and grew its own recreational drugs, and local bands figured out ways to make records, which often meant driving south to Tampa or Miami. Gainesville was also a party town, and those in the surrounding areas of midland Florida flocked toward the city to attend.

There it is, hidden in the deepest corner of the South: Gainesville, Florida. Diverse. Geographically isolated. Southern, yet liberal and relatively progressive in politics, with a long tradition of supporting music. A city with equal parts higher education and hedonistic behavior. These are some of the aspects of Gainesville that helped make the city an ideal breeding ground for musicians. As a result, the city has produced some of the greatest rock and roll songwriters and musicians of our time.

But there is another reason, often referred to as the "X" factor. Sometimes a place just happens naturally of its own accord.

Gainesville has brought a lot of musical soul to the world, and Gainesville continues to nurture the musical spirit of those who live and play music there. It's the hippie city and retains the best of that era.

Gainesville will continue to sustain musical artists. Based on what we have learned about the city, there will always be musicians and bands gettin' down in Gatortown.

ACKNOWLEDGMENTS

The birth of this book can be traced to a panel discussion at the Matheson Historical Museum in Gainesville in August 2006, addressing the city's thriving band scene of the sixties and seventies, an event created and organized by Barry Baumstein, the president of the museum's board of directors. The panel was moderated by writers William McKeen and Bill DeYoung and consisted of Mike Boulware, Gary Gordon, Tom Holtz, and myself. I was inspired by the large, enthusiastic turnout for what seemed to be no more than a bunch of musicians reminiscing about the old days. People arrived with band business cards, concert posters, photos, memories, and—thanks to Mike Boulware—Duane Allman's 1957 Les Paul, which I was allowed to briefly strum.

The research for the book was aided greatly by the assistance of Carl Van Ness, curator of the Manuscripts and Archives Department in the University of Florida Library's Special and Area Studies Collections, who arranged access to back issues of the *Florida Alligator*. The eighteen consecutive years of issues I reviewed (1959–1976) became the core of the book's chronology and served as the framework for the ensuing narrative.

For allowing me to interview them, I thank Jimmy Tutten, Tom Laughon, Boomer Hough, David "Lefty" Wright, Tom Leadon, Michael Hitchcock, Trantham Whitley, Don Felder, Benmont Tench III, Stan Lynch II, Jeffrey Meldon, Bruce Nearon, Jeff Goldstein, Charlie Ramirez, Jim Lenahan, Nancy Luca, Randall Marsh, Jeff Jourard, Dean Lowry, Charles Steadham, Lonnie Morris, Rick Reed, Charlie

Souza, Bill Killeen, Bill Carter, Joe Folsom, Jim Garcia, Geoffrey May, Vinnie Fiorello, Drew Copeland, and Codi Lazar. Did I forget someone? Thanks for your help, too!

Red Slater provided photos from the early days of Mudcrutch and the local music scene, and these contributed greatly to the project. Carl Chambers's website dizzyrambler.com provided archival information about Ron and the Starfires. Melanie Barr helped me with 1968. Ale Gasso helped me with aspects of chapter 11. Jeff Goldstein contributed memorabilia from the Rose Community concert promotion years, an organization that brought a lot of great music to Gainesville audiences.

Special thanks also to Gary Gordon and Steve Soar, for giving me my start playing in bands.

And last but most likely most, my thanks to University Press of Florida acquisitions editor Sian Hunter, whose organizational suggestions were vital to the form of the book and whose inherent tact and knowledge were the very thing we were looking for.

Live Performances, 1960–1976

Imagine growing up in a small college town that routinely presented national acts on a variety of stages and settings. The University of Florida presented the most popular musical acts at three venues: University Auditorium, the Florida Gym, and Florida Field. In addition there were outdoor music festivals, shows at Citizens' Field and the Suburbia Drive-In and various outdoor locales on the university's two thousand acres, and indoor shows, many of them free shows, in addition to bands playing keg parties, frat parties, private parties, the Halloween Ball at the Plaza of the Americas, shows at the Great Southern Music Hall, bands in bars, clubs, taverns, beer joints . . . you get the drift? Music was in the air and at times seemed to be everywhere.

Here is a list of music events of varied musical genres, from acts as legendary as Louis Armstrong down to a teen band playing a recreation center. All listings are documented, the main source being sixteen consecutive years of the *Florida Alligator*, the weekday college-based newspaper. Secondary sources include concert posters from the UF digital collection and posters that managed to survive through the years for shows that were not university-sponsored. Of the many fraternity and sorority gigs that bands played, none is listed, because of a lack of documentation. Add a countless amount of these to get a more accurate total of musical performances in Gainesville. A few key events in rock history are also added.

Local and regional acts are listed in italics.

Venue abbreviations are as follows:

CR	Club Rendezvous (at Florida Hub)
GFA	Greer Farm (near Alachua)
GMFS	Gainesville Music Festival site
GSMH	Great Southern Music Hall
HMB	Halloween Masquerade Ball (followed by number)
HSTF	High Springs Tobacco Festival
POTA	Plaza of the Americas
RCP	Rose Community Presents
RUB	Reitz Union Ballroom
SFCC	Santa Fe Community College

Date	Artist	Venue	Ticket
1960			
May 30, 1960	Louis Armstrong	University of Florida	$1.50
July 16, 1960	*Little Johnny Ace*	Florida Union	
1961			
April 23, 1961	Dave Brubeck Quartet	Florida Gym	$1.00
April 28, 1961	Jimmy Reed/Limeliters/Pete Fountain	Florida Gym	
July 22, 1961	Jimmy Clanton		
November 8, 1961	Brothers Four	Florida Gym	
1962			
September 22, 1962	*The Playboys*	Florida Union Ballroom	$1.50
November 9, 1962	Ray Charles	Florida Gym	
November 17, 1962	Peter, Paul, and Mary	Florida Gym	$1.00
November 17, 1962	*The Playboys*	Florida Gym basement	Free
1963			
July 20, 1963	Johnny Nash	University Inn	
September 26, 1963	Hootenanny [various artists]	Florida Union	Free
November 15, 1963	The Smothers Brothers	Florida Gym	
November 20, 1963	*The Playboys*	CR	Free

Date	Artist	Venue	Ticket
1964			
January 17, 1964	*The Playboys*	CR	
January 19, 1964	Carlos Montoya	University Auditorium	
January 29, 1964	*The Continentals/The Playboys/Southgate Singers*	State Theater	$1.00
February 9, 1964	BEATLES' FIRST APPEARANCE ON *ED SULLIVAN SHOW*		
February 15, 1964	Paul Winter Sextet	University Auditorium	
February 21, 1964	Journeymen/Ian and Sylvia		
February 28, 1964	*The Playboys*	CR	
March 23, 1964	*Fred Neil/Vince Martin*	University Auditorium	$0.50
April 3, 1964	*The Hi-Fi's*	CR	Free
May 22, 1964	*The Pink Panthers*	CR	Free
July 10, 1964	GHS ADMITS THREE AFRICAN-AMERICAN STUDENTS		
September 1, 1964	*The Playboys*	CR	Free
September 18, 1964	*The Four Scores*	South Side Florida Union	Free
October 5, 1964	Chad Mitchell Trio	Florida Gym	
November 13, 1964	The Lettermen/Bud and Travis		
November 14, 1964	*The Playboys/The Four Scores*	Graham Hall	
November 20, 1964	*The Hustlers*	Broward Recreation Room	Free
1965			
February 20, 1965	Ferrante and Teicher		
April 2, 1965	*The Dynamics*	Broward Recreation Room	Free
April 8, 1965	*The 5 of Us*	Union Social Room	Free
July 16, 1965	New Christy Minstrels		
September 25, 1965	Henry Mancini/Four Preps	Florida Gym	
November 1, 1965	*The Eight Balls*		
November 4, 1965	The Platters/Lesley Gore	Florida Gym	
1966			
March 5, 1966	Simon and Garfunkel/The Four Saints	Florida Gym	
March 18, 1966	Count Basie/Peter Nero	Florida Gym	

Date	Artist	Venue	Ticket
March 24, 1966	*Nation Rocking Shadows/Odds Against*	Hume Hall	$1.50
March 29, 1966	John Jacob Niles	University Auditorium	
June 3, 1966	*Odds Against*	Jennings Hall	Free
July 23, 1966	The Highwaymen/The Cyrkle/*Maundy Quintet*		
October 25, 1966	*The Birdwatchers*	Hub	
November 18, 1966	James Brown	Florida Gym	
1967			
February 22, 1967	Al Hirt		
February 24, 1967	*The Better Half*	Florida Union	
March 17, 1967	The Righteous Brothers	Florida Gym	
March 31, 1967	*Maundy Quintet*	The Place	$1.50
March 31, 1967	Glenn Yarborough		
May 26, 1967	*The Essex*	Gainesville Recreation Center	
October 6, 1967	Allen and Rossi/The Brothers Four		
October 13, 1967	*The Metrics*	The Place	
October 21, 1967	*U.S. Males/Limits of Persuasion/The Centurys*	Woman's Club	
November 10, 1967	Wilson Pickett/Rufus Thomas	Florida Gym	
1968			
January 12, 1968	Peter, Paul, and Mary/Paul Winter	University Auditorium	
January 27, 1968	*City Steve/Gingerbread*	RUB	
February 16, 1968	The Hollies	Florida Gym	
February 22, 1968	The Five Americans	The Place	
March 31, 1968	John Fred and His Playboy Band	The Place	$2.00
April 10, 1968	The Beach Boys/Buffalo Springfield/ Strawberry Alarm Clock	Florida Field	
April 19, 1968	Ray Charles	Florida Gym	
May 3, 1968	Jack Jones/Buddy Rich	Florida Gym	
May 25, 1968	*Thana Renshaw/Relatively Straight String Band*	Bent Card	$0.50
June 6, 1968	*Rare Breed*	Union Hub	Free
June 22, 1968	*The Certain Amount*	Union Terrace	Free

Date	Artist	Venue	Ticket
June 28, 1968	Dion	Florida Gym	
July 27, 1968	*The Wrong Numbers*	Lake Wauburg	Free
October 3, 1968	The Fifth Dimension	Florida Gym	
October 11, 1968	*Styrophoam Soule*	RUB	Free
October 11–12, 1968	*Noah's Ark*	White Rabbit	$0.50
October 25, 1968	The Four Tops	Florida Gym	$2.50
October 28, 1968	James Brown	Citizens Field	
December 10, 12, 1968	*Styrophoam Soule*	RUB	Free
December 27, 1968	*The Brothers Grymm*	Woman's Club	
1969			
January 10, 1969	*The Whatnots*	Dub's	
February 21, 1969	Vanilla Fudge	Florida Gym	
April 2, 1969	The Supremes/Gladys Knight and the Pips	Florida Gym	
May 23–24, 1969	Dion	Rat	
May 23, 1969	The Four Seasons	Florida Gym	
October 18, 1969	*The Tropics*	Union	Free
October 31, 1969	The Lettermen	Florida Gym	
1970			
January 9, 1970	*Celebration*	Rat	$0.50
February 1, 1970	*RGF/Frosted Glass*	Union	
February 13–14, 1970	Dion	Rat	
February 14, 1970	*Dead or Alive/Two Shades of Soul/ Emergency Exit/Celebration*	POTA	Free
February 19–21, 1970	Pacific Gas and Electric	Rat	
March 6, 1970	Johnny Rivers/Sweetwater/*Celebration*	Florida Gym	$2.75
April 3, 1970	*Power*	Dub's	
April 6–11, 1970	*Royal Guardsmen*	Dub's	
April 10–11, 1970	*Blues Image*	Rat	
April 24–25, 1970	Brewer and Shipley/Duckbutter		
April 30, 1970	Biff Rose	Rat	
May 4, 1970	KENT STATE SHOOTINGS		

Date	Artist	Venue	Ticket
May 16, 1970	CELEBRATION '70	Florida Field	$5.50
	Sly and the Family Stone		
	Grand Funk Railroad		
	The Youngbloods		
	Genya Ravan and Ten Wheel Drive		
	Mecki Mark Men		
	Sweetwater		
	James Cotton		
	Ewing St. Times		
	Crow		
May 29, 1970	Janis Joplin	Florida Gym	
August 5, 1970	*Tropics*	RUB	
August 6, 1970	*Blues Image/Riff*	Florida Gym	$2.00
September 18, 1970	JIMI HENDRIX DIES		
October 2, 1970	Chambers Brothers	Florida Gym	$2.75
October 4, 1970	JANIS JOPLIN DIES		
October 9, 1970	*Celebration/Image*	University Auditorium	$0.75
October 9–10, 1970	*Riff*	Rat	
October 15, 1970	Ravi Shankar	University Auditorium	
October 28, 1970	Johnny Winter/*Power*	Suburbia	$3.00
October 30, 1970	*RGF*	RCP HMB1 POTA	Free
October 31, 1970	The Tams	Florida Gym	
November 6, 1970	*Bethlehem Asylum*	Reitz Union	Free
November 15, 1970	*Boys in Blue*	University Auditorium	Free
November 21, 1970	Temptations	Florida Gym	
November 21, 1970	*RGF*	Union Mall	Free
December 13, 1970	*Mudcrutch Farm Festival*	Mudcrutch Farm	Free

1971

Date	Artist	Venue	Ticket
January 16, 1971	The Association	Florida Gym	$2.75
January 22, 1971	*Stonehenge*	University Auditorium	
January 23, 1971	*Mudcrutch Farm Festival*	Mudcrutch Farm	Free
January 31, 1971	Joan Baez	Florida Gym	$2.00
February 12, 1971	*Mudcrutch/RGF*	SFCC Auditorium	$1.00
February 13, 1971	*Celebration*/The Brotherhood	University Auditorium	$0.50
February 13, 1971	*Mudcrutch*	Rat	$0.75/$0.50
February 19, 1971	*Blackfoot*	Rat	

Date	Artist	Venue	Ticket
February 19, 1971	*Lynard Skynard*	University Auditorium	$0.50
February 20, 1971	Sugarloaf/Pacific Gas and Electric	Florida Gym	$2.25
February 27, 1971	*Mudcrutch*	Union Terrace	Free
March 3–4, 1971	*Mudcrutch/Rare Bird/Dreyfus*	SFCC West Campus	
March 5, 1971	*RGF*	University Auditorium	$0.50
March 5, 1971	*Blackfoot*	Rat	$0.75
March 12, 1971	*RGF*	Union Terrace	Free
April 2, 1971	*Power*	University Auditorium	$0.75
April 7, 1971	*Doug Clark and the Hot Nuts*	Rat	
April 9, 1971	The Echo	University Auditorium	$0.75
April 14, 1971	The New Folk	RUB	$1.00
April 16, 1971	*RGF*	Rat	$1.00
April 17, 1971	Bill Cosby/Nitty Gritty Dirt Band	Florida Field	$3.00
April 17, 1971	*Lynard Skynard*	Rat	$1.00
April 23–24, 1971	*Ewing St. Times*	Rat	
April 24, 1971	*Bethlehem Asylum*	SFCC	$0.75
April 27, 1971	*RGF*	Rat	Free
April 30, 1971	Game	Rat	$1.00
May 6, 1971	Jerry Jeff Walker	Rat	
May 7–8, 1971	Dion		
May 8, 10, 12, 1971	Oliver	Rat	
May 14, 1971	*Power/Celebration/Mudcrutch*	University Auditorium	$1.00
May 16, 1971	Brewer and Shipley	University Auditorium	
May 22–23, 1971	GAINESVILLE MUSIC FESTIVAL	GFA	$2.50
	Power/RGF/Mudcrutch/Celebration/ Lynnard Skynnard/Grean		
	Shoe Shine Boy/*Weston Prim*/Image/ Beloved		
	Sparrow/Blues South/*Dark Star*		
May 29–30, 1971	DUSSERAH MUSIC FESTIVAL	GFA	$6.00/$10.00
	Amboy Dukes/Mother's Milk/NYRR Ensemble/*Mudcrutch*		
	Dion/Tom Paxton/*Lynard Skynard*/Game/ *Hogtown Creek*		
June 24, 1971	*Hogtown Creek*	Union Terrace	Free
July 10, 1971	*Mudcrutch*/Howard Segal	University Auditorium	$0.75

Date	Artist	Venue	Ticket
July 14–15, 1971	*Doug Clark and the Hot Nuts*	Rat	
July 22, 1971	*Weston Prim Show/Johnny Hines*	University Auditorium	$1.00
July 22, 1971	Alex Taylor	Rat	
July 27, 1971	Goose Creek Symphony		
July 31, 1971	*Power*/Joe Taylor	University Auditorium	$1.00
August 3–4, 1971	*Cowboy*	Rat	$0.50
August 5, 1971	*Swingin' Medallions*	Rat	$1.50
August 7, 1971	*Stonehenge*	University Auditorium	$1.00
August 13, 1971	*RGF/Longreen Toad/Pete Einhorn*	University Auditorium	$1.00
August 21, 1971	*Mudcrutch/Lynyrd Skynyrd*	University Auditorium	$1.00
September 24, 1971	Goose Creek Symphony/Joe Taylor	University Auditorium	$1.50
October 1, 1971	*Mudcrutch*	Rat	
October 1, 1971	*Lynyrd Skynyrd*/Dixie Ramblers	University Auditorium	$1.00
October 8, 1971	*Power*	University Auditorium	$1.00
October 14, 1971	Drifters	Rat	
October 15, 1971	*Weston Prim*	University Auditorium	$1.00
October 21, 1971	*Mudcrutch/Road Turkey*	Museum Terrace	Free
October 30, 1971	*Mudcrutch*/Goose Creek Symphony	RCP HMB2 POTA	Free
October 31, 1971	Blood, Sweat, and Tears/Bill Withers	Florida Field	$3.00
November 5, 1971	*Cowboy/Mudcrutch*	University Auditorium	$1.50
November 22, 1971	Guess Who/Gypsy	Florida Gym	$3.25
1972			
January 28, 1972	Don McLean	Florida Gym	$2.50
January 28, 1972	*Bacchus*	RUB	$0.50
February 4, 1972	Hampton Grease Band	Rat	$1.00
February 5, 1972	*Rare Bird*	GMFS	Free
February 10–11, 1972	Archie Bell and the Drells	Rat	$1.00
February 12, 1972	*Mudcrutch*	GMFS	Free
February 18, 1972	Richie Havens/Jimmy Spheeris	Florida Gym	$3.00
February 18, 1972	*Lynyrd Skynyrd*/Round House/Jonah/ Birnum Wood	Rat	$1.00
February 19, 1972	*Mudcrutch/Dreyfus*	GMFS	$1.00
February 26, 1972	*M. Jourard Band/Dreyfus/Dark Star*	GMFS	
March 3–4, 1972	*Mudcrutch/Rare Bird (Fri.)/Dreyfus (Sat.)*	SFCC	$1.00
March 4–6, 1972	Bette Midler	Rat	$1.50

Date	Artist	Venue	Ticket
March 11, 1972	*Road Turkey/Dark Star*	GMFS	Free
April 7–8, 1972	The Box Tops	Rat	$1.50
April 21, 1972	Stephen Stills and Manassas	Florida Field	$2.50
April 28, 1972	The Carpenters	Florida Gym	$3.50
April 29, 1972	Son of Super Show: Tower of Power/Stillwater/six others	Lake Alice	Free
May 12, 1972	*Mudcrutch*	Rat	$0.50
May 21, 1972	Victor Borge	Florida Gym	
May 30, 1972	Goose Creek Symphony	Rat	
July 8, 1972	Charlie and Inezz Foxx	RUB	$1.25
July 14–15, 1972	*Mudcrutch*	HSTF	
July 15, 1972	*Road Turkey*	Rat	$0.75
July 21–22, 1972	*White Witch/Homer*	Rat	$0.75
July 28, 1972	*RGF*	University Auditorium	$1.50
July 29, 1972	*RGF*	Rat	$1.50
August 18–19, 1972	*Mudcrutch*	Rat	$1.50
August 19, 1972	*Weston Prim*	RUB	$0.50
September 24, 1972	Image/*Froggy and the Magic Twangers*	Union Terrace	Free
October 5, 1972	Lowell Correctional Institution Pop and Jazz Band	Union North Lawn	Free
October 6, 1972	Isaac Hayes	Florida Gym	$4.00
October 13, 1972	*Road Turkey*/Company/*Backwater Blues Band*	Behind Hub	Free
October 21, 1972	*Clear Blue Sky/Froggy and the Magic Twangers/Image*	Union North Lawn	Free
October 28, 1972	*Mudcrutch/RoadTurkey/Midnight Machete/John Jones/Danny Roberts*	RCP HMB3 POTA	Free
November 3, 1972	Beck, Bogart, and Appice	Florida Gym	$3.50
November 18, 1972	Drifters/Little Anthony and the Imperials	Florida Gym	$2.50
December 7, 1972	Ted Nugent and the Amboy Dukes/Cactus/Ramatam	Florida Gym	$3.00

1973

Date	Artist	Venue	Ticket
January 12–13, 1973	*Mudcrutch*	Rat	$1.00
January 26–27, 1973	Gary and the U.S. Bonds	Rat	$1.50
February 2, 1973	Preservation Hall Jazz Band	RUB	
February 3, 1973	*Mudcrutch*	Behind Hub	Free

Date	Artist	Venue	Ticket
February 9, 1973	*Mudcrutch*	Rat	$1.00
February 10, 1973	*New Days Ahead*	University Auditorium	$1.00
February 16, 1973	*Blackfoot*	Tolbert Area	Free
February 23, 1973	Goose Creek Symphony/Rare Earth	Florida Gym	$3.50
February 24, 1973	*Blackfoot/Mudcrutch*	University Auditorium	$1.00
March 2–3, 1973	*Image/Randy Kidd/Mr. Poundit and the Master Race*	Rat	$1.00
March 3–4, 1973	*Mudcrutch/Dreyfus/Rare Bird*	SFCC	$1.00
March 8, 1973	[Leon Russell cancelled]	Florida Field	$5.00
March 9, 1973	*University of Florida Jazz Band*	Rat	
March 31, 1973	Nitty Gritty Dirt Band/Charles Lloyd/Homer	Citizens' Field	$3.00
April 12, 1973	The Beach Boys	Florida Field	
April 28, 1973	Seals and Crofts	Florida Gym	$3.00
May 4, 1973	Jimmie Spheeris/*Nate and John*	University Auditorium	$1.50
May 10, 1973	Stevie Wonder	Florida Gym	$4.00
May 26, 1973	Brownsville Station/*Cowboy*	Hub Mall	Free
June 28, 1973	*Road Turkey/Color*	Hub Mall	Free
July 7, 1973	Dr. Hook/Unicorn	University Auditorium	
July 13, 1973	*New Days Ahead*	University Auditorium	
July 20, 1973	Earl Scruggs Revue	Florida Gym	
July 30–August 11, 1973	*Mudcrutch/Road Turkey*	The Keg	
August 3, 1973	*Shotgun*	Hub Mall	Free
August 19, 1973	*Gamble Rogers/Eric Quincy Tate*	Union North Lawn	Free
September 19–20, 1973	*Mudcrutch/Purlee/Catworth Fox/Road Turkey*	Suburbia	$3.00
September 29, 1973	Jimmy Spheeris	POTA	Free
October 4, 1973	Carlos Montoya	RUB	
October 6, 1973	*Flood*	Graham Pond	Free
October 12, 1973	*New Days Ahead*	University Auditorium	$1.50
October 21, 1973	Elton John	Florida Gym	$6.00
October 22, 1973	*Road Turkey*	Cin City	Free
October 27, 1973	*White Witch/New Days Ahead/Mudcrutch*	Hume Hall	Free
October 30, 1973	*Gamble Rogers*	Beef and Bottle	
November 2, 1973	John Mayall/Taj Mahal	Florida Gym	

Date	Artist	Venue	Ticket
November 3, 1973	Country Joe McDonald/Sky Lake/ *Fat Chance*		
	Randy Kidd/Dr. Bell Wizard Oil Review with G.R.I.T.S.	RCP HMB4 SFCC	Free

1974

Date	Artist	Venue	Ticket
January 19, 1974	Goose Creek Symphony	University Auditorium	
January 20, 1974	*Eric Quincy Tate*	Union North Lawn	Free
January 24–26, 1974	Freddie King	Longbranch	$3.50
February 2, 1974	Hydra	POTA	Free
February 7, 1974	Yes	Florida Gym	$5.00
February 24, 1974	*Road Turkey*	Union North Lawn	Free
February 24, 1974	Virgil Fox	Florida Gym	
February 25, 1974	Ike and Tina Turner Revue	Florida Gym	$5.00
March 4, 1974	Todd Rundgren	University Auditorium	$3.50
March 4, 1974	Bob Seger	Dub's	$3.00
March 31, 1974	Grand Funk Railroad	Florida Gym	$6.00
April 11, 1974	Al Kooper/*Mose Jones*	Hilton Ballroom	$3.50
April 14, 1974	The Doobie Brothers	Florida Gym	$5.00
April 26, 1974	Earl Scruggs Revue	GSMH	$4.00
April 29, 1974	*Fat Chance*	Longbranch	$0.50
May 2, 1974	The Temptations	Florida Gym	
May 3, 1974	Brewer and Shipley	GSMH	$4.00
May 4, 1974	Climax Blues Band	POTA	Free
May 8, 1974	Goose Creek Symphony	GSMH	$2.50
May 9, 1974	*The Outlaws*/The Jam Factory	Longbranch	
May 16, 1974	Nitty Gritty Dirt Band	GSMH	
May 18, 1974	John Hartford	POTA	Free
May 19, 1974	John Sebastian	Florida Gym	$2.50
May 28, 1974	Ray Charles	GSMH	$5.00
May 29, 1974	Two Generations of Brubeck	GSMH	$3.00
May 30, 1974	*Eric Quincy Tate*	Longbranch	
June 1, 1974	Gainesville Community Festival of Music and Arts	Citizens Field	$2.00
	Richie Havens/*Laurie Powers/New River Station*		

Date	Artist	Venue	Ticket
	Paul Hillis Jazz Group/Johnny Ace and the Percolators/Slow Poke		
	Breeze/Linda Hoover Willingham/ Gainesville Classic Guitar Society/Treat Gary and Rusty/Randy Kidd/Clinch Mountain Belly/Amos and Jarret		
June 21–22, 1974	Bo Diddley	GSMH	
June 28, 1974	*Purlee/Road Turkey/Linda Hoover Willingham*	GSMH	
June 29, 1974	Jerry Lee Lewis	GSMH	$5.50
July 28, 1974	*Road Turkey*	Union Lawn	Free
August 13, 1974	*Riff*	Lamplighter	Free
September 25–26, 1974	Doug Kershaw	GSMH	
September 26, 1974	Ted Nugent	Longbranch	$4.50
October 1–6, 1974	John Hammond/*Fat Chance Band*	Longbranch	
October 5, 1974	*Cowboy*	POTA	Free
October 10, 1974	Muddy Waters	GSMH	$5.00
October 18–19, 1974	Minnie Riperton	GSMH	
October 20, 1974	Paco de Lucia	RUB	Free
October 26, 1974	*Greg Allman/Boyer and Talton*	Florida Gym	$5.50
November 2, 1974	[Michael Murphy cancelled]/Johnny Jones Band/Hook and Ladder	RCP HMB5 GFA	Free
November 2, 1974	America	Florida Gym	$4.50
November 14, 1974	Jimmy Buffett	GSMH	
November 15, 1974	Loggins and Messina	Florida Gym	$5.00
November 25, 1974	Souther-Hillman-Furay Band/ Dan Fogelberg	GSMH	$5.50
December 4, 1974	The Shirelles	GSMH	

1975

Date	Artist	Venue	Ticket
January 6, 1975	*Gamble Rogers*	Beef and Bottle	
January 10, 1975	Richie Havens	GSMH	$4.50
January 16, 1975	Barry Meldon	Longbranch	
January 17–18, 1975	*Doug Clark and the Hot Nuts*	Rat	
January 20, 1975	Severin Browne	Beef and Bottle	$1.00
January 24, 1975	Two Generations of Brubeck	GSMH	$5.00
January 26, 1975	Loudon Wainright III	Graham Pond	Free

Date	Artist	Venue	Ticket
January 29, 1975	Eric Burdon Band	GSMH	$4.00
February 8, 1975	*Atlanta Rhythm Section*	Union Lawn	Free
February 11–15, 1975	Steve Martin	Beef and Bottle	$2.00
February 13, 1975	Spinners	Florida Gym	$5.00
February 14, 1975	Weather Report	GSMH	
February 18, 1975	Red White, and Blue(Grass)	Beef and Bottle	
February 22, 1975	Spirit	GSMH	$4.00
February 23, 1975	Herbie Mann and the Family of Mann	Union Lawn	Free
March 1, 1975	Melissa Manchester	GSMH	$4.00
March 2, 1975	Johnny Cash Family	Florida Gym	$3.50
March 10–12, 1975	*Micanopy Jam Band*	Connection Lounge	Free
April 3, 1975	Baker Gurvitz Army/Trapeze	GSMH	$4.50
April 5, 1975	Carol Douglas	Melody Club	$5.00
April 10, 1975	Ramsey Lewis	GSMH	$5.00
April 11, 1975	Friley Creek	ROTC Field	Free
April 11–12, 1975	Dion	Beef and Bottle	$3.00
April 12, 1975	Stix River Rounders	ROTC Field	Free
April 15, 1975	The Dillards	Beef and Bottle	$2.00
April 16–17, 1975	Tim Weisberg	Longbranch	
April 19, 1975	*Cowboy*	GSMH	$3.50
April 24–26, 1975	Leon Redbone	Beef and Bottle	
April 25, 1975	The Earl Scruggs Revue	GSMH	
April 26, 1975	Nitty Gritty Dirt Band and Steve Martin	Union Lawn	Free
May 1, 1975	John Mayall	GSMH	$5.00
May 3, 1975	Jimmy Buffett	Union Lawn	Free
May 7, 1975	Kraftwerk	GSMH	$4.00
May 8, 1975	*Southpaw*	Connection	Free
May 10, 1975	Chick Corea/Larry Coryell/Strider	Union Lawn	Free
May 25, 1975	David Bromberg	Union Lawn	Free
May 30–31, 1975	Doc Watson	Beef and Bottle	$3.50
June 27, 1975	Ike and Tina Turner Revue	GSMH	$6.00
July 3, 1975	The Vogues	Dub's	
July 22, 1975	Chuck Mangione	GSMH	$5.00
July 24, 1975	Nitty Gritty Dirt Band	GSMH	$4.00
July 27, 1975	*Boyer and Talton (Cowboy)*	Union Lawn	Free

Date	Artist	Venue	Ticket
August 19, 1975	*Gamble Rogers/Eric Quincy Tate*	Union Lawn	Free
September 19–21, 1975	*Hatchett Creek Music Festival '75/Gamble Rogers and others*	Near Archer	$10.00
October 3, 1975	Elvin Bishop	GSMH	$4.50
October 5, 1975	Two Generations of Brubeck featuring Dave Brubeck	Union Lawn	Free
October 10, 1975	Muddy Waters	GSMH	$3.50
October 17, 1975	Jimmy Buffett	Union Lawn	Free
October 17, 1975	Return to Forever	GSMH	$5.00
October 17, 1975	*The Jazz Project*	Keg	$1.00
October 25, 1975	James Taylor	Florida Gym	$5.00
October 30, 1975	Climax Blues Band	RCP HMB6 POTA	Free
November 2, 1975	David Crosby and Graham Nash	Florida Gym	$5.00
November 5, 1975	Blood, Sweat, and Tears	GSMH	
November 16, 1975	Chicago	Florida Field	$5.00
November 20, 1975	Labelle	GSMH	
November 22, 1975	Melissa Manchester	GSMH	
December 3–5, 1975	Doc Watson	Beef and Bottle	$3.50

1976

Date	Artist	Venue	Ticket
January 15, 1976	BEEF AND BOTTLE CLOSES ENTERTAINER LOUNGE, GOES DISCO		
January 23, 1976	*Wet Willie/Blackfoot*	GSMH	$4.50
January 31, 1976	*Outlaws*	Union Lawn	Free
February 7, 1976	Harry Chapin	Florida Gym	$4.50
February 11, 1976	B. B. King	GSMH	$6.50
February 14, 1976	Tim Weisberg	GSMH	
February 21, 1976	Billy Cobham/George Duke and Spectrum/Tone	Union Lawn	Free
February 21, 1976	Count Basie	GSMH	
February 27, 1976	Earl Scruggs Revue	GSMH	$5.00
February 28, 1976	Pure Prairie League	Schnell Field	Free
March 5, 1976	Leo Kottke/Rosewater Blue	GSMH	$4.50
March 13, 1976	Chuck Mangione	GSMH	$5.00
March 29, 1976	Ramsey Lewis	GSMH	$5.00
April 9, 1976	*Sandy Valley Boys*	ROTC Field	Free

Date	Artist	Venue	Ticket
April 10, 1976	Sneaky Pete	ROTC Field	Free
April 10, 1976	Hatchett Creek 76	Near Archer	
April 11, 1976	Brian Auger's Oblivion Express	GSMH	$4.50
April 14, 1976	Taj Mahal	GSMH	$5.00
April 15, 1976	Jimmy Buffett/Gamble Rogers	Florida Gym	$3.50
April 23, 1976	*Autumn*	Bilbo and Gandalf's	$1.00
April 23, 1976	Dizzy Gillespie/[Oscar Peterson cancelled]/*The Jazz Project*	Union Lawn	Free
April 25, 1976	Bob Dylan/Joan Baez/Rolling Thunder Review	Florida Field	$8.75
April 29, 1976	Weather Report	GSMH	$5.00
May 7, 1976	Jesse Colin Young	Union Lawn	Free
May 8, 1976	Richie Havens	GSMH	$4.00
May 19, 1976	*Riff/Beloved/Saucer/Southern Comfort/ Bluesberry Jam/Flyer*	Rat	Free
May 20, 1976	Ray Charles	GSMH	$7.50
May 22, 1976	Doc and Merle Watson	Union Lawn	Free
May 29, 1976	Chris Hillman	GSMH	$3.00
July 14, 1976	Roy Buchanan	GSMH	$3.50
July 19, 1976	Savoy Brown	GSMH	$4.50
July 28, 1976	Sea Level	GSMH	$4.00
August 13, 1976	Earl Scruggs Revue	Union Lawn	Free
October 1–2, 1976	*Archer Road Band*	Cockney's	
October 8, 1976	Dr. Hook	Union Lawn	Free
October 8–9, 1976	*Archer Road Band*	Cockney's	
October 15–16, 1976	*Archer Road Band*	Orange and Brew	
October 22, 1976	David Bromberg Band	GSMH	
October 22–23, 1976	*Archer Road Band*	Orange and Brew	
October 31, 1976	Commander Cody	RCP HMB7 POTA	Free
November 5, 1976	Stephen Stills	Florida Gym	$5.00
November 13, 1976	Thunderbird with Roger McGuinn	Union Lawn	Free
November 14, 1976	Leon and Mary Russell	Florida Field	
November 15, 1976	Tim Weisberg	GSMH	
November 18, 1976	José Feliciano	GSMH	
December 2, 1976	Melissa Manchester	GSMH	

NOTES ON SOURCES

Chapter 1. See You Later, Alligator

Gainesville musician named Tommy Durden . . . Thomas Russell Durden (1919–1999) was born in Georgia and lived in Jacksonville before moving to Gainesville in the early fifties, where he was a member of Smilin' Jack Herring and His Swingbillies, a country music band that performed regularly throughout north-central Florida.

Elvis was even . . . www.rockabilly.nl/references/messages/glenn_reeves.htm.

In the northwest part of the city . . . *Polk's Gainesville City Directory, 1955* (Richmond, VA: R. L. Polk, 1955).

"My father was basically" . . . Bill DeYoung, "The Boy Who Would Be Stills," *Gainesville Sun*, August 5, 2001.

Four blocks to the south . . . Ibid.

In 1867, Civil War Veteran . . . Benmont Tench Jr., oral history, Samuel Proctor Oral History, Florida State Museum, University of Florida, August 8, 1986, http://ufdc.ufl.edu/UF00024774/00001/1j.

Three miles northeast . . . *Polk's Gainesville City Directory, 1955.*

The Petty patriarch . . . www.findagrave.com/cgi-bin/fg.cgi?page=gr&GRid=30493277.

Three blocks west of the Petty house . . . *Polk's Gainesville City Directory, 1955.*

with their two sons . . . Don Felder interview, October 30, 2013.

annual Homecoming Parade . . . www.gatorgrowl.org.

My Cross to Bear . . . Gregg Allman, *My Cross to Bear* (New York: William Morrow, 2012), 143.

Chapter 2. From *Hootenanny* to *A Hard Day's Night*

The first place I did anything . . . Jimmy Tutten interview, April 2012.

The buzzword for . . . David Hajdu, *Positively 4th Street: The Lives and Times of Joan Baez, Bob Dylan, Mimi Baez Fariña, and Richard Fariña* (New York: Picador, 2001).

a place called the Blue Eagle . . . A club that stayed in business through the early
    seventies. From a 1964 ad in the *Gainesville Daily Sun*: "Alachua County's
    Newest Lounge BLUE EAGLE. Dance to the music of THE CASANOVAS
    Friday nights 9 'til. Featuring Ray Parrish, Pat Kee, Aubray Deen and Dean
    Bass. From G'ville drive to Grove Park, turn right on Magnesia Springs Rd.
    and go ¼ Mile. Fully Air Conditioned With Comfortable Seating."
They wouldn't issue . . . Don Felder interview, October 30, 2013.
Don formed his band . . . Don Felder, *Heaven and Hell: My Life in the Eagles
    (1974–2001)* (Hoboken: John Wiley, 2008), 25.
one of the most distinctive . . . Ibid.
After his initial few . . . Dave Zimmer, *Crosby, Stills, and Nash: The Authorized
    Biography* (Boston: Da Capo Press, 2008).
I was the drummer . . . Bill DeYoung, "The Boy Who Would Be Stills," *Gainesville
    Sun*, August 5, 2001.
John Scarritt . . . E-mail to author.
"There were four" . . . E-mail to author.
It was weird how . . . http://www.ourmusicalstory.com/bios/FrankBirdsong.
    html.
The Beatles had taken . . . *Billboard* magazine singles charts for these weeks.

Chapter 3. London Calling

One spring afternoon . . . Personal recollection of author.
The music just hypnotized . . . *Runnin' Down a Dream*, directed by Peter Bogda-
    novich (Warner Brothers, 2007), DVD.
The minute I saw the Beatles . . . Paul Zollo, *Conversations with Tom Petty* (New
    York: Omnibus Press, 2005), 15.
We were working guys . . . Ibid., 23.
obsessed with it . . . Bernie Leadon oral interview, Matheson Historical Society,
    http://ufdc.ufl.edu/MH00001785/00001.
Bernie and I had . . . Don Felder interview, October 30, 2013.
Crider recalls Leadon . . . Dale Crider e-mail to author, February 7, 2015.
My mom made us . . . Tom Laughon interview, April 27, 2011.
When the group added . . . Ibid.
That was the craziest . . . Boomer Hough interview, February 19, 2013.
I met him in high school . . . Zollo, *Conversations with Tom Petty*, 29.
Petty and I went . . . Jim Lenahan interview, May 20, 2011. The performance
    he mentions was either October 22 or December 10, 1965, based on the
    datebook of Ron Whitney, http://dizzyrambler.com/features/GarageBands/
    Ron_Starfires/63_datebook.htm.
Buster Lipham was born . . . Buster Lipham interview, February 27, 2012.

Chapter 4. People Got to Be Free

A Human Be-In . . . Neville Powis, *The Human Be-In and the Hippy Revolution* (Radio Netherlands, 2001), documentary, www.youtube.com/watch?v=RAt26TawHCw.

I walked in with two guys . . . Melanie Barr Facebook posting.

I think everyone back then . . . James Hellegaard, "Remember 1968?" *Gainesville Sun,* September 5, 1993, 6a.

They moved the station . . . Boomer Hough interview, February 19, 2013.

The harmony singing . . . Tom Laughon interview, April 27, 2011.

There was a guy . . . Don Felder interview, October 30, 2013.

I had a six-month draft . . . Bernie Leadon interview, Matheson Historical Society, http://ufdc.ufl.edu/MH00001785/00001?search=bernie+=leadon.

bands that had record deals . . . Ibid.

In the fall of 1967 . . . Bill Killeen interview, March 27, 2011.

Rodney came by . . . Tom Leadon interview, February 10, 2014.

That's where I kind of . . . Paul Zollo, *Conversations with Tom Petty,* 25.

I was partying with Tom . . . Jim Lenahan interview, May 20, 2011.

For those of us . . . Jerry Silberberg, "Light Show Freaks Out," *Florida Alligator,* January 27, 1968.

I wore a green Pierre Cardin . . . Bill DeYoung, "The Boy Who Would Be Stills," *Gainesville Sun,* August 5, 2001.

Bernie Leadon, who was raised . . . www.floridamemory.com/fpc/memory/collections/folklife/festival_programs/1968/1968-04.jpg.

Less than a month . . . John Einarson and Richie Furay, *For What It's Worth* (New York: Cooper Square Press, 2004), 255.

About ten blocks above the northern . . . Charles Steadham interview, June 8, 2015, and www.gainesville.com/article/20030514/DAYBREAK/205140309.

It was a predominantly . . . Harold Fethe e-mail to author.

Linda did a television show . . . Charles Steadham interview, January 19, 2012.

Of the nine musicians . . . *Muscle Shoals* (New York: Magnolia Pictures, 2013), DVD.

Chapter 5. I Can Hear Music

I go to Buster Lipham . . . Trevor Pinch and Frank Trocco, *Analog Day: The Invention and Impact of the Moog Synthesizer* (Cambridge: Harvard University Press, 2004), 244.

The instrumental track includes . . . http://www2.gibson.com/News-Lifestyle/Features/en-us/10-Great-Songs-That-Make-Use-of-Tremolo.aspx.

We'd been having bands . . . Buster Lipham interview, February 27, 2012.

One day the Allman Brothers . . . Michael Hitchcock interview, March 22, 2012.

Another band we liked . . . Aerosmith and Stephen Davis, *Walk This Way: The Autobiography of Aerosmith* (New York: Harper Entertainment, 1997).

If you were there on . . . *Florida Alligator*, January 28, 1970.

Most of the members of Celebration . . . Deborah Shane interview, December 5, 2013.

I moved up to Gainesville . . . Randall Marsh interview, March 12, 2013.

And I heard him yell . . . *Runnin' Down a Dream.*

The Epics and all the bands . . . Tom Leadon interview, February 10, 2014.

Away from the hubbub . . . *Gainesville Sun*, October 30, 1964, 3.

Nine years ago . . . Jim McGee, "Dub's: Signet of Success," *Florida Alligator*, May 28, 1974.

Dub's was still considered . . . E-mail to author.

Tom and I got a job . . . Tom Leadon interview, February 10, 2014.

Grand Funk Railroad, a rock trio . . . Billy James, *An American Band: The Story of Grand Funk Railroad* (London: SAF Publishing, 1999).

Dan Ryals of Ryals Plumbing . . . Jeffrey Meldon interview, August 26, 2011.

We did the second one . . . Tom Leadon interview, February 10, 2014.

Chapter 6. Getting Better

He was renowned . . . Cathy DeWitt, e-mail to author.

It was when I was fourteen . . . Nancy Luca interview, December 13, 2013.

[Felder] would sit down with me . . . Paul Zollo, *Conversations with Tom Petty*, 26.

In less than six months . . . Don Felder, *Heaven and Hell: My Life in the Eagles (1974–2001)*, 53.

Robert was kind of esteemed . . . Jeff Jourard interview, April 2, 2014.

I started him with my . . . Oral interview with Judge Benmont Tench Jr., by Nancy Steigner, http://ufdc.ufl.edu/UF00024774/00001.

Before his family's move . . . Stan Lynch interview, January 20, 2013.

The Tropics played all over . . . Charlie Souza interview, November 7, 2011.

The approach was my insistence . . . Trantham Whitley interview, December 12, 2013.

I personally witnessed Herbie . . . William Crawford e-mail to author, June 4, 2014.

I remember that they sang . . . Stan Lynch interview, January 20, 2013.

Styrophoam Soule was a busy . . . Lonnie Morris interview, April 23, 2012.

The kit that was so great . . . Stan Lynch interview, January 20, 2013.

in playing drums and being right behind . . . Bill Dean, "Stills Gives Back to Musical Roots," *Gainesville Sun*, November 22, 2008.

I played rhythm guitar for a band . . . "Sounding Out: Stephen Stills" (BBC, 1972), documentary.

The collective discographies . . . www.discogs.com.

I would ride my bike past . . . Trantham Whitley interview, December 12, 2013.

Playing cover songs in a club . . . Malcolm Gladwell, *Outliers* (New York: Little, Brown, 2008), and the work of Dr. K. Anders Ericcson.

I think there was a lot . . . Don Felder interview, October 30, 2013.

On our way back my buddy said . . . Bruce Nearon interview, January 14, 2014.

I meet Father Gannon . . . Ibid.

There used to be a bicycle store . . . Ibid.

Early in the morning . . . Charlie Ramirez e-mail, February 27, 2014.

Three local music promoters . . . Mel Libby, director of the Rathskeller; Tom Tedrow, chairman of SGP; and Bill Cate. *Florida Alligator*, March 24, 1971, 7.

Some of the police were . . . *Florida Alligator*, May 31, 1971, 1.

if anybody provoked . . . *Florida Alligator*, June 1, 1971, 1.

no redeeming value in sending . . . *Florida Alligator*, June 1, 1971, 3.

Far from being a sleepy . . . http://www.afn.org/~iguana/archives/2002_05/20020509.html.

Chapter 7. Stoned Soul Picnic

In surrounding rural areas . . . Brandon Mattey, "Gainesville Green," *Orange and Blue Magazine*, Fall 2003, http://www.jou.ufl.edu/pubs/onb/fo3/gainesvillegreen.htm.

Some topless places . . . Carl Hiaasen, "The Only Game in Town," *Florida Alligator*, January 29, 1974, 4.

We'd book six weeks at a time . . . Randall Marsh interview, March 12, 2013.

We were at Dub's . . . Tom Leadon interview, February 10, 2014.

We were playing one night . . . Randall Marsh interview, March 12, 2013.

about this Halloween Ball . . . Bruce Nearon interview, January 14, 2014.

As we drove around looking . . . Jon and Sue Jacobs, "Happy Hippy Halloween," *Great Speckled Bird* 4, no. 46, 12.

A few days before we planned . . . Jeff Goldstein e-mail, January 30, 2014.

I played a set . . . Danny Roberts interview, January 14, 2014.

We did one out at Santa Fe . . . Charlie Ramirez interview, January 24, 2014.

driving all the way from . . . Jeff Goldstein interview, January 28, 2014.

Gainesville was so different . . . Randall Marsh interview, March 12, 2013.

You would take 200–300 . . . Jeff Goldstein interview, January 28, 2014.

Despite this abundance . . . Janice Pritchard, "Entertainment, Where Have You Gone?" *Florida Independent Alligator*, February 21, 1973. Miles Wilkin is now CEO of Broadway across America.

It was very tight . . . Joe Folsom interview, April 12, 2013.

It was a long drive . . . Randall Marsh interview, March 12, 2013.

The Mudcrutch session . . . Rick Reed interview, November 7, 2011.

Chapter 8. Something in the Air

Ray Stevens's latest novelty . . . http://www.raystevens.com/about.

Todd Rundgren's band Utopia . . . March 4, 1974.

Freddie King . . . January 24–26, 1974.

Dion . . . May 7–8, 1971.

Steve Martin . . . February 11–15, 1975.

The whole point of the band . . . *Runnin' Down a Dream.*

The label representative listened . . . Ibid.

I do remember having to talk . . . Ibid.

Denny Cordell took us . . . Danny Roberts interview, January 14, 2014.

On the other side of Lincoln . . . All Meldon quotes are from Jeffrey Meldon interview, August 26, 2011.

"Lovin' You" was written . . . Four years later Minnie Riperton (1947–1979) succumbed to cancer. Her Gainesville-born daughter, Maya Rudolph, played and sang in the Rentals, a nineties rock band, was a member of the *Saturday Night Live* cast for seven years, and is now a comedienne and actress.

I met Frank Zappa . . . Roger Schliefstein e-mail to author.

When you're young . . . Dave Grohl, *Sound City* (Variance Films, 2013), DVD.

Gregg Allman also recalls . . . Gregg Allman, *My Cross to Bear*, 143.

Glenn wanted to speed things up . . . Don Felder, *Heaven and Hell: My Life with the Eagles*, 115.

Chapter 9. Disco Inferno

One likely candidate is . . . Peter Shapiro, *Turn the Beat Around: The Secret History of Disco* (London: Faber and Faber, 2005), 35.

"Will It Go Round in Circles" . . . Billy Preston was a childhood musical prodigy who had met the Beatles in 1962 in Hamburg as an organist in Little Richard's band, performed with Ray Charles as a band member, and played keyboards on two sides of a Beatles hit record: "Get Back" and the flip side, "Don't Let Me Down." Preston performed with the Beatles in their famous rooftop concert, as seen in the movie *Let It Be,* followed by a solo career that included five songs that hit the Top Five, including two number ones: "Will It Go Round in Circles" and "Nothing from Nothing" the following year. Preston is one of only two musicians ever credited as playing on a Beatles track (the other is Tony Sheridan).

For one week in July 1979 . . . From the *Billboard* singles chart of that week: "Bad Girls" (Donna Summer), "Ring My Bell" (Anita Ward), "Hot Stuff" (Donna Summer), "Good Times" (Chic), "Makin' It" (David Naughton), "Boogie Wonderland" (Earth, Wind, and Fire).

Audio engineer Jim Nygaard . . . E-mail to author.

Stan Bush, a singer and guitarist . . . E-mail to author, May 31, 2014.

As the youngest player . . . Stan Lynch interview, January 20, 2013.

soon joined Slip of the Wrist . . . Myrick left the band to pursue a solo career as a songwriter and performer and had his initial success in 1980 with the song "She Talks in Stereo."

I moved out to L.A. at the end of 1972 . . . Tom Leadon phone interview, May 18, 2014.

where I met Johnny Rivers . . . Johnny Rivers released nine songs that made the Top Ten between 1964 and 1977, charting at 2, 9, 7, 3, 1, 3, 10, 6, and 10.

The band's fourth album . . . Patti Davis, Ronald Reagan's daughter, cowrote "I Wish You Peace" with Bernie Leadon, her boyfriend at the time.

Petty's "Louisiana Rain" . . . This version of the song was not released.

My first place in L.A. . . . . Stan Lynch interview, January 20, 2013.

Ron's sister Janice was married . . . Janice Blair was married to Gregg Allman from 1973 to 1975.

Drummer Michael Hitchcock explains the arrival . . . Michael Hitchcock interview, March 22, 2012.

In Petty's own words . . . Paul Zollo, *Conversations with Tom Petty,* 46–47.

One afternoon while enjoying . . . Don Felder, *Heaven and Hell: My Life in the Eagles,* 169.

Chapter 10. Golden Years

recording engineer Bill Halverson . . . www.soundonsound.com/sos/aug10/articles/classic-tracks-0810.htm.

At Gibbs's request Stills . . . http://www.independent.co.uk/arts-entertainment/music/features/stephen-stills-interview-were-still-here-haha-haha-ha-8772387.html.

During dedication ceremonies in 2008 . . . Bill Dean, "Stills Gives Back to Musical Roots," *Gainesville Sun,* November 22, 2008.

You eventually pick a place . . . Dave Schlenker, "Rock Star Stills Buys House in Area," *Gainesville Sun,* March 12, 2004.

such an exhilarating thing . . . *Runnin' Down a Dream.*

The place was absolutely packed . . . Ibid.

The group's videos . . . Lenahan directed "Woman in Love," "You Got Lucky," "Letting You Go," "The Waiting," "Insider," "Runnin' Down a Dream," and "Jammin' Me."

Chapter 11. Go Your Own Way

kind of a Top Forty band . . . Stan Bush interview, March 4, 2014.

Sister Hazel is a Gainesville rock band . . . "Sister Hazel's Diner Always Serving," *Florida Alligator,* October 3, 1974, 12.

Copeland recounts how Sister Hazel . . . Drew Copeland interview, April 17, 2014.

When I first went down to . . . Chuck Taylor, "Airwaves," *Billboard,* September 20, 1997, 76.

Mark remembers the audition . . . Chris Michie, "The Complete Mark Pinske Interview," *Mix Magazine,* January 1, 2003.

In addition to his solo performances . . . Soni Veliz, "Laundromat 'refreshes sensibilities,'" *Independent Florida Alligator,* May 9, 1973.

I was in a band in Gainesville . . . Codi Lazar interview, January 30, 2015.

Lazar and Marshall then formed . . . A few years later the word *alternative* was dropped, and the organization was renamed Gainesville Music Alliance.

Geoffrey May recalls the process . . . Geoffrey May interview, April 18, 2014.

Micanopy is a small town . . . www.micanopytown.com.

I recorded River for . . . Mark Pinske e-mail, May 8, 2014.

If you're living in Florida . . . Brian Raftery, "Sunshine State," *Spin,* August 2007, www.spin.com.

I had come up to Gainesville in . . . Vinnie Fiorello interview, May 5, 2014.

Chapter 12. A Place in the Sun

in that void of pointless leisure . . . W. J. Cash, *The Mind of the South* (New York: Vintage Books, 1941), 51.

known primarily as the largest . . . The cotton-ginning business established on South Main Street by H. F. Dutton and Company was for several years the largest dealer in Sea Island cotton in the South.

tung oil . . . In 1928, L. P. Moore, nephew of the Benjamin Moore Paints founder, built the first mechanized tung oil compressing mill in the world, located in Gainesville, Florida, http://www.se-eppc.org/wildlandweeds/pdf/Winter2005-Brown-pp4-6.pdf.

children of university faculty members . . . Bernie Leadon, Stan Lynch, Jeff and Marty Jourard, and Ken Block, respectively.

However, in the only music lecture . . . Maurice Ravel, "Contemporary Music," Rice Institute Pamphlet 15, no. 2 (April 1928), 129–45.

An annual music festival . . . www.thefestfl.com, http://store.noidearecords.com.

Coastal Plains map . . . Charles B. Hunt, *Physiography of the United States* (San Francisco: W. H. Freeman, 1967), 138.

MARTY JOURARD was born in Atlanta and raised in Gainesville, Florida, where at 15 he began playing in rock bands. Two years after his 1976 move to Los Angeles he became a member of the Motels, an eighties pop group whose recordings include two gold albums and two Top Ten singles. Marty is the author of *Start Your Own Band* and *The Marty Method*, a music instruction book. He lives in Seattle where he plays and writes music and writes about playing music. www.martyjourard.com

CPSIA information can be obtained
at www.ICGtesting.com
Printed in the USA
LVOW08*0516160117

521063LV00003B/20/P

9 780813 062587